Ultimate Pandas for Data Manipulation and Visualization

*Efficiently Process and Visualize
Data with Python's Most Popular
Data Manipulation Library*

Tahera Firdose

www.orangeava.com

First published: June 2024

Published by: Orange Education Pvt Ltd, AVA™

Address: 9, Daryaganj, Delhi, 110002, India

275 New North Road Islington Suite 1314 London, N1 7AA, United Kingdom

ISBN: 978-81-97256-24-0

www.orangeava.com

Dedicated To

My Husband:

Nasrulain Mohamed

My Strength and Support System

My Parents:

Maqbool Ahmed and Yasmeen Begum

My Guiding Lights

My Daughter:
Alina Nasrulain
My Inspiration

About the Author

Tahera Firdose holds a postgraduate degree in Artificial Intelligence and has made significant strides in the fields of data analysis and machine learning. Her academic background, combined with her passion for these domains, has propelled her into a prominent position as an educator, blogger, and community influencer.

Tahera's expertise in Artificial Intelligence extends beyond theoretical knowledge; she has applied her skills in various practical and impactful projects. Her work in machine learning, particularly in developing innovative algorithms and predictive models, has been recognized for its excellence and practical applications. She is known for her ability to simplify complex concepts and make them accessible to a broader audience.

An avid writer, Tahera frequently shares her insights and discoveries through her well-regarded blog. Her articles cover a wide range of topics within data analysis and machine learning, providing valuable resources for both beginners and seasoned professionals. Her writing is characterized by its clarity, depth, and practical relevance, making her blog a go-to source for anyone looking to deepen their understanding of these fields.

Beyond her professional and academic pursuits, Tahera has a rich personal life that she balances with her career. She loves to cook and often experiments with new recipes, finding joy in the culinary arts. This hobby allows her to unwind and express her creativity in a different medium. Family time is also incredibly important to Tahera. She cherishes moments spent with her loved ones, finding them to be a source of inspiration and support.

Tahera's commitment to education, her contributions to the field of Artificial Intelligence, and her ability to maintain a well-rounded life serve as an inspiration to many. Her journey reflects a blend of professional excellence and personal fulfillment, making her a respected and admired figure in the tech community.

About the Technical Reviewers

Nehaa Bansal is a pioneering thought leader and data scientist with a passion for early innovation. She has extensive experience across banking, finance, telecom, and insurance, excelling in predictive modeling. Nehaa's skills shine both as an individual contributor and team player. Academically, she graduated top of her class with a bachelor's in computer science and a master's in data science from BITS Pilani.

Her professional ethos is defined by ownership, prioritizing people, and questioning the "why" before starting any endeavor. Nehaa's agile mindset drives her to act swiftly, learn from failures, iterate continuously, and maintain fairness. Her passion for solving user problems fuels her expertise in analytics, product strategy, and leadership, leading to innovative solutions.

Outside of work, Nehaa values continuous learning, stays ahead of emerging trends, and advocates for inclusivity and diversity. Her dedication to excellence and empathy for others has established her as a thought leader and catalyst for positive change in technology and data science.

Pratik Kotian is a seasoned professional with 8 years of expertise in Natural Language Processing (NLP), Machine Learning (ML), Generative AI, and Python programming. Based in Mumbai, India, Pratik has dedicated his career to advancing AI technology and applications.

Starting with a focus on neural networks during his academic years, Pratik has since developed cutting-edge solutions for data-intensive enterprise applications, both on-premises and in the cloud. His career spans multiple sectors, including technology, telecommunications, finance, and retail, where he has excelled in leadership roles. Currently, Pratik is a Manager at Deloitte, leading the Generative AI Team to create innovative solutions and drive AI-driven strategies for clients. He is committed to building high-performing teams and supporting organizational goals. In his spare time, Pratik actively engages in the AI community, sharing knowledge and contributing to advancements in the field, cementing his reputation as a respected leader in AI.

Acknowledgements

Embarking on the journey of writing *Ultimate Pandas for Data Manipulation and Visualization* has been an extraordinary experience, and I am deeply grateful to the individuals who have played a crucial role in bringing this book to fruition. This endeavor wouldn't have been possible without the unwavering support, guidance, and expertise generously shared by many.

Firstly, my heartfelt thanks go to the Pandas community and Wes McKinney, the creator of Pandas, whose dedication to the library has shaped this book. The Pandas documentation, an invaluable resource at https://pandas.pydata.org/docs/, served as a guiding light, enriching the content and ensuring accuracy. Special gratitude is extended to the technical reviewers whose meticulous reviews and insightful feedback enhanced the book. Their dedication and expertise have been invaluable in refining the content and ensuring its accuracy.

To my family, thank you for your unwavering support. In particular, I want to express deep appreciation to my husband, Nasrulain Mohamed, whose encouragement and understanding have been a constant source of strength throughout this writing journey. Special thanks to my parents, Maqbool Ahmed and Yasmeen Begum, my guiding lights, for their steadfast support, and to my daughter, Alina Nasrulain, my joy and inspiration, for bringing immense happiness and motivation into my life. I also extend my gratitude to my siblings, whose support and encouragement have been invaluable.

To all those at the publication house who have contributed in various capacities, your collective efforts have enriched this endeavor. I appreciate the collaborative spirit that has fueled the creation of *Ultimate Pandas for Data Manipulation and Visualization.*

Finally, to the readers, thank you for choosing this book as your source of knowledge. May it be a valuable companion on your journey to mastering Pandas and navigating the dynamic world of data manipulation.

Preface

In the ever-evolving field of data science, mastering a versatile and powerful tool like Pandas is essential. Welcome to *Ultimate Pandas for Data Manipulation and Visualization*, your comprehensive guide to harnessing the full potential of this remarkable Python library. Whether you're a data analyst, scientist, or newcomer eager to delve into data analysis, this book will elevate your skills and empower you to handle data with finesse.

This book consists of 11 chapters, each serving as a complete module designed to help you understand and apply Pandas in real-world scenarios. From the basics of data handling to advanced techniques, this guide ensures you have everything you need to become proficient in data manipulation using Pandas.

Chapter 1. Introduction to Pandas and Data Analysis: This chapter sets the foundation for your journey into data analysis with Pandas. It introduces the library, discusses its significance, and guides you through the installation and setup process. You'll also learn about IPython Notebooks and how they integrate seamlessly with Pandas. The chapter covers the two core Pandas objects: Series and DataFrame, and shows you how to load data from various sources.

Chapter 2. Pandas Series: Dive deep into the Pandas Series, a one-dimensional labeled array capable of holding any data type. This chapter covers creating Series, indexing, selecting data, and performing operations. You'll learn the differences between Series and other data structures, how to handle NaN values, and perform arithmetic and filtering operations on Series.

Chapter 3. Pandas DataFrame: Explore the Pandas DataFrame, a two-dimensional labeled data structure. Learn how to create, manipulate, and transform DataFrames, and perform various operations on them. The chapter includes methods for viewing DataFrames, adding and removing columns and rows, renaming and reordering columns, and selecting data using loc[] and iloc[].

Chapter 4. Data Cleaning with Pandas: Data cleaning is crucial for quality data analysis. This chapter covers techniques to identify and handle missing data using functions such as isna() and dropna(), and manage duplicates with duplicated() and drop_duplicates(). You'll also learn about the importance of data cleaning in the analysis process.

Chapter 5. Data Filtering with Pandas: Learn to extract specific subsets of data based on conditions. This chapter covers filtering techniques to refine your datasets using equality, inequality, and logical operators. You'll explore methods for numeric, date, and time filtering, as well as handling null values during filtering.

Chapter 6. Grouping and Aggregating Data: Aggregation helps summarize and analyze data. This chapter explores grouping data and applying functions to obtain summary statistics. You'll learn about the split-apply-combine strategy, built-in aggregation methods, and user-defined function aggregation. The chapter also covers discretization and binning.

Chapter 7. Reshaping and Pivoting in Pandas: Reshaping and pivoting are essential for data manipulation. This chapter covers techniques to reshape and pivot data, including stacking, unstacking, melting, and exploding data. You will also learn how to create pivot tables to summarize data effectively.

Chapter 8. Joining and Merging Data in Pandas: Joining and merging data are fundamental for combining datasets. This chapter covers techniques for various types of joins and merges, including inner, outer, and left joins, as well as concatenating data along rows and columns. You will also learn to join dataframes on their index and merge on multiple columns.

Chapter 9. Introduction to Time Series Analysis in Pandas: Time series analysis deals with data indexed by time. This chapter covers techniques to handle and analyze time series data, including working with the Timestamp object, datetime handling in Python and Pandas, resampling time series, and using datetime as an index.

Chapter 10. Visualization Using Matplotlib: Visualizing data helps in understanding and communicating insights. This chapter covers Pandas' plotting capabilities using Matplotlib. You'll learn about the components of a plot, creating various types of plots, customizing plot aesthetics, and plotting time series data. The chapter also covers exporting and saving plots.

Chapter 11. Analyzing Bank Customer Churn Using Pandas: To culminate your learning, this chapter guides you through a real-world scenario where you'll apply the concepts learned to analyze bank customer churn data, reinforcing your understanding and skills.

This hands-on guide, filled with practical examples, real-world scenarios, and best practices, will empower you to leverage Pandas for effective data manipulation and analysis. Embrace this journey to enhance your data handling capabilities and become proficient in the dynamic field of data science. Happy analyzing!

Downloading the code bundles and colored images

Please follow the links or scan the QR codes to download the
Code Bundles and Images of the book:

https://github.com/ava-orange-education/Ultimate-Pandas-for-Data-Manipulation-and-Visualization

The code bundles and images of the book are also hosted on
https://rebrand.ly/exx0xgg

In case there's an update to the code, it will be updated on the existing
GitHub repository.

Errata

We take immense pride in our work at **Orange Education Pvt Ltd,** and follow best practices to ensure the accuracy of our content to provide an indulging reading experience to our subscribers. Our readers are our mirrors, and we use their inputs to reflect and improve upon human errors, if any, that may have occurred during the publishing processes involved. To let us maintain the quality and help us reach out to any readers who might be having difficulties due to any unforeseen errors, please write to us at :

errata@orangeava.com

Your support, suggestions, and feedback are highly appreciated.

DID YOU KNOW

Did you know that Orange Education Pvt Ltd offers eBook versions of every book published, with PDF and ePub files available? You can upgrade to the eBook version at **www.orangeava.com** and as a print book customer, you are entitled to a discount on the eBook copy. Get in touch with us at: **info@orangeava.com** for more details.

At **www.orangeava.com**, you can also read a collection of free technical articles, sign up for a range of free newsletters, and receive exclusive discounts and offers on AVA™ Books and eBooks.

PIRACY

If you come across any illegal copies of our works in any form on the internet, we would be grateful if you would provide us with the location address or website name. Please contact us at **info@orangeava.com** with a link to the material.

ARE YOU INTERESTED IN AUTHORING WITH US?

If there is a topic that you have expertise in, and you are interested in either writing or contributing to a book, please write to us at **business@orangeava.com**. We are on a journey to help developers and tech professionals to gain insights on the present technological advancements and innovations happening across the globe and build a community that believes Knowledge is best acquired by sharing and learning with others. Please reach out to us to learn what our audience demands and how you can be part of this educational reform. We also welcome ideas from tech experts and help them build learning and development content for their domains.

REVIEWS

Please leave a review. Once you have read and used this book, why not leave a review on the site that you purchased it from? Potential readers can then see and use your unbiased opinion to make purchase decisions. We at Orange Education would love to know what you think about our products, and our authors can learn from your feedback. Thank you!

For more information about Orange Education, please visit **www.orangeava.com**.

Table of Contents

CHAPTER 1
Introduction to Pandas and Data Analysis

Introduction

In today's data-driven era, organizations of all sizes and across various industries are faced with the challenge of extracting meaningful information from the vast amounts of data available to them. Making sense of this data requires powerful tools and techniques that enable efficient data manipulation, pre-processing, and exploration. This is where pandas truly shine.

We will dive deep into the capabilities of pandas, exploring their countless functionalities for data manipulation, exploration, and analysis. We will start with the basics, learning how to load data into pandas from various sources, handle missing values, and clean messy datasets. From there, we will progress to more advanced techniques, such as reshaping and pivoting data, merging and joining datasets, and applying statistical computations.

Structure

In this chapter, we will cover the following essential topics that form the foundation of pandas and data analysis:

- Overview of Pandas and Their Role in Data Analysis
- Installation and Setup of Pandas
- Introduction to IPython Notebooks and how They Integrate with Pandas
- Understanding the two Core Pandas Objects: Series and DataFrame
- Understanding Data Types
- Loading Data from Files and the Web

Overview of Pandas and Their Role in Data Analysis

Pandas, an open-source Python library, was first developed by Wes McKinney in 2008 while working at AQR Capital Management. Wes created pandas to address the limitations he encountered while working with data in Python, aiming to provide a powerful and efficient tool specifically designed for data manipulation and analysis.

Initially, pandas was primarily used in the financial industry, where it quickly gained traction due to its ability to handle large and complex datasets. Its intuitive data structures and comprehensive set of functionalities made it a game-changer for quantitative analysts, traders, and researchers who needed to process and analyze vast amounts of financial data efficiently.

Over time, pandas expanded beyond the financial sector and gained popularity across various domains and industries. Today, it is widely used in academia, scientific research, marketing, social sciences, healthcare, and more. Any field that deals with data analysis, exploration, and pre-processing can benefit from pandas' capabilities.

Pandas Popularity

The popularity of pandas can be attributed to several factors. First, its user-friendly interface and intuitive syntax make it accessible to both novice and experienced Python users. The DataFrame and Series data structures mimic the tabular structure of data, resembling what users are already familiar with in spreadsheets or SQL tables.

Furthermore, pandas' rich set of functions and methods for data manipulation, cleaning, and analysis streamline the workflow of data professionals. It provides concise and efficient ways to handle common data tasks, allowing users to focus on the analysis itself rather than the intricacies of data manipulation.

The community support surrounding pandas has also contributed to its popularity. The open-source nature of the library has encouraged contributions from a vast number of developers worldwide. This has led to the rapid development of new features, bug fixes, and enhancements, ensuring that pandas stays up-to-date with the evolving needs of data analysts and scientists.

Moreover, the seamless integration of pandas with other popular libraries in the Python ecosystem, such as NumPy, Matplotlib, and scikit-learn, has further propelled its popularity. This integration allows users to combine the strengths of different libraries, enabling powerful data analysis, visualization, and machine-learning workflows.

Advantages of Pandas over Traditional Data Analysis Methods

Here are the advantages of Pandas over traditional data analysis methods:

- **Efficient Data Handling:** Pandas provides highly efficient data structures, such as DataFrames and Series, which are optimized for handling large datasets. These structures allow for fast data manipulation operations, such as filtering, aggregation, and sorting, resulting in improved performance compared to traditional methods like manual looping or using spreadsheets.

- **Broad Data Format Support:** Unlike traditional methods that often rely on specific data formats, Pandas supports a wide range of data formats, including CSV, Excel, SQL databases, and JSON. This versatility enables seamless integration and analysis of data from various sources, eliminating the need for manual data conversion or preprocessing.

- **Advanced Data Manipulation:** Pandas offers a rich set of functions and methods for data manipulation, transformation, and cleaning. It provides easy-to-use functionalities for handling missing values, reshaping data, merging datasets, and performing complex operations, reducing the complexity and time required for data preprocessing.

- **Time Series Analysis:** Pandas provides specialized tools and functions for working with time series data. It offers built-in support for time-based indexing, resampling, and time shifting operations, making it particularly well-suited for analyzing and modelling time-dependent data.

- **Integration with the Python Ecosystem:** Pandas seamlessly integrates with other popular libraries in the Python ecosystem, such as NumPy, Matplotlib, asci-kit-learn. This integration allows for efficient data exchange and collaboration between different tools, enhancing the capabilities and flexibility of data analysis workflows.

Installation and Setup

Pandas require Python 3.7 or later versions to run properly. It is recommended to use the latest stable version of Python available at the time of installation. Pandas is compatible with both Python 2.x and Python 3.x, but Python 2.x is no longer actively supported, so it's strongly advised to use Python 3.x.

Before installing Pandas, ensure that you have Python installed on your system. You can check the Python version by opening a command prompt or terminal and running the following command:

```
python –version
```

```
C:\Users\Alina>python --version
Python 3.10.11
```

Figure 1.1: *Python version*

If you have Python installed and the version displayed is 3.7 or later, you meet the Python requirement to run Pandas. If you don't have Python installed or have an older version, you can download and install the latest version of Python from the official Python website (https://www.python.org).

Once you have Python installed, you can proceed with installing Pandas using the appropriate method, such as pip or Anaconda.

Installing Pandas on Windows

To install Pandas on Windows, follow these steps:

Using pip:

1. Open the command prompt by pressing *Win* + R and typing **cmd**.

2. Enter the following command to install Pandas:

    ```
    pip install pandas
    ```

Using Anaconda:

1. Download Anaconda from the official website (https://www.anaconda.com/products/individual) and run the installer.

2. Follow the installation instructions, selecting the desired options.

3. Open Anaconda Prompt from the **Start** menu.

4. Enter the following command to install Pandas:

    ```
    conda install pandas
    ```

Installing Pandas on MaCOS

To install Pandas on MaCOS, follow these steps:

Using pip:

1. Open the terminal by going to "**Applications**" > "**Utilities**" > "**Terminal**".

2. Enter the following command to install Pandas:

    ```
    pip install pandas
    ```

Installing Pandas on Linux

To install Pandas on Linux, follow these steps:

Using pip:

1. Open the terminal.

2. Enter the following command to install Pandas:

```
pip install pandas
```

If you're using Pandas and it is already installed, but you want to update it to the latest version, use the following command:

```
pip install --upgrade pandas
```

IPython Notebooks and its Integration with Pandas

IPython Notebooks, now known as Jupyter Notebooks, provide an interactive computing environment for creating and sharing documents that combine code, visualizations, and explanatory text. Jupyter Notebooks have become immensely popular in the data science community and seamlessly integrate with Pandas, a powerful data analysis library in Python.

Overview of IPython/Jupyter Notebooks:

1. Jupyter Notebooks are web-based environments that allow you to create and execute code, visualize data, and document your analysis in a single document.

2. The notebooks are organized into cells, each of which can contain code (Python, in this case), markdown text, or raw text.

3. Code cells can be executed independently, allowing for an interactive and iterative data analysis process.

4. Notebooks provide a rich interface that supports the inclusion of charts, tables, mathematical equations, images, and more.

5. Jupyter Notebooks foster reproducibility by combining code, visualizations, and explanations in a shareable format.

Installing Jupyter Notebooks

To install Jupyter Notebooks, you can follow these steps:

1. Ensure that you have Python installed on your system. You can download

Python from the official website (https://www.python.org) and follow the installation instructions.

2. Open a command prompt or terminal.

3. Install Jupyter Notebooks using pip, which is a package manager for Python. Enter the following command:

```
pip install jupyter
```

4. Wait for the installation to complete. Jupyter Notebooks and its dependencies will be installed in your Python environment.

To check if Jupyter Notebook is already installed on your system, you can follow these steps:

1. Open a command prompt or terminal.

2. Type the following command and press *Enter*

```
jupyter notebook -version
```

If Jupyter Notebook is installed, the command will display the version number. For example, you might see something like this:

```
6.4.0
```

Let's run Jupyter notebook, assuming you already have installed Anaconda.

Open the Anaconda Navigator application. You can typically find it in your system's application launcher or start menu. Once opened, the Anaconda Navigator window will appear.

In the Anaconda Navigator window, you will see several tools and environments. Click the "**Launch**" button under the Jupyter Notebook tile. This action will open a new window or tab in your default web browser.

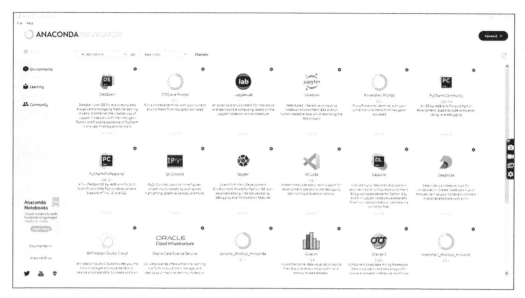

Figure 1.2: *Anaconda navigator*

The web browser will display the Jupyter Notebook interface. It will show a file browser on the left side and the list of available notebooks in the selected directory.

Figure 1.3: *Jupyter Notebook*

To create a new notebook, click the "**New**" button located at the top-right corner of the interface. From the drop-down menu, select "**Python 3**" to create a new Python notebook.

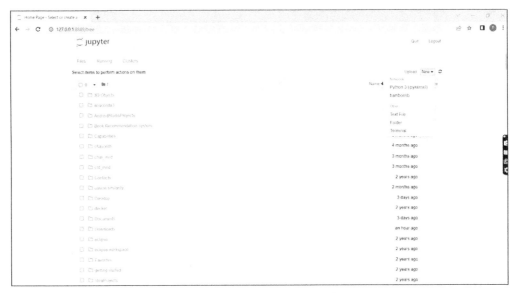

Figure 1.4: *Create new Python file*

The notebook dashboard will appear, showing the newly created notebook. It will have the file extension **.ipynb**. You can see the notebook's name at the top, and it can be renamed by clicking the title.

Figure 1.5: *New Notebook*

1. In the notebook, you will find an empty cell where you can write and execute Python code.

2. To add a new cell, click the "**+**" button in the toolbar or use the keyboard shortcut B to insert a cell below the currently selected cell.

3. You can change the cell type from "**Code**" to "**Markdown**" by selecting the appropriate option from the drop-down menu in the toolbar. Markdown cells allow you to include formatted text, headings, bullet points, and more.

4. You can write Python code in the cell and execute it by pressing *Shift+Enter* or by clicking the "**Run**" button in the toolbar.

5. To save the notebook, click the floppy disk icon in the toolbar or go to "**File**" > "**Save and Checkpoint**".

6. To exit the notebook, close the browser tab containing the notebook interface or go to "**File**" > "**Close and Halt**".

Understanding Pandas Objects: Series and DataFrame

In this section, we will explore the two core Pandas objects: **Series** and **DataFrame**. These are powerful tools for working with data in one or two dimensions, with labels and types. We will show you how to create them using Python.

Before we can work with Series and DataFrame, we need to import pandas, which is a library of useful functions and methods for data analysis. We can do this by typing: **import pandas as pd**. This will give us a shortcut to use pandas by typing **pd** before any pandas function or method.

```
Import pandas as pd
```

Series

A Series is a one-dimensional labeled array capable of holding any data type (integers, strings, floating-point numbers, Python objects, and more). It consists of two main components: the data and the index.

- **Data**: The data component of a Series represents the values or elements that the Series holds. These values can be of any data type, such as numbers, text, or even more complex objects. The data can be provided using a NumPy array, a Python list, or a scalar value.

- **Index:** It is a sequence of labels which identifies each element in the Series. By default, the index starts from 0 and increments by 1, but you can customize it.

Example 1: We will start with a basic example using a Python list. Suppose you have a list of weekly temperatures: [**25**, **28**, **30**, **26**, **29**, **31**, **27**]. Pandas offers a data structure called a **Series**, which is ideal for storing and working with this type of data.

```
Temperatures = [25, 28, 30, 26, 29, 31, 27]
series = pd.Series(temperatures)
print(series)
```

Output:

```
0      25
1      28
2      30
3      26
4      29
5      31
6      27
dtype: int64
```

Figure 1.6: Series output

Example 2: In this example, we are using a scalar value. Suppose you want to create a **Series** with the same value repeated multiple times. Let's say you want a **Series** with the value **10** repeated 5 times.

```
Value = 10
series = pd.Series(value, index=[0, 1, 2, 3, 4])
print(series)
```

Output:

```
0      10
1      10
2      10
3      10
4      10
dtype: int64
```

Figure 1.7: Output: creating a series with repeated scalar value

This example demonstrates that the data component of the Series is the scalar value 10, which is repeated 5 times.

Index: The index component of a Series represents the labels or names assigned to each element in the Series. It helps to identify and access specific elements of the Series. By default, the index starts from 0 and increments by 1 for each element, but you can customize it to any sequence of labels.

Example 1: Using default index

Let's consider the previous example of the temperature Series. The default index labels are assigned automatically when we create the Series.

```
Temperatures = [25, 28, 30, 26, 29, 31, 27]
series = pd.Series(temperatures)
print(series)
```

Output:

```
0    25
1    28
2    30
3    26
4    29
5    31
6    27
dtype: int64
```

Figure 1.8: *Series with default index labels*

In this example, the default index labels are 0, 1, 2, 3, 4, 5, and 6.

Example 2: Using custom index

Suppose you have a Series representing the ages of different people, and you want to assign custom labels to each age.

```
Ages = [25, 30, 35, 28, 32]
index_labels = ['John', 'Jane', 'Mike', 'Emily', 'Alex']
series = pd.Series(ages, index=index_labels)
print(series)
```

Output:

```
John     25
Jane     30
Mike     35
Emily    28
Alex     32
dtype: int64
```

Figure 1.9: *Series with custom index labels*

In this example, we assigned custom index labels (names) to each age in the Series, making it easier to identify the age of each person.

The data and index components together form a Series, where each element has both a value and a corresponding label. This makes it convenient to work with and access specific elements in the Series based on their labels.

DataFrame

A DataFrame in Pandas is a two-dimensional labeled data structure that can hold multiple columns. It can be thought of as a table or spreadsheet where each column represents a variable or attribute, and each row represents a specific observation or record.

A DataFrame consists of three main components: data, index, and columns.

Data: The data component of a DataFrame represents the actual values in the table. It can be created from various data structures, such as Python dictionaries, NumPy arrays, or other DataFrames.

Example 1: Creating a DataFrame from a Python dictionary:

```
data = {'Name': ['John', 'Jane', 'Mike'],
        'Age': [25, 30, 35],
        'City': ['New York', 'Paris', 'London']}
df = pd.DataFrame(data)
print(df)
```

Output:

```
    Name  Age       City
0   John   25   New York
1   Jane   30      Paris
2   Mike   35     London
```

Figure 1.10: Output: dataFrame created from a Python dictionary

In this example, we create a DataFrame named "**df**" from a Python dictionary. The dictionary keys represent column names (**'Name'**, **'Age'**, **'City'**), and the corresponding values represent the data for each column. The resulting DataFrame has three columns: **'Name'**, **'Age'**, and **'City'**, and each row represents a person's information.

Index: The index component of a DataFrame represents the labels assigned to each row. It helps to uniquely identify and access specific rows in the DataFrame. By default, Pandas assigns a numeric index starting from 0, but you can customize it with your own labels.

Example 2: Customizing the index labels of a DataFrame:

```
data = {'Name': ['John', 'Jane', 'Mike'],
        'Age': [25, 30, 35],
        'City': ['New York', 'Paris', 'London']}
```

```
df = pd.DataFrame(data, index=['A', 'B', 'C'])
print(df)
```

Output:

```
    Name  Age      City
A   John   25  New York
B   Jane   30     Paris
C   Mike   35    London
```

Figure 1.11: Customizing the index labels of a DataFrame

In this example, we create a DataFrame named "**df**" with custom index labels ('**A**', '**B**', '**C**'). Now each row in the DataFrame has a unique identifier based on the assigned index labels.

Datatypes of Pandas

Pandas data structures: Series and DataFrame can store different types of data, such as numbers, strings, booleans, and dates. In this section, we will learn how to use the datatypes of pandas in Series and DataFrame.

Defining Datatypes

Datatypes are the categories of data that tell us how the data is stored and what operations can be performed on it. For example, integers are a datatype that can store whole numbers and can be added, subtracted, multiplied, and so on. Strings are a datatype that can store text and can be concatenated, sliced, searched, and more.

Python has several built-in datatypes, such as **int**, **float**, **str**, **bool**, and so on. However, pandas borrows its datatypes from another Python library called NumPy, which is a library for scientific computing. NumPy has more datatypes than Python, such as **int8**, **int16**, **int32**, **int64**, **uint8**, **uint16**, **uint32**, **uint64**, **float16**, **float32**, **float64**, **complex64**, **complex128**, and so on. These datatypes allow us to specify the size and precision of the data.

Pandas also has some datatypes that are specific to pandas, such as **datetime64**, **timedelta64**, and category. These datatypes allow us to work with dates and times and categorical data.

Using the Datatypes of Pandas in Series and DataFrame

Pandas will automatically assign a suitable datatype to each column or Series based on the values in it. We can also specify our own datatype by using the dtype argument in the constructor.

Here are some examples of how to create and use different datatypes in pandas:

Object

The object datatype is used to store any type of data that is not numeric or boolean. It can store strings, mixed types or Python objects. The object datatype is also used when pandas cannot infer a specific datatype for a column or **Series**.

For example:

```
# Create a Series of strings
s = pd.Series(["apple", "banana", "cherry"])


# Check the datatype of the Series
print(s.dtype)
```

Output:

```
# Create a Series of strings
s = pd.Series(["apple", "banana", "cherry"])

# Check the datatype of the Series
print(s.dtype)

object
```

Figure 1.12: *Series with datatype object*

We can also create a DataFrame with object columns by using a dictionary of lists or Series. For example:

```
# Create a DataFrame with object columns
df = pd.DataFrame({"name": ["Alice", "Bob", "Charlie"],
                   "gender": ["F", "M", "M"],
                   "hobby": ["reading", "gaming", "cooking"]})


# Check the datatypes of all the columns
print(df.dtypes)
```

Output:

```
# Create a DataFrame with object columns
df = pd.DataFrame({"name": ["Alice", "Bob", "Charlie"],
                   "gender": ["F", "M", "M"],
                   "hobby": ["reading", "gaming", "cooking"]})

# Check the datatypes of all the columns
print(df.dtypes)

name      object
gender    object
hobby     object
dtype: object
```

Figure 1.13: *Dataframe with datatype object*

Int64

The **int64** datatype is used to store 64-bit integers. It can store whole numbers from -9223372036854775808 to 9223372036854775807. It is the default datatype for numeric columns or Series that do not have decimal points or missing values.

For example:

```
# Create a Series of integers
s = pd.Series([1, 2, 3, 4])


# Check the datatype of the Series
print(s.dtype)
```

```
# Create a Series of integers
s = pd.Series([1, 2, 3, 4])

# Check the datatype of the Series
print(s.dtype)
```

Figure 1.14: *Series with datatype integer64*

We can also create a DataFrame with **int64** columns by using a list of lists or a dictionary of lists or Series. For example:

```
# Create a DataFrame with int64 columns
df = pd.DataFrame({"id": [1, 2, 3],
                   "age": [25, 30, 35],
                   "score": [80, 90, 100]})


# Check the datatypes of all the columns
print(df.dtypes)
```

Output:

```
# Create a DataFrame with int64 columns
df = pd.DataFrame({"id": [1, 2, 3],
                   "age": [25, 30, 35],
                   "score": [80, 90, 100]})

# Check the datatypes of all the columns
print(df.dtypes)

id       int64
age      int64
score    int64
dtype: object
```

Figure 1.15: DataFrame with datatype integer64

Float64

The **float64** datatype is used to store 64-bit floating-point numbers. It can store decimal numbers with up to 15 digits of precision. It is the default datatype for numeric columns or Series that have decimal points or missing values.

For example:

```
# Create a Series of floats
s = pd.Series([1.0, 2.5, 3.2])


# Check the datatype of the Series
print(s.dtype)
```

Output:

```
# Create a Series of floats

s = pd.Series([1.0, 2.5, 3.2])

# Check the datatype of the Series

print(s.dtype)
```

Figure 1.16: Series with datatype float64

We can also create a DataFrame with **float64** columns by using a list of lists or a dictionary of lists or Series. For example:

```
df = pd.DataFrame({"price": [10.0, np.nan, 15.0],
                   "discount": [0.1, np.nan, np.nan],
                   "final_price": [9.0,np.nan, np.nan]})
```

```
# Check the datatypes of all the columns
print(df.dtypes)
```

Output:

```
df = pd.DataFrame({"price": [10.0, np.nan, 15.0],

                   "discount": [0.1, np.nan, np.nan],

                   "final_price": [9.0,np.nan, np.nan]})

# Check the datatypes of all the columns
print(df.dtypes)

price           float64
discount        float64
final_price     float64
dtype: object
```

Figure 1.17: DataFrame with datatype float64

Boolean

The boolean datatype is used to store **True** or **False** values. It can be used to represent logical conditions or binary choices. It is the default datatype for columns or Series that contain only **True** or **False** values.

For example:

```
# Create a Series of booleans
s = pd.Series([True, False, True])
```

```
# Check the datatype of the Series
print(s.dtype)
```

Output:

```
# Create a Series of booleans
s = pd.Series([True, False, True])

# Check the datatype of the Series
print(s.dtype)

bool
```

Figure 1.18: Series with datatype boolean

We can also create a DataFrame with bool columns by using a list of lists or a dictionary of lists or Series. For example,

```
# Create a DataFrame with bool columns
df = pd.DataFrame({"is_even": [True, False, True],
                   "is_positive": [True, True, False],
                   "is_prime": [False, True, False]})
```

```
# Check the datatypes of all the columns
print(df.dtypes)
```

Output:

```
# Create a DataFrame with bool columns
df = pd.DataFrame({"is_even": [True, False, True],
                   "is_positive": [True, True, False],
                   "is_prime": [False, True, False]})

# Check the datatypes of all the columns
print(df.dtypes)

is_even        bool
is_positive    bool
is_prime       bool
dtype: object
```

Figure 1.19: *DataFrame with datatype boolean*

Loading Data from Files and the Web for Pandas

One of the most common tasks in data analysis is loading data from various sources, such as files and the web. Pandas provides several functions and methods to help you read and write data in different formats, such as CSV, Excel, JSON, HTML, and SQL.

In this section, we will explore the most common ways to load data using Pandas. Specifically, we will learn how to use the **read_csv** and **read_excel** functions to load data from CSV and Excel files, respectively. Additionally, we will learn how to use the **read_html** function to load data from web pages

Loading Data from CSV Files Using `pandas.read_csv()`

Comma-S Values (CSV) is a common file format for storing tabular data. A CSV file consists of rows and columns separated by commas or other delimiters. Pandas provides the **pandas.read_csv()** function to read data from CSV files into a DataFrame object. A DataFrame is a two-dimensional table of data with rows and columns.

To use **pandas.read_csv()**, you need to pass the file path or file-like object as the first argument. You can also specify other optional arguments to customize the behavior of the function.

Here are some of the most commonly used parameters:

- **filepath_or_buffer:** This parameter specifies the path of the CSV file to be read.

- **sep:** This parameter specifies the delimiter used in the CSV file. The default value is ',.

- **header:** This parameter specifies which row of the CSV file should be used as the column names. The default value is 0.

- **index_col:** This parameter specifies which column of the CSV file should be used as the index. The default value is None.

- **Use cols:** This parameter specifies which columns of the CSV file should be read into the DataFrame. The default value is None, which means all columns are read.

- **dtype:** This parameter specifies the data type of each column in the DataFrame. The default value is None, which means pandas will try to infer the data types automatically.

- **skiprows:** This parameter specifies how many rows should be skipped from the beginning of the CSV file. The default value is 0.

- **nrows:** This parameter specifies how many rows should be read from the CSV file. The default value is None, which means all rows are read.

Here is an example of how to use **pandas.read_csv()** to load a CSV file into a DataFrame:

```
# Read data from a CSV file
df = pd.read_csv("housing.csv")


# Print the first 5 rows of the DataFrame
df.head()
```

Output:

```
# Read data from a CSV file
df = pd.read_csv("housing.csv")

# Print the first 5 rows of the DataFrame
df.head()
```

	Suburb	Address	Rooms	Type	Price	Method	SellerG	Date	Distance	Postcode	...	Bathroom	Car	Landsize	BuildingArea	YearBuilt
0	Abbotsford	85 Turner St	2	h	1480000.0	S	Biggin	3/12/2016	2.5	3067.0	...	1.0	1.0	202.0	NaN	NaN
1	Abbotsford	25 Bloomburg St	2	h	1035000.0	S	Biggin	4/02/2016	2.5	3067.0	...	1.0	0.0	156.0	79.0	1900.0
2	Abbotsford	5 Charles St	3	h	1465000.0	SP	Biggin	4/03/2017	2.5	3067.0	...	2.0	0.0	134.0	150.0	1900.0
3	Abbotsford	40 Federation La	3	h	850000.0	PI	Biggin	4/03/2017	2.5	3067.0	...	2.0	1.0	94.0	NaN	NaN
4	Abbotsford	55a Park St	4	h	1600000.0	VB	Nelson	4/06/2016	2.5	3067.0	...	1.0	2.0	120.0	142.0	2014.0

5 rows × 21 columns

Figure 1.20: *Load the data and print the first five rows of the DataFrame*

Now, let's see how we can use some of the parameters to customize the reading process.

- **header**: If we want to use a different row as the column names, we can pass the row number to this parameter. For example, if we want to use the second row as the column names, we can pass **header=1**.

```
# Read data from the CSV file with a different header row
df = pd.read_csv("housing.csv", header=1)


# Print the first 5 rows of the DataFrame
df.head()
```

Output:

Figure 1.21: *Read data with different header*

We can see that pandas used the second row as the column names and skipped the first row. Note that this will also change the number of rows in the DataFrame.

- **index_col**: If we want to use a specific column as the index, we can pass the column name or number to this parameter. For example, if we want to use the name column as the index, we can pass **index_col="Date"**.

```
# Read data from the CSV file with a specific index column
df = pd.read_csv("housing.csv", index_col="Date")


# Print the first 5 rows of the DataFrame
df.head()
```

Output:

Date	Suburb	Address	Rooms	Type	Price	Method	SellerG	Distance	Postcode	Bedroom2	Bathroom	Car	Landsize	BuildingArea
3/12/2016	Abbotsford	85 Turner St	2	h	1480000.0	S	Biggin	2.5	3067.0	2.0	1.0	1.0	202.0	NaN
4/02/2016	Abbotsford	25 Bloomburg St	2	h	1035000.0	S	Biggin	2.5	3067.0	2.0	1.0	0.0	156.0	79.0
4/03/2017	Abbotsford	5 Charles St	3	h	1465000.0	SP	Biggin	2.5	3067.0	3.0	2.0	0.0	134.0	150.0
4/03/2017	Abbotsford	40 Federation La	3	h	850000.0	PI	Biggin	2.5	3067.0	3.0	2.0	1.0	94.0	NaN
4/06/2016	Abbotsford	55a Park St	4	h	1600000.0	VB	Nelson	2.5	3067.0	3.0	1.0	2.0	120.0	142.0

Figure 1.22: *Read data with specific index column*

We can see that pandas used the Date column as the index and dropped it from the columns.

- **usecols**: If we want to read only selected columns from the CSV file, we can pass a list of column names or numbers to this parameter. For example, if we want to read only the name and age columns, we can pass **usecols=["Rooms", "age"]**.

```
# Read data from the CSV file with only selected columns
df = pd.read_csv("housing.csv", usecols=["Rooms", "Landsize"])


# Print the first 5 rows of the DataFrame
df.head()
```

Output:

	Rooms	Landsize
0	2	202.0
1	2	156.0
2	3	134.0
3	3	94.0
4	4	120.0

Figure 1.23: *Read data with selected columns*

We can see that pandas read only the Rooms and Landsize columns and ignored the gender column.

- **dtype**: If we want to specify the data type of each column in the DataFrame, we can pass a dictionary of column names and data types to this parameter. For example, if we want to convert the age column to float and the gender column to category, we can pass **dtype={"Landsize": int, "Type": "category"}**.

```
df = pd.read_csv("housing.csv")
```

```
df.info()
```

Output:

```
<class 'pandas.core.frame.DataFrame'>
RangeIndex: 13580 entries, 0 to 13579
Data columns (total 21 columns):
 #   Column         Non-Null Count  Dtype
---  ------         --------------  -----
 0   Suburb         13580 non-null  object
 1   Address        13580 non-null  object
 2   Rooms          13580 non-null  int64
 3   Type           13580 non-null  object
 4   Price          13580 non-null  float64
 5   Method         13580 non-null  object
 6   SellerG        13580 non-null  object
 7   Date           13580 non-null  object
 8   Distance       13580 non-null  float64
 9   Postcode       13580 non-null  float64
 10  Bedroom2       13580 non-null  float64
 11  Bathroom       13580 non-null  float64
 12  Car            13518 non-null  float64
 13  Landsize       13580 non-null  float64
 14  BuildingArea   7130 non-null   float64
 15  YearBuilt      8205 non-null   float64
 16  CouncilArea    12211 non-null  object
 17  Lattitude      13580 non-null  float64
 18  Longtitude     13580 non-null  float64
 19  Regionname     13580 non-null  object
 20  Propertycount  13580 non-null  float64
dtypes: float64(12), int64(1), object(8)
memory usage: 2.2+ MB
```

Figure 1.24: *Displaying DataFrame information*

We can see that the dtype of **Landsize** is **Float** and **Type** is Object. The following example shows how to change the dtype of columns by passing the columns **Landsize** and **Type** as dictionary.

```
# Read data from the CSV file with specific data types for each column
df = pd.read_csv("housing.csv", dtype={"Landsize": int, "Type": "category"})
```

```
df[['Landsize','Type']].dtypes
```

Output:

```
Landsize        int32
Type         category
dtype: object
```

Figure 1.25: *Changing the data type of columns*

We can see that pandas has converted the **Landsize** column to integer and the Type column to category.

- **skiprows**: If we want to skip some rows from the beginning of the CSV file, we can pass a number or a list of numbers to this parameter. For example, if we want to skip the first two rows, we can pass **skiprows=2**.

Before skip rows:

```
#Read data from csv file
df = pd.read_csv("housing.csv")
```

```
# Print the first 5 rows of the DataFrame
df.head()
```

Output:

	Suburb	Address	Rooms	Type	Price	Method	SellerG	Date	Distance	Postcode	...	Bathroom	Car	Landsize	BuildingArea	YearBuilt
0	Abbotsford	85 Turner St	2	h	1480000.0	S	Biggin	3/12/2016	2.5	3067.0	...	1.0	1.0	202.0	NaN	NaN
1	Abbotsford	25 Bloomburg St	2	h	1035000.0	S	Biggin	4/02/2016	2.5	3067.0	...	1.0	0.0	156.0	79.0	1900.0
2	Abbotsford	5 Charles St	3	h	1465000.0	SP	Biggin	4/03/2017	2.5	3067.0	...	2.0	0.0	134.0	150.0	1900.0
3	Abbotsford	40 Federation La	3	h	850000.0	PI	Biggin	4/03/2017	2.5	3067.0	...	2.0	1.0	94.0	NaN	NaN
4	Abbotsford	55a Park St	4	h	1600000.0	VB	Nelson	4/06/2016	2.5	3067.0	...	1.0	2.0	120.0	142.0	2014.0

5 rows × 21 columns

***Figure 1.26**: Displays the first five rows*

After skipping the first two rows:

```
# Read data from the CSV file with some rows skipped from the beginning
df = pd.read_csv("housing.csv", skiprows=2)
```

```
# Print the first 5 rows of the DataFrame
df.head()
```

Output:

	Suburb	Address	Rooms	Type	Price	Method	SellerG	Date	Distance	Postcode	...	Bathroom	Car	Landsize	BuildingArea	YearBuilt			
	Abbotsford	25 Bloomburg St	2	h	1035000.0	S	Biggin	4/02/2016	2.5	3067.0	...	1.0	0.0	156.0	79.0	1900.0	Yarra	-37.8079 144.9934	Northern Metropolitan
0	Abbotsford	5 Charles St	3	h	1465000.0	SP	Biggin	4/03/2017	2.5	3067.0	...	2.0	0.0	134.0	150.0	1900.0	Yarra	-37.8093 144.9944	Northern Metropolitan
1	Abbotsford	40 Federation La	3	h	850000.0	PI	Biggin	4/03/2017	2.5	3067.0	...	2.0	1.0	94.0	NaN	NaN	Yarra	-37.7969 144.9969	Northern Metropolitan
2	Abbotsford	55a Park St	4	h	1600000.0	VB	Nelson	4/06/2016	2.5	3067.0	...	1.0	2.0	120.0	142.0	2014.0	Yarra	-37.8072 144.9941	Northern Metropolitan
3	Abbotsford	129 Charles St	2	h	941000.0	S	Jellis	7/05/2016	2.5	3067.0	...	1.0	0.0	181.0	NaN	NaN	Yarra	-37.8041 144.9953	Northern Metropolitan
4	Abbotsford	124 Yarra St	3	h	1876000.0	S	Nelson	7/05/2016	2.5	3067.0	...	2.0	0.0	245.0	210.0	1910.0	Yarra	-37.8024 144.9993	Northern Metropolitan

Figure 1.27: Skipping the first two rows

We can see that pandas has skipped the first two rows and read the rest of the CSV file.

- **nrows**: If we want to read only a certain number of rows from the CSV file, we can pass a number to this parameter. For example, if we want to read only the first two rows, we can pass **nrows=2**.

```
# Read data from the CSV file with only a certain number of rows
df = pd.read_csv("housing.csv", nrows=2)


# Print the first 5 rows of the DataFrame
df.head()
```

Output:

	Suburb	Address	Rooms	Type	Price	Method	SellerG	Date	Distance	Postcode	...	Bathroom	Car	Landsize	BuildingArea	YearBuilt
0	Abbotsford	85 Turner St	2	h	1480000.0	S	Biggin	3/12/2016	2.5	3067.0	...	1.0	1.0	202.0	NaN	NaN
1	Abbotsford	25 Bloomburg St	2	h	1035000.0	S	Biggin	4/02/2016	2.5	3067.0	...	1.0	0.0	156.0	79.0	1900.0

2 rows × 21 columns

Figure 1.28: Reading the first two rows

We can see that pandas has read only the first two rows and ignored the rest of the CSV file.

Loading Data from Excel Files Using `pandas.read_excel()`

Excel is a popular spreadsheet application that can store and manipulate tabular data. Excel files have the extension **.xls** or **.xlsx** and can contain multiple sheets or tabs. Pandas provides the **pandas.read_excel()** function to read data from Excel files into a DataFrame object.

To use **pandas.read_excel()**, you need to pass the file path or file-like object as the first argument. You can also specify other optional arguments to customize the behavior of the function, such as **sheet_name**, **header**, **index_col**, **names**, **usecols**, **skiprows**, **na_values**, and so on.

Here is an example of how to use **pandas.read_excel ()** to load an Excel file into a DataFrame:

```
# Read data from an Excel file
df = pd.read_excel("people.xlsx")
```

```
# Print the first 5 rows of the DataFrame
df.head()
```

Output:

	Name	Age	Gender
0	Alice	25	F
1	Bob	30	M
2	Charlie	35	M
3	Melanie	55	F

Figure 1.29: *Load an Excel file into a DataFrame*

We can see that pandas have automatically inferred the column names and datatypes from the Excel file. We can also access the attributes and methods of the DataFrame object to explore and manipulate the data further.

To access a specific sheet use **sheet_name** as an optional parameter

```
# Read data from a specific sheet of an Excel file
df = pd.read_excel("people.xlsx", sheet_name="female")
```

```
# Print the rows of the DataFrame
df.head()
```

Output:

	Name	Age	Gender
0	Alice	25	F
1	Bobby	30	F
2	Melanie	55	F
3	Jerry	18	F

Figure 1.30: *Load an Excel file from a specific sheet*

All the parameters we looked for **read_csv** also applies to **read_excel**.

Loading Data from HTML Tables Using `pandas.read_html()`

HyperText Markup Language (HTML) is a common file format for creating web pages. HTML files consist of tags that define the structure and content of the web page. HTML tables are used to display data in rows and columns. Pandas provides the **pandas.read_html()** function to read data from HTML tables into a list of DataFrame objects.

To use **pandas.read_html()**, you need to pass the file path, file-like object, or web URL as the first argument. You can also specify other optional arguments to customize the behavior of the function, such as **attrs**, **header**, **index_col**, **names**, **usecols**, **skiprows**, **na_values**, and so on.

Here is an example of how to use **pandas.read_html()** to load an HTML table from a web URL into a list of DataFrame objects:

```
# Read data from an HTML table from a web URL
```

```
dfs =pd.read_html("https://en.wikipedia.org/wiki/List_of_countries_by_
population")
```

```
# Print the number of DataFrames in the list
```

```
print(len(dfs))
```

```
# Print the first DataFrame in the list
```

```
dfs[1]
```

Output:

	Rank	Country / Dependency	Population		Date	Source (official or from the United Nations)	Notes
	Rank	Country / Dependency	Numbers	% of the world	Date	Source (official or from the United Nations)	Notes
0	–	World	8035830000	100%	14 Jun 2023	UN projection[3]	NaN
1	1	China	1411750000	NaN	31 Dec 2022	Official estimate[4]	[b]
2	2	India	1392329000	NaN	1 Mar 2023	Official projection[5]	[c]
3	3	United States	334886000	NaN	14 Jun 2023	National population clock[7]	[d]
4	4	Indonesia	277749853	NaN	31 Dec 2022	Official estimate[8]	NaN
...	...	...	...	...	...	...	...
237	–	Tokelau (New Zealand)	1647	NaN	1 Jan 2019	2019 Census [211]	NaN
238	–	Niue	1549	NaN	1 Jul 2021	National annual projection[96]	NaN
239	195	Vatican City	825	NaN	1 Feb 2019	Monthly national estimate[212]	[af]
240	–	Cocos (Keeling) Islands (Australia)	593	NaN	30 Jun 2020	2021 Census[213]	NaN
241	–	Pitcairn Islands (United Kingdom)	47	NaN	1 Jul 2021	Official estimate[214]	NaN

242 rows × 7 columns

Figure 1.31: *Load an HTML file from a web URL*

Conclusion

This chapter provides a comprehensive overview of pandas and its role in data analysis. It covers the usage of IPython Notebooks, explores the core objects Series and DataFrame, explains data types in pandas, and guides through loading data from files and the web in various formats.

In the next chapter, we will take a closer look at Pandas Series. We will learn how to create a Series from different data structures, assigning custom index labels, analyzing size, shape, uniqueness, and value counts. We will even explore arithmetic operations, filtering, and handling special cases, such as NaN values.

Questions

1. What are the steps involved in installing and setting up pandas on your system?

2. Install Jupyter Notebook and explore the Jupyterlab Interface.

3. What is the difference between Series and DataFrame?

4. Name three common data types supported by pandas and explain their characteristics.

5. True or False: Pandas supports loading data from Excel files. Justify your answer.

CHAPTER 2
Pandas Series

In the previous chapter, we explored the fundamentals of the pandas library and learned about its key data structures: the Series and Dataframes object. Now, let's delve deeper into what a Series object is and its significance in data analysis.

In this chapter, we will explore the concept of a Pandas Series and cover a range of topics related to its creation, manipulation, and analysis.

Structure

In this chapter, we will discuss the following topics:

- Pandas Series
- Key Differences between Pandas Series and Python List or NumPy Array
- Creating a Series from a List, Array, Dictionary, or other Data Structure
- Series Custom Index Labels
- Assigning a Name to a Series
- Analyzing Size, Shape, Uniqueness, and Value Counts in a Pandas Series
- Analyzing Data with Head, Tail, and Sample
- Indexing and Selecting Data
- Arithmetic Operations with Series
- Filtering Data with Series
- The special case of Not-A-Number (NaN)

Pandas Series

As a quick recap, a Series is a one-dimensional labeled array provided by the pandas library. It is capable of holding data of any type, including integers, floats, strings, and so on. The primary components of a Series are the index and the data array.

The index serves as the labels or identifiers for each element in the Series. By default, the index is a sequence of integers starting from 0, but it can be customized to use any hashable type, such as strings or dates. The index allows for intuitive access and manipulation of the data based on meaningful labels rather than just numeric positions.

The data array, on the other hand, holds the actual values or observations associated with each index label. This array can be a NumPy array, a Python list, or any other sequence-like object. The data array is aligned with the index, meaning that each element in the data array corresponds to a specific label in the index. This alignment enables efficient and intuitive data manipulation and analysis.

The key features of a Pandas Series include:

- **Size and Shape:** A Series has a fixed size and shape once created. It can hold a specific number of elements and is immutable.

- **Data Alignment:** Series automatically aligns data based on the index labels, allowing for efficient and consistent operations even when working with multiple Series objects.

- **Flexible Indexing:** Series supports various indexing techniques, including positional indexing, label-based indexing, and Boolean indexing, enabling easy data retrieval and manipulation.

- **Vectorized Operations:** Series leverages the underlying NumPy array and provides vectorized operations, allowing for efficient computations on large datasets.

- **Missing Data Handling**: Series handles missing data by representing them as NaN (Not-a-Number) values, providing methods to handle and manipulate missing values effectively.

- **Integration with Pandas Ecosystem:** Series seamlessly integrates with other Pandas data structures, such as DataFrames, enabling comprehensive data analysis and manipulation.

Furthermore, the Series object provides a wide range of functionalities and methods to manipulate and analyze the data. We can perform operations such as indexing, slicing, filtering, sorting, aggregating, and computing statistics on the Series. These operations enable us to extract meaningful insights, identify patterns, and make informed decisions based on the data contained within the Series.

Key Differences Between Pandas Series and Python List or NumPy Array

In this section, we will explore the key differences between Pandas Series and Python lists or NumPy arrays. While Python lists and NumPy arrays are fundamental data structures in Python, Pandas Series offers additional functionality and optimizations specifically designed for data analysis tasks. Understanding the following differences is crucial for leveraging the power and capabilities of Pandas Series effectively:

- **Heterogeneous Data:** While both Python lists and NumPy arrays can contain elements of different data types, Pandas Series is designed to handle homogeneous data. It allows for efficient storage and manipulation of data of a single type. This specialization enables optimized computations and operations on the data within a Series.

- **Labeled Indexing:** One of the distinctive features of Pandas Series is the ability to assign labels, known as the index, to each element. This labeled indexing provides meaningful and intuitive access to data points, making it easier to retrieve and manipulate specific values based on their index labels. In contrast, Python lists and NumPy arrays primarily use positional indexing.

- **Additional Functionality:** Pandas Series offers a wide range of additional functionality compared to Python lists and NumPy arrays. It includes powerful data manipulation and analysis methods, such as data alignment, missing data handling, statistical functions, time series functionality, etc. These features make Pandas Series a versatile and efficient tool for data analysis and manipulation tasks.

- **Performance:** Pandas Series, being built on top of NumPy, provides high-performance data structures and operations. While Python lists offer flexibility, they may be slower when dealing with large datasets due to their dynamic nature. NumPy arrays and Pandas Series, on the other hand, provide optimized operations that leverage low-level optimizations for faster computations.

- **Missing Data Handling:** Pandas Series has built-in support for handling missing data through the use of NaN (Not-a-Number) values. It provides methods to easily detect, filter, fill, or drop missing values, allowing for robust data analysis and manipulation. Python lists and NumPy arrays do not have native support for missing data handling.

Creating a Series from a List, Array, Dictionary, or Other Data Structure

Pandas Series provides a convenient way to create a one-dimensional labeled data structure from various data types. You can pass lists, arrays, dictionaries, sets, tuples, or other iterable objects to the **pd.Series()** function, and it will convert them into a Series object with default or custom index labels. This flexibility allows you to work with different data structures seamlessly within the Pandas framework.

Following are the import statements. In Python, most functionality is provided by modules. To use a module in your program, you first have to import it. Here we're importing two modules – pandas and numpy. The as **pd** and as **np** parts are optional and serve to give aliases to these modules for convenience. Now you can use **pd** and **np** in your code instead of writing out pandas and numpy.

```
Import pandas as pd
```

```
Import numpy as np
```

Creating a Series from a List

A list is a built-in data type that can be used to store multiple items in a single variable. Lists are created by placing all the items (elements) inside square brackets [], separated by commas. It can have any number of items and they may be of different types (integer, float, string, and so on).

Here's an example of a list:

```
my_list = ["Apple", "Banana", "Cherry"]
```

You can create a Pandas Series from a list. The elements of the list become the values in the Series, and an index will be automatically created. Here's an example:

```
my_list = ["Apple", "Banana", "Cherry"]
my_series = pd.Series(my_list)
print(my_series)
```

Output:

```
0      Apple
1      Banana
2      Cherry
dtype: object
```

Figure 2.1: *Creating a Series from the list*

In this code, we first create a list, **my_list,** containing three elements. We then pass this list to the **pd.Series()** function, which converts it into a Series object. The indices are generated automatically, starting from 0 to n-1.

The left column of the output displays the index of the Series. By default, when creating a Series from a list, an index is automatically generated as a sequence of integers starting from 0.

The right column of the output displays the values of the Series. These values were created from the elements of the list.

The **dtype:** object at the bottom indicates the data type of the Series. This Series contains strings, so the dtype is object, which is the name pandas uses for strings.

Creating a Series from an Array

An array is a data structure that can hold values of the same type. In Python, arrays are not as widely used as lists, but they can be more efficient for numerical operations if the items in the array are of a uniform type, like integers or floating-point numbers.

However, in the context of data analysis in Python, when we refer to arrays, we are usually referring to numpy arrays. NumPy is a library in Python that provides a multidimensional array object and a variety of routines for fast operations on arrays, including mathematical, logical, shape manipulation, sorting, selecting, and so on.

Here's an example of a numpy array:

```
my_array = np.array([10, 20, 30, 40, 50])
```

You can create a Pandas Series from a numpy array. The elements of the array become the values in the Series, and an index will be automatically created. Here's an example:

```
# Creating a numpy array
my_array = np.array([10, 20, 30, 40, 50])


# Creating a Series from the numpy array
series_from_array = pd.Series(my_array)
print(series_from_array)
```

Output:

```
0    10
1    20
2    30
3    40
4    50
dtype: int32
```

Figure 2.2: *Creating a Series from numpy array*

Numpy array is created with the **np.array()** function, which contains the elements **[10, 20, 30, 40, 50]** and is stored in the **my_array** variable. This numpy array is then converted into a pandas Series using the **pd.Series()** function and assigned to the **series_from_array** variable.

The left column of the output displays the index of the Series. By default, when creating a Series from a numpy array, an index is automatically generated as a sequence of integers starting from 0.

The right column of the output displays the values of the Series. These values were created from the values of the numpy array.

The **dtype: int64** at the bottom indicates the data type of the Series. This Series contains integers, so the dtype is int64, which represents 64-bit integer types.

Creating a Series from a Dictionary

A dictionary is an unordered collection of items. Each item is stored as a key-value pair. The keys in a dictionary are unique and are used to access the corresponding values. The keys and values can be of any data type. Here's a simple example of a dictionary:

```
my_dict = {
    "Name": "Alice",
    "Age": 25,
    "Occupation": "Engineer"
}
```

In this dictionary, "**Name**", "**Age**", and "**Occupation**" are the keys, and "**Alice**", **25**, and "**Engineer**" are the corresponding values.

You can create a Pandas Series from a dictionary. The keys of the dictionary become the index (or labels) of the Series, and the values of the dictionary become the corresponding values in the Series. Here's an example:

```
my_dict = {
    "Name": "Alice",
    "Age": 25,
    "Occupation": "Engineer"
}


my_series = pd.Series(my_dict)
print(my_series)
```

Output:

```
Name          Alice
Age              25
Occupation   Engineer
dtype: object
```

Figure 2.3: *Output: creating a Series from a dictionary*

A dictionary is created with key-value pairs where "**Name**" maps to "**Alice**", "**Age**" maps to 25, and "**Occupation**" maps to "**Engineer**". This dictionary is stored in the **my_dict** variable. The dictionary **my_dict** is then converted into a pandas Series using the **pd.Series()** function and the result is assigned to the **my_series** variable.

The left column of the output displays the index of the Series. The index was created from the keys of the dictionary.

The right column of the output displays the values of the Series. These values were created from the values of the dictionary.

The **dtype: object** at the bottom indicates the data type of the Series. The "**object**" dtype is used in pandas to denote a column that contains strings (or more generally, any Python object), but in this case, it's used because the Series contains mixed data types. "**Alice**" is a string, and 25 is an integer. If a Series contains mixed types, pandas will default to using the "**object**" type.

Creating a Series from a Tuple

A tuple is similar to a list. The difference between the two is that a tuple is immutable, which means you can't change the elements of a tuple once it is assigned. A tuple is a collection of Python objects separated by commas. In some ways, a tuple is similar to a list in terms of indexing, nested objects, and repetition. However, unlike lists, tuples are immutable.

Tuples are created by placing all the items (elements) inside parentheses **()**, separated by commas.

Here's an example of a tuple:

```
my_tuple = ("Apple", "Banana", "Cherry")
```

You can create a Pandas Series from a tuple. The elements of the tuple become the values in the Series, and an index will be automatically created. Here's an example:

```
my_tuple = ("Apple", "Banana", "Cherry")
my_series = pd.Series(my_tuple)
print(my_series)
```

Output:

```
0    Apple
1    Banana
2    Cherry
dtype: object
```

Figure 2.4: Creating a series from tuple

A tuple is created with the elements "**Apple**", "**Banana**", and "**Cherry**" and is stored in the **my_tuple** variable. This tuple is then converted into a pandas Series using the **pd.Series()** function and the result is assigned to the **my_series** variable. In the resultant pandas Series, the index is automatically generated starting from 0, and the corresponding values from the tuple become the data in the Series.

Creating a Series from a CSV files

To create a Series from a CSV file, pandas library provides the **read_csv()** function, which allows you to read data from a CSV file and convert it into a Series.

1. **Load the CSV file**: Use the **read_csv()** function provided by pandas to load the CSV file into a DataFrame:

   ```
   df = pd.read_csv("housing.csv")
   df.head()
   ```

Output:

	Suburb	Address	Rooms	Type	Price	Method	SellerG	Date	Distance	Postcode	...	Bathroom	Car	Landsize	BuildingArea	YearBuilt
0	Abbotsford	85 Turner St	2	h	1480000.0	S	Biggin	3/12/2016	2.5	3067.0	...	1.0	1.0	202.0	NaN	NaN
1	Abbotsford	25 Bloomburg St	2	h	1035000.0	S	Biggin	4/02/2016	2.5	3067.0	...	1.0	0.0	156.0	79.0	1900.0
2	Abbotsford	5 Charles St	3	h	1465000.0	SP	Biggin	4/03/2017	2.5	3067.0	...	2.0	0.0	134.0	150.0	1900.0
3	Abbotsford	40 Federation La	3	h	850000.0	PI	Biggin	4/03/2017	2.5	3067.0	...	2.0	1.0	94.0	NaN	NaN
4	Abbotsford	55a Park St	4	h	1600000.0	VB	Nelson	4/06/2016	2.5	3067.0	...	1.0	2.0	120.0	142.0	2014.0

5 rows × 21 columns

Figure 2.5: *Reading a CSV file and storing in a Dataframe*

2. **Create a Series from a column**: Extract a specific column from the DataFrame and convert it into a Series. You can use the column name or index position to specify the column:

   ```
   series = df['Rooms']
   series.head()
   ```

Output:

```
0    2
1    2
2    3
3    3
4    4
Name: Rooms, dtype: int64
```

Figure 2.6: *Creating a Series from CSV file*

Alternatively, you can use the column index to create the Series. For example, if the column you want to extract is at index 1:

```
series = df.iloc[:, 2]
series.head()
```

Output:

```
0    2
1    2
2    3
3    3
4    4
Name: Rooms, dtype: int64
```

Figure 2.7: Creating a Series using column index

Series Custom Index Labels

In pandas, a custom index refers to user-defined labels or identifiers assigned to the elements of a Series. It allows us to assign labels that have specific meaning or context in their data domain. Instead of relying on default numerical indices, custom labels enhance data representation, accessibility, and interpretability.

Creating Custom Index Labels

Creating custom index labels for a Series in pandas is straightforward. It can be done during the initialization of the Series or by modifying an existing Series. Here's an example of creating a custom index:

```
data = [10, 20, 30, 40]
index = ['A', 'B', 'C', 'D']

series = pd.Series(data, index=index)
series
```

Output:

```
A    10
B    20
C    30
D    40
dtype: int64
```

Figure 2.8: Creating a Series using custom index labels

In the aforementioned example, we define a list of data values **[10, 20, 30, 40]** and assign custom index labels **['A', 'B', 'C', 'D']** to create a Series. We use the index parameter of the **pd.Series()** constructor to specify the custom index labels.

Utilizing Custom Index Labels

Once the custom index labels are assigned, they can be utilized for various operations on the Series, including data retrieval, slicing, mathematical operations, merging, and so on.

```
print(series['A'])
print(series['C'])

10
30
```

Figure 2.9: *Retrieving series using custom indexes*

We can see from the preceding figure that the data retrieve at Index A is 10 and Index C is 30.

Importance of Custom Index Labels

Custom index labels refer to the practice of assigning user-defined or custom names or identifiers to the indices of data elements within a data structure, such as arrays, data frames, or database tables. The theory behind the importance of custom index labels lies in enhancing the readability, interpretability, and usability of the data, which, in turn, can lead to more effective data analysis and decision-making. Here are some key aspects of why custom index labels are considered essential:

- **Improved Readability**: Custom index labels provide a more descriptive representation of the data, making it easier to understand and interpret. They allow users to quickly identify and refer to specific data points without relying on numeric positions.

  Let's consider the following example:

```
# Create a Series with default numerical indices
   series_default = pd.Series([85, 92, 78, 90, 88])


# Create a Series with custom index labels
   series_custom = pd.Series([85, 92, 78, 90, 88], index=['Math',
   'English',   'Science', 'History', 'Art'])


print("Series with default numerical indices:")
print(series_default)
print("\nSeries with custom index labels:")
print(series_custom)
```

Output:

```
Series with default numerical indices:
0    85
1    92
2    78
3    90
4    88
dtype: int64

Series with custom index labels:
Math       85
English    92
Science    78
History    90
Art        88
dtype: int64
```

Figure 2.10: *Creating Series with custom labels to improve readability*

In the aforementioned example, we create two Series: one with default numerical indices **(series_default)** and another with custom index labels **(series_custom)**.

By assigning custom index labels such as **'Math'**, **'English'**, **'Science'**, **'History'**, and **'Art'** to the elements of **series_custom**, the code becomes more readable and self-explanatory. The custom labels provide a clear indication of what each element represents, in this case, representing grades in different subjects.

With the custom index labels, it is easier to understand and interpret the data. For example, it is clear that the **series_custom** grade **'92'** in the represents the grade in **'English'**. This makes the code more intuitive and eliminates the need to remember or reference numerical indices.

- **Contextual Information**: Contextual information refers to additional details or metadata associated with data that provide a deeper understanding of its meaning or relevance. In the context of a pandas Series, custom index labels can serve as a source of contextual information, offering insights into the data domain. Here's an example that demonstrates contextual information using Python code:

```
# Define stock prices
prices = [100.50, 102.20, 98.75, 101.80, 99.45]


# Define custom index labels as dates
dates = ['2023-06-20', '2023-06-21', '2023-06-22', '2023-06-23',
'2023-06-24']


# Create a Series with custom index labels representing stock
prices
```

```
stocks = pd.Series(prices, index=pd.to_datetime(dates))


print("Stock prices with contextual information:")
print(stocks)
```

Output:

```
Stock prices with contextual information:
2023-06-20    100.50
2023-06-21    102.20
2023-06-22     98.75
2023-06-23    101.80
2023-06-24     99.45
dtype: float64
```

Figure 2.11: Creating Series with custom labels to improve readability

In the aforementioned example, we define a list of stock prices (**prices**) and a list of corresponding dates (**dates**). We use **pd.to_datetime()** to convert the dates to a datetime format (we will be looking into pandas datetime in the upcoming chapter so, for now, ignore the **to_datetime()**), ensuring the proper handling of dates in the Series. The resulting Series, stocks, incorporate custom index labels representing the dates.

By incorporating custom index labels that represent dates, the **stocks** Series gains contextual information. Each stock price now corresponds to a specific date, facilitating time-based analysis and providing temporal context to the data. This enables us to understand the historical trend, identify price fluctuations, or perform time series analysis with ease.

For example, we can retrieve the stock price for a specific date:

```
print(stocks['2023-06-21'])

102.2
```

Figure 2.12: Retrieving stock price for a specific date

By using custom index labels that provide contextual information, we gain a better understanding of the data and can perform meaningful analysis.

- **Enhanced Data Accessibility**: Custom index labels enable more natural and intuitive access to data elements. Users can retrieve specific values using labels that are familiar to them, making the code more readable and reducing the chance of errors. Here's an example that demonstrates Enhanced Data Accessibility using Python code:

```
# Create a Series with default numerical indices
series_default = pd.Series([10, 20, 30, 40])
```

```
# Create a Series with custom index labels
series_custom = pd.Series([10, 20, 30, 40], index=['A', 'B', 'C',
'D'])

print("Series with default numerical indices:")
print(series_default)
print("\nSeries with custom index labels:")
print(series_custom)
```

Output:

```
Series with default numerical indices:
0    10
1    20
2    30
3    40
dtype: int64

Series with custom index labels:
A    10
B    20
C    30
D    40
dtype: int64
```

Figure 2.13: Numeric and custom index

In the aforementioned example, we create two Series: one with default numerical indices (**series_default**) and another with custom index labels (**series_custom**).

Custom index labels enhance data accessibility by allowing us to retrieve specific elements using intuitive labels. This makes the code more readable and reduces the chances of errors.

For example, let's say we want to access the second element of the Series. With the custom index labels, it is more intuitive and straightforward:

```
print(series_custom['B'])
20
```

Figure 2.14: Retrieving second element with custom index

Using custom index labels, we can directly refer to the data point associated with a specific label. This simplifies data retrieval and makes the code more readable and self-explanatory.

On the other hand, if we want to access the second element in the Series with default numerical indices, we will need to remember and reference the index position:

```
print(series_default[1])

20
```

Figure 2.15: *Retrieving second element with default index*

By utilizing custom index labels, we improve data accessibility by providing a more intuitive and direct way to access specific elements. This can be particularly useful when working with large datasets or when the data points have meaningful labels that are easier to remember and work with.

Assigning a Name to a Series

In data analysis, assigning a name to a Series is a fundamental task that enhances the clarity and context of the data. By providing a descriptive label or identifier, a named Series improves code readability, facilitates data interpretation, and simplifies collaborative efforts. In this section, we will explore the importance of assigning a name to a Series and discuss various approaches to accomplish this task.

Approaches to Assigning a Name

There are multiple ways to assign a name to a **Series** in pandas. Here are a few common approaches:

1. **Assigning a Name During Initialization:**

   ```
   series = pd.Series([10, 20, 30, 40], name='MySeries')
   ```

In this approach, the **name** parameter is used during the initialization of the Series to assign a name directly.

2. **Assigning a Name Using the name Attribute:**

   ```
   series = pd.Series([10, 20, 30, 40])
   series.name = 'MySeries'
   ```

This approach involves assigning a **name** to the name attribute of an existing Series.

3. **Assigning a Name When Extracting a Series from a DataFrame:**

   ```
   df = pd.DataFrame({'A': [10, 20, 30, 40]})
   series = df['A']
   series.name = 'MySeries'
   ```

This approach involves extracting a Series from a DataFrame and assigning a name to the extracted Series using the **name** attribute.

Analyzing Size, Shape, Uniqueness, and Value Counts in a Pandas Series

In this section, we will explore the concepts of size, shape, uniqueness, and value counts, which are essential for understanding the characteristics of the data stored within a Series. By examining these aspects, we can extract valuable information and draw meaningful conclusions from our data.

Size of a Series

The size of a **Series** refers to the total number of elements it contains. It provides a quick way to determine the overall quantity of data present in the **Series**. The size of a **Series** can be obtained using the **len()** function or the **Series.size** attribute.

```
series = pd.Series([10, 20, 30, 40, 50])

size = len(series)

print("Size of the Series:", size)
```

Output:

```
Size of the Series: 5
```

Figure 2.16: Size of a series

In the above example, we create a Pandas Series with five elements. To determine the size of the **Series**, we use the **len()** function, which returns the total number of elements in the **Series**. The size of the Series is then printed, resulting in an output of 5.

The size of a Series is an important metric as it indicates the amount of data available for analysis. It helps in understanding the extent of the dataset and can be used for various purposes, such as determining memory usage or evaluating the scale of the data.

It's important to note that the size of a Series does not refer to the memory size or the number of bytes consumed by the Series. Instead, it represents the count of elements in the Series. If you need to check the memory usage of a Series, you can utilize the **Series.memory_usage()** method.

Shape of a Series

The shape of a Series represents its dimensions, indicating the number of rows and columns in the Series. Since a Series is one-dimensional, its shape consists of only one dimension. The shape of a Series can be obtained using the **Series.shape** attribute.

```
series = pd.Series([10, 20, 30, 40, 50])
```

```
# Obtaining the shape of the Series
shape = series.shape
print("Shape of the Series:", shape)
```

Output:

```
Shape of the Series: (5,)
```

Figure 2.17: Shape of a series

The shape attribute returns a tuple that represents the dimensions of the Series. Since a Series is one-dimensional, its shape consists of only one dimension. In this case, the output is (**5,**), indicating that the Series has 5 elements in its single dimension.

The shape of a Series can be particularly useful when working with multidimensional data structures like DataFrames, where you may have multiple rows and columns. However, since a Series is one-dimensional, its shape will always consist of only one element.

Uniqueness in a Series

Uniqueness refers to the presence of unique elements within a Series. It allows us to identify distinct values and understand the variety or diversity in the data. We can check the uniqueness of a Series using the **Series.unique()** method, which returns an array of unique values.

```
series = pd.Series([10, 20, 30, 40, 50, 10, 20])
```

```
# Obtaining the unique values in the Series
unique_values = series.unique()
print("Unique values in the Series:", unique_values)
```

Output:

```
Unique values in the Series: [10 20 30 40 50]
```

Figure 2.18: Unique values in a series

In the preceding code, we create a Pandas Series **series** with seven elements, including some duplicate values. To identify the unique values in the Series, we use the **Series.unique()** method.

The **unique()** method returns an array that contains only the unique elements from the Series. In this case, the output is **[10 20 30 40 50]**, indicating that these are the distinct values present in the Series. The duplicate values are eliminated, and only the unique values are retained.

The ability to determine unique values in a Series is crucial for understanding the variety and distribution of data. It allows you to identify the distinct elements and analyze their occurrence or frequency. This information can be valuable when performing data exploration, data cleaning, or when identifying patterns or anomalies within the dataset.

Value Counts in a Series

Value counts provide a tabulation of the frequency of each unique value in a Series. It helps in understanding the distribution and occurrence of different values. The **Series.value_counts()** method generates a new Series, where each unique value in the original Series is paired with its count.

```
series = pd.Series([10, 20, 30, 40, 50, 10, 20, 30, 20])
```

```
# Obtaining the value counts in the Series
value_counts = series.value_counts()
print("Value counts in the Series:\n", value_counts)
```

Output:

```
Value counts in the Series:
  20    3
  10    2
  30    2
  40    1
  50    1
  dtype: int64
```

Figure 2.19: Value counts

In the above example, the **value_counts()** method returns a new Series where each unique value from the original Series is paired with its count. The unique values become the index labels, and the count of each value becomes the corresponding data component. The resulting Series is sorted in descending order based on the count.

The output indicates that the value **20** occurs **three** times in the Series, **30** and **10** occur **twice**, while **50** and **40** occur only **once**.

Value counts are particularly useful for analyzing the distribution and occurrence of different values within a Series. It provides a quick summary of the data, highlighting the most common values and their frequencies. This information can help in understanding patterns, identifying outliers, or making data-driven decisions.

Analyzing Data with Head, Tail, and Sample

When working with data, it's essential to get a quick overview of the dataset before diving into further analysis. Pandas provides several methods to help you look at data, including **head()**, **tail()**, and **sample()**. These methods allow you to examine the initial rows, last rows, and obtain random samples from a DataFrame or Series.

head()

The **head()** method allows you to view the first few rows of the data. By default, it displays the top 5 rows, but you can specify the number of rows to display by passing an argument.

```
# Create a Series
series = pd.Series([10, 20, 30, 40, 50, 60, 70, 80, 90, 100])


# Display the default head (first 5 rows)
default_head = series.head()
print("Default head:\n", default_head)
```

Output:

```
Default head:
 0    10
 1    20
 2    30
 3    40
 4    50
dtype: int64
```

Figure 2.20: *Displaying the first five rows*

In the preceding code, we create a Pandas Series **series** with ten elements. By using the **head()** method without passing any argument, we retrieve the default head of the Series, which is the first 5 rows.

The output shows the **first 5** elements of the Series along with their corresponding index labels. In this case, the Series starts from index position 0 and continues up to index position 4.

You can also specify a different number of rows to display by passing an argument to the **head()** method. For example, if you want to display the first 3 rows, you can modify the code as follows:

```
custom_head = series.head(3)
print("Custom head:\n", custom_head)
```

Output:

```
Custom head:
 0    10
 1    20
 2    30
dtype: int64
```

Figure 2.21: Displaying three rows

In this case, the **head(3)** method returns the **first 3** rows of the Series, starting from index position 0.

tail()

The **tail()** method allows you to examine the last few rows of the data. By default, it displays the last 5 rows, but you can specify the number of rows to display. This is helpful when you want to check the concluding rows of the dataset.

```
# Display the default tail (last 5 rows)
default_tail = series.tail()
print("Default tail:\n", default_tail)
```

Output:

```
Default tail:
 5     60
 6     70
 7     80
 8     90
 9    100
dtype: int64
```

Figure 2.22: Displaying the last five rows

By using the **tail()** method without passing any argument, we retrieve the default tail of the Series, which is the last 5 rows.

The output shows the last 5 elements of the Series along with their corresponding index labels. In this case, the Series ends with index position **9** and goes backward up to index position **5**.

You can also specify a different number of rows to display by passing an argument to the **tail()** method. For example, if you want to display the last 3 rows, you can modify the code as follows:

```
custom_tail = series.tail(3)

print("Custom tail:\n", custom_tail)
```

Output:

```
Custom tail:
 7     80
 8     90
 9    100
dtype: int64
```

Figure 2.23: *Displaying three rows*

In this case, the **tail(3)** method returns the last 3 rows of the Series, starting from index position **7**.

sample()

The **sample()** method enables you to obtain random samples from the data. You can specify the number of samples to retrieve, allowing for randomized exploration of the dataset. This is beneficial for conducting exploratory analysis or verifying data patterns.

```
# Obtain a random sample of 3 elements

sample_data = series.sample(3)

print("Random sample from the Series:\n", sample_data)
```

Output:

```
Random sample from the Series:
 0    10
 3    40
 6    70
dtype: int64
```

Figure 2.24: *Displaying random rows*

In the preceding code, we create a Pandas Series **series** with ten elements. By using the **sample()** method and passing an argument of **3**, we obtain a random sample of 3 elements from the Series.

The output displays the randomly selected elements along with their corresponding index labels. In this case, three random elements from the Series are returned.

Indexing and Selecting Data

Indexing and selecting data in a Pandas Series involve accessing specific elements or subsets of elements based on various criteria such as labels, positions, conditions, or combinations thereof. The primary methods for indexing and selecting data in a Series are as follows:

- **Indexing with square brackets ([ ])**: The square bracket notation allows you to access elements in a **Series** using labels or positions.

  o **Label-based indexing**: You can use labels to retrieve specific elements or subsets of elements from a **Series**. For example:

  ```
  s = pd.Series([1, 2, 3, 4, 5], index=['A', 'B', 'C', 'D', 'E'])


  # Accessing a single element by label
  element = s['B']
  print('single element by label',element)
  print(' ')


  # Accessing multiple elements by labels
  subset = s[['A', 'C', 'E']]
  print('multiple elements by labels\n', subset)
  ```

Output:

```
single element by label 2

multiple elements by labels
 A    1
 C    3
 E    5
dtype: int64
```

Figure 2.25: Label-based indexing

In this example, we have a Series s with values **[1, 2, 3, 4, 5]** and corresponding labels **['A', 'B', 'C', 'D', 'E']**. Using square brackets, we can access specific elements. For instance, s['**B**'] retrieves the element with the label '**B**', which is 2. Similarly, **s[['A', 'C', 'E']]** returns a subset of the Series containing elements with labels '**A**', '**C**', and '**E**'.

  o **Position-based indexing: Position-based indexing involves accessing elements or subsets of elements from a Series using integer positions.**

```
# Accessing a single element by position
element = s[2]
print('single element by position', element)
print(' ')
# Accessing multiple elements by positions
subset = s[[0, 2, 4]]
print('multiple elements by positions\n', subset)
```

Output:

```
single element by position 3

multiple elements by positions
 A    1
 C    3
 E    5
dtype: int64
```

Figure 2.26: Position-based indexing

○ **loc:** The **loc** accessor allows for label-based indexing and selecting elements or subsets based on labels or label-based conditions. For example:

```
s = pd.Series([1, 2, 3, 4, 5], index=['A', 'B', 'C', 'D', 'E'])
```

```
# Accessing a single element by label
element = s.loc['B']
print('single element by label', element)
print(' ')
# Accessing multiple elements by labels
subset = s.loc[['A', 'C', 'E']]
print('multiple elements by labels\n',subset)
```

Output:

```
single element by label 2

multiple elements by labels
 A    1
 C    3
 E    5
dtype: int64
```

Figure 2.27: Fetching elements or subsets based on Label Indexing

In this example, we have a Series **s** with values **[1, 2, 3, 4, 5]** and corresponding labels **['A', 'B', 'C', 'D', 'E']**. The loc accessor allows us to access specific elements based on labels. Using **loc['B']** retrieves the element with the label 'B', which is 2. Similarly, **loc[['A', 'C', 'E']]** returns a subset of the Series containing elements with labels '**A**', '**C**', and '**E**'.

- o **iloc**: The **iloc** accessor enables position-based indexing and selecting elements or subsets based on integer positions or position-based conditions. For example:

```
# Accessing a single element by position
element = s.iloc[2]
print('single element by position',element)
print(' ')
# Accessing multiple elements by positions
subset = s.iloc[[0, 2, 4]]
print('multiple elements by positions/n',subset)
```

Output:

```
single element by position 3

multiple elements by positions/n A    1
C    3
E    5
dtype: int64
```

Figure 2.28: *Fetching elements or subsets based on position indexing*

In this example, we have a Series **s** with values **[1, 2, 3, 4, 5]**. The iloc accessor allows us to access specific elements based on their positions. Using **iloc[2]** retrieves the element at position 2, which is 3. Similarly, **iloc[[0, 2, 4]]** returns a subset of the Series containing elements at positions 0, 2, and 4.

Arithmetic Operations in Series

Arithmetic operations in Series refer to the mathematical computations we can perform on Series data structures. Just like you'd perform arithmetic operations on numbers, Pandas allows you to conduct these operations on Series, enabling you to add, subtract, multiply, or divide entire arrays of data in a single operation. It also supports more complex mathematical operations and functions.

Addition

The addition operator allows element-wise addition between two Series of the same length. Additionally, scalar addition can be performed, where a scalar value is added to each element of the Series.

Let's consider the following example:

```
# Create two pandas Series
s1 = pd.Series([2, 4, 6, 8, 10])
s2 = pd.Series([1, 3, 5, 7, 9])


# Perform addition operation
s3 = s1 + s2


# Print the result
print(s3)
```

Output:

```
0     3
1     7
2     11
3     15
4     19
dtype: int64
```

Figure 2.29: *Adding two series*

In this code, we create two Series: **s1** and **s2**. We then perform an addition operation on them and assign the result to **s3**. The result is a new Series, **s3**, where each element is the sum of the corresponding elements in **s1** and **s2**.

This operation is based on the index of the Series. So, the first element in **s1** (which is 2) is added to the first element in **s2** (which is 1), and the result (which is 3) is the first element in **s3**. This operation is repeated for every pair of corresponding elements in the two Series.

Subtraction (-)

Subtraction in Series is as simple as addition and works on an element-by-element basis. This means that the elements in the same positions (based on the index) in the series are subtracted from each other.

Let's look at the following example:

```
# Create two pandas Series
s1 = pd.Series([2, 4, 6, 8, 10])
s2 = pd.Series([1, 3, 5, 7, 9])


# Perform subtraction operation
```

```
s3 = s1 - s2


# Print the result
print(s3)
```

Output:

```
0    1
1    1
2    1
3    1
4    1
dtype: int64
```

Figure 2.30: *Subtracting two series*

In this code, we first create two Series: **s1** and **s2**. We then perform a subtraction operation on them and assign the result to **s3**. The resulting series, **s3**, contains elements that are the results of subtracting the corresponding elements in **s2** from **s1**.

This operation is based on the index of the Series. Therefore, the first element in s1 (which is 2) is subtracted by the first element in **s2** (which is 1), and the result (which is 1) is the first element in **s3**. This operation is repeated for every pair of corresponding elements in the two Series.

Multiplication (*)

Multiplication of Series in pandas can be performed by using the * operator. Similar to addition and subtraction, multiplication operates on an element-by-element basis. Here's an example:

```
s1 = pd.Series([2, 4, 6, 8, 10])
s2 = pd.Series([1, 3, 5, 7, 9])


# Perform multiplication operation
s3 = s1 * s2


# Print the result
print(s3)
```

Output:

```
0     2
1    12
2    30
3    56
4    90
dtype: int64
```

Figure 2.31: *Series multiplication*

In this code, we create two Series: **s1** and **s2**. We then perform a multiplication operation on them and assign the result to **s3**. The resulting series, **s3**, contains elements that are the product of the corresponding elements in **s1** and **s2**.

For instance, the first element in **s3** is the result of multiplying the first element in s1 by the first element in **s2** (2*1 = 2). This operation is repeated for every pair of corresponding elements in the two Series.

Division(/)

Division of Series in pandas can be performed by using the **/** operator and operates on an element-by-element basis. Here's an example:

```
s1 = pd.Series([2, 4, 6, 8, 10])
s2 = pd.Series([1, 2, 3, 4, 5])


# Perform division operation
s3 = s1 / s2


# Print the result
print(s3)
```

Output:

```
0    2.0
1    2.0
2    2.0
3    2.0
4    2.0
dtype: float64
```

Figure 2.32: Series division

In this code, we create two Series: **s1** and **s2**. We then perform a division operation on them and assign the result to **s3**. The resulting series, **s3**, contains elements that are the results of dividing the corresponding elements in **s1** by **s2**.

For instance, the first element in **s3** is the result of dividing the first element in s1 by the first element in **s2** (2 / 1 = 2.0). This operation is repeated for every pair of corresponding elements in the two Series.

Modulo Operation (%)

This operation will give the remainder of the division between two Series on an element-by-element basis. Here's an example:

```
s1 = pd.Series([10, 9, 8, 7, 6])
s2 = pd.Series([2, 3, 2, 3, 2])


# Perform modulo operation
s3 = s1 % s2


# Print the result
print(s3)
```

Output:

```
0    0
1    0
2    0
3    1
4    0
dtype: int64
```

Figure 2.33: *Modulo operation on series*

In this code, we create two Series: **s1** and **s2**. We then perform a modulo operation on them and assign the result to **s3**. The resulting series, **s3**, contains the remainder of the division of the corresponding elements in **s1** by **s2**.

For instance, the first element in **s3** is the result of finding the remainder of the first element in **s1** divided by the first element in **s2** (10 % 2 = 0). This operation is repeated for every pair of corresponding elements in the two Series.

Now let us see some negative scenarios:

Handling Mismatch in Series Length: When we try to perform arithmetic operations on two series of different lengths, Pandas fills missing values with NaN. This can create potential issues because NaN is a float, and thus the entire series will be converted to floats, even if it was initially an integer series.

For instance:

```
s1 = pd.Series([2, 4, 6, 8, 10])
s2 = pd.Series([1, 3, 5])
s3 = s1 + s2
print(s3)
```

Output:

```
0     3.0
1     7.0
2    11.0
3     NaN
4     NaN
dtype: float64
```

Figure 2.34: *Addition of two Series with different lengths*

As you can see, indices 3 and 4 have **NaN** as the operation could not be performed due to a lack of corresponding elements in **s2**.

Arithmetic Operation with Non-Numerical Series

Another scenario where arithmetic operations may lead to issues is when dealing with non-numeric series. A common mistake is to attempt arithmetic operations on series containing non-numeric values, such as strings or objects.

Consider the following example:

```
s1 = pd.Series(['a', 'b', 'c'])
s2 = pd.Series(['d', 'e', 'f'])
s3 = s1 + s2
print(s3)
```

Output:

```
0    ad
1    be
2    cf
dtype: object
```

Figure 2.35: Concatenation operation

Here, "+" leads to concatenation, not addition, because the series are composed of strings, not numbers. Attempting other operations like subtraction or division will throw an error.

Series with Different Indices

If two series have different indices and you perform an operation on them, the result will contain the union of the indices. If a label is not found in one series or the other, the result will be marked as missing, **NaN**. For example:

```
s1 = pd.Series([2, 4, 6], index=['a', 'b', 'c'])
s2 = pd.Series([1, 3, 5], index=['b', 'c', 'd'])
s3 = s1 + s2
print(s3)
```

Output:

```
a    NaN
b    5.0
c    9.0
d    NaN
dtype: float64
```

Figure 2.36: Series with different indices

Here, '**a**' and '**d**' indices don't have corresponding elements in both the series, and hence, they result in **NaN**.

Implicit Type Conversion

Implicit type conversion is a common pitfall that could lead to subtle bugs in your program. When performing arithmetic operations between integer and float series, the resulting series will be of type float, even if the result could be expressed as integers.

Consider this example:

```
s1 = pd.Series([2, 4, 6])
s2 = pd.Series([1.0, 2.0, 3.0])
s3 = s1 + s2
print(s3)
```

Output:

```
0    3.0
1    6.0
2    9.0
dtype: float64
```

Figure 2.37: Implicit type conversion

Although all numbers in the result can be expressed as integers, the resulting series is of type float.

Division by Zero

Division by zero is a common issue in any computing environment, and pandas Series are no exception. When dividing by zero in a Series, pandas will not raise an exception but will instead fill the offending division with inf if it's a float series or NaN if it's an integer series.

```
s1 = pd.Series([2.0, 4.0, 6.0])
s2 = pd.Series([0, 0, 0])
s3 = s1 / s2
print(s3)
```

Output:

```
0    inf
1    inf
2    inf
dtype: float64
```

Figure 2.38: Division by zero

Broadcasting in Series

Broadcasting in Python is a term borrowed from the field of broadcasting in telecommunications and refers to how NumPy (the Python library for scientific computing) handles operations between arrays of different shapes.

When you perform an operation between two arrays of equal sizes, the operation is carried out element-wise, which is straightforward. However, when the arrays in the operation are of different shapes, broadcasting comes into play to try to make these shapes compatible with the operation.

Let's look at a simple example:

```
a = np.array([1, 2, 3])
b = 2
c = a * b
print(c)
```

Output:

```
import numpy as np

a = np.array([1, 2, 3])
b = 2
c = a * b
print(c)

[2 4 6]
```

Figure 2.39: *Broadcasting in series*

In this example, **b** is a scalar and a is an array. They have different shapes: **a** is of shape (3,) and **b** is of shape (). Thanks to broadcasting, **b** is 'stretched' into an array of the same shape as a for the multiplication operation. The operation is equivalent to a being multiplied by an array [2, 2, 2].

Let's see one more addition example:

```
s = pd.Series([1, 2, 3, 4, 5])


# Broadcasting addition
result = s + 1
print(result)
```

Output:

```
0    2
1    3
2    4
3    5
4    6
dtype: int64
```

Figure 2.40: *Broadcasting addition*

Here, we have the same Pandas Series **s** [1, 2, 3, 4, 5]. We perform an addition operation with a scalar value 1 using the + operator. Broadcasting takes place, and the scalar value 1 is broadcast across the Series, adding 1 to each element. The resulting Series result contains the updated values [2, 3, 4, 5, 6].

In both cases, broadcasting allows us to perform the operation between a Series and a single value without explicitly creating a new Series or using loops. The operation is applied element-wise, and the scalar value is effectively extended or stretched to match the shape of the Series.

Here are the following rules of broadcasting:

- If the arrays do not have the same rank, then a 1 will be prepended to the smaller ranking arrays until their ranks match.
- When the shape of the arrays is not the same, the array with a shape equal to 1 in that dimension is stretched to match the other shape.
- If in any dimension the sizes disagree and neither has a size equal to 1, an error is raised, and the arrays are said to be incompatible.

It's important to note that broadcasting can be applied to various arithmetic operations, including multiplication, addition, subtraction, division, and so on, allowing efficient element-wise computations between a Series and a single value.

You will have the opportunity to explore broadcasting in more depth when you work with DataFrames in the upcoming chapters of your learning journey.

Filtering Data with Series

Filtering data is an essential task in data analysis, allowing us to extract specific subsets of information from a larger dataset. In the context of Pandas Series, filtering data refers to selecting elements or subsets of elements based on certain conditions or criteria. By filtering data with Pandas Series, we can focus on the specific data points that meet our requirements and perform further analysis or manipulations on them. In this section, we will explore different techniques and methods for filtering data using Pandas Series to effectively extract and work with the data that matters most to you.

Filtering Data Using Comparison Operators

Filtering data using comparison operators in Pandas Series involves applying operators such as >, <, >=, <=, ==, and != to create Boolean masks. These masks indicate whether each element in the Series satisfies the specified condition. Let's dive into some examples to illustrate how to filter data using comparison operators:

Example 1: Filtering data greater than a threshold:

```
s = pd.Series([10, 20, 30, 40, 50])


# Filter data greater than 30
filtered_data = s[s > 30]
print(filtered_data)
```

Output:

```
3    40
4    50
dtype: int64
```

Figure 2.41: Filtering data using comparison operators

In this example, we have a Series **s** with values **[10, 20, 30, 40, 50]**. By using the comparison operator **>**, we create a Boolean mask that checks if each element is greater than 30. Applying this mask to the Series (**s** > 30) returns a filtered subset of data containing only the elements that satisfy the condition.

Example 2: Filtering data equal to a specific value:

```
s = pd.Series(['apple', 'banana', 'cherry', 'apple', 'kiwi'])


# Filter data equal to 'apple'
filtered_data = s[s == 'apple']
print(filtered_data)
```

Output:

```
0    apple
3    apple
dtype: object
```

Figure 2.42: Filtering data equal to a specific value

In this example, we have a Series s with string values [**'apple'**, **'banana'**, **'cherry'**, **'apple'**, **'kiwi'**]. By using the comparison operator **==**, we create a Boolean mask that checks if each element is equal to **'apple'**. Applying this mask (**s == 'apple'**) filters the Series, retaining only the elements that match the specified value.

By leveraging comparison operators, you can create Boolean masks to filter data based on various conditions, such as greater than, less than, equal to, or not equal to specific values. This allows you to extract subsets of data from a Series that meet your desired criteria for further analysis or manipulation.

Filtering Data Using Logical Operators

Filtering data using logical operators in Pandas Series involves combining multiple conditions using operators such as **&** (AND) and **|** (OR). These operators allow you to create more complex filtering conditions. Let's explore how to filter data using logical operators with Python code examples:

Example 1: Filtering data with AND operator (&): Suppose you have a Series with numeric values and want to filter elements that are both greater than 2 and less than 7. You can use the logical AND operator **&** to combine the conditions.

```
s = pd.Series([1, 5, 3, 9, 4])


# Filtering values greater than 2 and less than 7
filtered_data = s[(s > 2) & (s < 7)]
print(filtered_data)
```

Output:

```
1    5
2    3
4    4
dtype: int64
```

Figure 2.43: Filtering data using logical operators

To filter the data, we apply two conditions using comparison operators: (**s > 2**) and (**s < 7**). These conditions create two separate Boolean masks. The first mask checks if each element is greater than 2, and the second mask checks if each element is less than 7.

Next, we combine these two masks using the logical AND operator **&** inside square brackets: (**s > 2**) & (**s < 7**). The logical AND operator evaluates the conditions for each element and returns a Boolean mask, indicating which elements satisfy both conditions.

Finally, we apply this combined mask to the original Series s using square brackets to extract the subset of elements that satisfy both conditions. The resulting filtered data is assigned to the variable **filtered_data**.

The **print(filtered_data)** statement displays the filtered data, which consists of elements that are greater than 2 and less than 7.

Example 2: Filtering data with **OR** operator (|): Let's consider a scenario where you want to filter elements that are either equal to "**apple**" or "**banana**". You can use the logical OR operator | to combine the conditions. For example:

```
s = pd.Series(['apple', 'banana', 'cherry', 'kiwi', 'orange'])


# Filtering elements equal to "apple" or "banana"
filtered_data = s[(s == 'apple') | (s == 'banana')]
print(filtered_data)
```

Output:

```
0       apple
1       banana
dtype: object
```

Figure 2.44: Filtering data with OR operator

In this example, we start by creating a Pandas Series s with string values **['apple', 'banana', 'cherry', 'kiwi', 'orange']**.

To filter the data, we apply two conditions using comparison operators: **(s == 'apple')** and **(s == 'banana')**. These conditions create two separate Boolean masks. The first mask checks if each element is equal to **'apple'**, and the second mask checks if each element is equal to **'banana'**.

Next, we combine these two masks using the logical OR operator | inside square brackets: **(s == 'apple') | (s == 'banana')**. The logical OR operator evaluates the conditions for each element and returns a Boolean mask, indicating which elements satisfy either of the conditions.

Finally, we apply this combined mask to the original Series s using square brackets to extract the subset of elements that satisfy either of the conditions. The resulting filtered data is assigned to the variable filtered_data.

The **print(filtered_data)** statement displays the filtered data, which consists of elements that are either equal to **'apple'** or **'banana'**.

By utilizing logical operators, you can combine multiple conditions and create more intricate filtering conditions for your data. Whether using the AND operator (**&**) to require all conditions to be true or the OR operator (|) to satisfy at least one condition, you have the flexibility to construct complex filtering conditions tailored to your specific requirements.

Filtering Data Using Methods

Pandas Series provides various built-in methods for filtering data. For example, the **isin()** method allows you to check if elements in a Series match any of the specified values, while the **between()** method helps filter data within a given range. These methods provide convenient ways to filter data based on specific values or ranges.

Example 1: Filtering data using the isin() method: The **isin()** method allows you to filter data based on whether each element is present in a specified list of values. This method is useful when you want to filter data based on multiple specific values.

```
s = pd.Series(['apple', 'banana', 'cherry', 'kiwi', 'orange'])


# Filtering elements in ['apple', 'kiwi', 'grape']
filtered_data = s[s.isin(['apple', 'kiwi', 'grape'])]
print(filtered_data)
```

Output:

```
0    apple
3    kiwi
dtype: object
```

Figure 2.45: Filtering data using the isin() method

The **isin()** method is applied to the Series s with the list of values **['apple', 'kiwi', 'grape']**. This method checks whether each element in the Series is present in the specified list of values. It returns a Boolean mask, marking True for elements that match any of the specified values and False for the rest.

Next, we apply this Boolean mask **s.isin(['apple', 'kiwi', 'grape'])** to the Series **s** using square brackets **[]**. This filters the Series and retains only the elements that match any of the specified values.

In this case, the output shows that the filtered data contains elements **'apple'** and **'kiwi'**, which are the elements that matched the specified values **['apple', 'kiwi', 'grape']**.

Example 2: Filtering data using the between() method: The **between()** method allows you to filter data within a given range. This method is useful when you want to filter numeric or datetime data based on a specific range of values.

```
s = pd.Series([1, 3, 5, 7, 9])


# Filtering values between 3 and 7
```

```
filtered_data = s[s.between(3, 7)]

print(filtered_data)
```

Output:

```
1    3
2    5
3    7
dtype: int64
```

Figure 2.46: *Filtering data using the between() method*

The **between()** method is applied to the Series s with the range of values from 3 to 7, specified as **s.between(3, 7)**. This method checks whether each element in the Series falls within the given range. It returns a Boolean mask, marking True for elements that are within the range and False for the rest.

Next, we apply this Boolean mask **s.between(3, 7)** to the Series **s** using square brackets **[]**. This filters the Series and retains only the elements that fall within the specified range.

In this case, the output shows that the filtered data contains elements 3, 5, and 7, which are elements that fall within the range of 3–7.

NaN Values in Pandas Series

NaN (Not a Number) is a special value that represents the result of an undefined or unrepresentable numerical computation. It is commonly encountered when performing calculations involving missing or invalid data. NaN serves as a placeholder to indicate that a value is not available or cannot be represented accurately.

The significance of NaN lies in its ability to identify and handle exceptional cases in numerical computations. It allows programmers and data analysts to detect and address missing or undefined values without disrupting the overall computation process.

Arithmetic Operations with `np.nan`

Let's explore how addition and multiplication operations behave when using NumPy arrays and Pandas Series, and let's examine the differences between the two.

```
arr = np.array([1, 2, np.nan, 4, 5])


# Addition

result_add = arr + 2

print(result_add)
```

Output:

```
[ 3.   4.  nan  6.   7.]
```

Figure 2.47: Addition with np.nan on Numpy

```
# Multiplication
result_mul = arr * 2
print(result_mul)
```

Output:

```
[ 2.   4.  nan  8.  10.]
```

Figure 2.48: Multiplication with np.nan on Numpy

Addition and Multiplication using Pandas Series

```
s = pd.Series([1, 2, np.nan, 4, 5])


# Addition
result_add = s + 2
print(result_add)
```

Output:

```
0    3.0
1    4.0
2    NaN
3    6.0
4    7.0
dtype: float64
```

Figure 2.49: Addition on Series with np.nan

```
# Multiplication
result_mul = s * 2
print(result_mul)
```

Output:

```
0     2.0
1     4.0
2     NaN
3     8.0
4    10.0
dtype: float64
```

Figure 2.50: Multiplication on Series with np.nan

In Pandas Series, arithmetic operations with **np.nan** values behave similarly to NumPy arrays. The resulting Series will contain **NaN** elements when the corresponding element in the operation involves **np.nan**. This behavior ensures consistency in handling missing or undefined values in arithmetic operations.

Mean and Median Calculation Using NAN

When calculating the mean and median using the aggregate function with NaN values, NumPy and Pandas behave differently.

In NumPy, functions like **np.mean()** and **np.median()** return nan when NaN values are present. NumPy ignores the **NaN** values and provides the result based on the non-**NaN** values.

```
arr = np.array([1, 2, np.nan, 4, 5])
```

```
# Mean calculation using np.mean() in NumPy
mean_np = np.mean(arr)
print(mean_np)
```

Output:

```
Nan
```

```
# Median calculation using np.median() in NumPy
median_np = np.median(arr)
print(median_np)
```

Output:

```
Nan
```

In Pandas, the **mean()** and **median()** method handles NaN values differently. By default, it excludes the **NaN** values and computes the mean and median based on the non-**NaN** values.

```
s = pd.Series([1, 2, np.nan, 4, 5])
```

```
# Mean calculation using mean() in Pandas Series
mean_pd = s.mean()
print(mean_pd)
```

Output:

```
3.0
```

```
# Median calculation using median() in Pandas Series
median_pd = s.median()
print(median_pd)
```

Output:

```
3.0
```

Therefore, if you have **NaN** values in your data and want to calculate the mean or median, NumPy will return **NaN**, while Pandas will compute the mean or median excluding the NaN values.

We will look deeper into the handling of NaN values in subsequent sections, discussing various techniques and methods to effectively handle NaN values using Pandas.

Conclusion

In this chapter, we explored Pandas Series and its distinctions from Python lists or NumPy arrays. We learned that a Series is a one-dimensional labeled data structure in Pandas, providing homogeneous data storage and powerful data analysis capabilities. We discussed creating Series from various data structures and assigning custom index labels and names. Analyzing the size, shape, uniqueness, and value counts in a Series was covered, along with examining data using methods like head, tail, and sample. We also explored indexing and selecting data, performing arithmetic operations, filtering data, and handling NaN values. Understanding these concepts equips us with the tools to effectively work with and analyze data using Pandas Series.

The upcoming chapter will look into DataFrames in Pandas. Topics include creating DataFrames, and selecting columns, rows, and subsets. We will also explore how to view data, adding/removing columns and rows, and performing arithmetic operations on DataFrames.

Exercise Questions

- Create a Pandas Series from a given list, array, dictionary, or another data structure of your choice. Demonstrate how the Series retains the data's original structure.

- Take a Pandas Series and customize the index labels to make them more meaningful. Provide an example illustrating how these custom index labels can be used to access specific elements.

- Show how to assign a name to a Pandas Series and explain why this can be beneficial for data analysis tasks.

- Given a Pandas Series, use appropriate methods to analyze its size, shape, uniqueness, and value counts. Provide an example and describe the insights gained from each analysis.

- Use the **head()**, **tail()**, and **sample()** methods on a Pandas Series to explore and gain insights from the data. Discuss the purpose and usefulness of these methods in data analysis.

- Perform arithmetic operations on two Pandas Series objects and observe how the operations are applied element-wise based on the aligned index labels. Show an example and discuss any potential challenges or considerations.

CHAPTER 3

Pandas DataFrame

In this chapter, we will delve into the powerful Pandas DataFrame, a two-dimensional labeled data structure capable of holding data of different types. We will cover various aspects of working with DataFrames, including creating, manipulating, and transforming them. Additionally, we will explore how to perform a wide range of operations and calculations on DataFrames to extract valuable insights from the data.

Structure

In this chapter, we will discuss the following topics:

- Pandas DataFrame
  - Advantages of Using DataFrames
  - Comparing DataFrames With Other Data
- Creating a DataFrame from Scratch
  - Creating a DataFrame from a Dictionary
  - Creating a DataFrame from a NumPy ndarray
- Similarities Between Series and DataFrames
- Exploring a DataFrame
- Selecting Columns and Rows of a DataFrame
- `loc[]` and `iloc[]` to Select Rows and Columns in a DataFrame
- Adding and Removing Columns in a DataFrame
- Adding and Removing Rows in a DataFrame
- Renaming Columns in a DataFrame
- Reordering Columns in a DataFrame
- Data Filtering Using Boolean Expressions
- Arithmetic Operations on DataFrames

Pandas DataFrame

Pandas DataFrame is a two-dimensional labeled data structure that is widely used for data analysis and manipulation in Python. It provides a tabular format to organize and analyze data, similar to a table in a relational database or a spreadsheet.

Key points:

- **Concept and Structure:** A DataFrame consists of rows and columns, where each column can have a different data type. It is a mutable, size-mutable, and heterogeneous data structure.

- **Labeled Data:** DataFrames have labeled axes (rows and columns) that enable easy indexing and manipulation. Each column has a unique column label, and each row has a unique row label (index).

- **Versatility**: DataFrames can hold various types of data, including numeric, string, boolean, and more. This flexibility allows you to handle diverse datasets and perform a wide range of operations on the data.

- **Built on Series:** DataFrames are built on top of Pandas Series, which are one-dimensional labeled arrays. Each column in a DataFrame is a Series, sharing a common index.

- **Integration with Other Libraries:** DataFrames integrate seamlessly with other popular Python libraries like NumPy, Matplotlib, and scikit-learn, making it convenient for data analysis, visualization, and machine learning tasks.

Advantages of using DataFrames:

- **Easy Data Manipulation:** DataFrames provide convenient methods and functions to handle data cleaning, transformation, filtering, and aggregation. These operations can be performed efficiently on large datasets.

- **Efficient Memory Usage:** Pandas optimizes memory usage and provides efficient data structures, enabling you to work with large datasets even on machines with limited resources.

- **Flexible Data Representation:** DataFrames offer flexible ways to represent and store data. They can handle missing values, support hierarchical indexing, and allow reshaping and pivoting operations.

- **Powerful Data Analysis:** DataFrames provide a vast array of functions and methods for data analysis, including statistical computations, grouping and aggregation, time series analysis, and more.

- **Data Integration:** DataFrames allow seamless integration with various data sources and formats, such as CSV files, Excel spreadsheets, SQL databases, and JSON/XML data.

Comparing DataFrames with other data structures:

- **DataFrames versus Series:** DataFrames are two-dimensional structures consisting of multiple Series objects. Series represent a single column or a single row within a DataFrame. DataFrames provide a tabular structure, while Series are one-dimensional labeled arrays.

- **DataFrames versus NumPy ndarrays:** NumPy ndarrays are multidimensional arrays that store homogeneous data. DataFrames, on the other hand, can store heterogeneous data with labeled axes, providing a more versatile and convenient structure for data manipulation and analysis.

Now, let's go ahead and create a DataFrame from scratch. To do this, we need to import the pandas library and then use one of its functions to construct the DataFrame.

Creating a DataFrame from a Dictionary

Creating a DataFrame from a dictionary is a common and straightforward method. The keys of the dictionary represent the column names, and the values represent the data for each column.

```
data = {'Name': ['John', 'Emma', 'Lisa', 'David'],
        'Age': [25, 28, 22, 30],
        'City': ['New York', 'London', 'Paris', 'Tokyo']}
```

In this example, we have three keys: **'Name', 'Age',** and **'City'**. The corresponding values are lists that contain the data for each column.

Once you have the dictionary with the column names and values, you can create the DataFrame using the pandas **pd.DataFrame()** function. Pass the dictionary as an argument to the function.

```
import pandas as pd

df = pd.DataFrame(data)
```

By calling **pd.DataFrame(data),** you create a DataFrame named df using the dictionary data. Pandas automatically aligns the data based on the keys of the dictionary, and each key becomes a column in the DataFrame.

Finally, you can display the resulting DataFrame using the **print()** function or by directly calling the DataFrame variable.

```
print(df)
```

```
print(df)
```

Figure 3.1: *Print the dataframe*

This will output the DataFrame:

```
     Name  Age       City
0    John   25   New York
1    Emma   28     London
2    Lisa   22      Paris
3   David   30      Tokyo
```

Figure 3.2: *Dataframe output*

The resulting DataFrame has three columns (**'Name'**, **'Age'**, and **'City'**) and four rows. Each column contains the corresponding data from the lists in the dictionary. The row index starts from 0 and increases incrementally.

Creating a DataFrame from a NumPy ndarray

Creating a DataFrame from a NumPy ndarray is another method to construct a DataFrame. A NumPy ndarray is a multi-dimensional array that can hold homogeneous data. Each column in the ndarray will correspond to a column in the DataFrame.

In this example, we create a 2D ndarray called data with four rows and three columns.

```
import numpy as np
```

```
data = np.array([['John', 25, 'New York'],
                 ['Emma', 28, 'London'],
                 ['Lisa', 22, 'Paris'],
                 ['David', 30, 'Tokyo']])
```

First, you need to define a list of column names that will be used to label the **columns** in the DataFrame. The number of column names should match the number of columns in the ndarray.

Let's define columns with name '**Name**', '**Age**' and '**City**' that correspond to the three columns in the data ndarray.

```
columns = ['Name', 'Age', 'City']
```

By calling **pd.DataFrame(data, columns=columns)**, you create a DataFrame named **df** using the ndarray data and the column names **columns**. Each column in the ndarray will align with the respective column in the DataFrame.

```
df = pd.DataFrame(data, columns=columns)
```

The resulting DataFrame has three columns (**'Name'**, **'Age'**, and **'City'**) and four rows. Each column contains the corresponding data from the ndarray. The row index starts from 0 and increases incrementally.

Output:

```
df

      Name   Age      City
0     John   25    New York
1     Emma   28      London
2     Lisa   22       Paris
3    David   30       Tokyo
```

Figure 3.3: Dataframe output

Similarities Between Series and DataFrames

Series and DataFrames are both data structures commonly used in data analysis and manipulation, particularly in the context of the Python programming language and its data manipulation libraries such as pandas. Here are some similarities between Series and DataFrames:

- **Tabular Structure**: Both Series and DataFrames have a tabular structure, representing data in rows and columns. They are designed to handle structured data in a way that is similar to spreadsheet-like structures.

- **Built on NumPy**: Both Series and DataFrames are built on top of the NumPy library, which provides efficient and high-performance numerical operations. This underlying integration allows for seamless interoperability with other numerical libraries in the Python ecosystem.

- **Indexing and Labeling**: Both Series and DataFrames support indexing and labeling of rows and columns. They allow you to assign meaningful labels or indices to the data elements, making it easier to access and manipulate specific data points.

- **Data Alignment**: Both Series and DataFrames automatically align data based on their indices or labels. This alignment ensures that operations between multiple Series or DataFrames are performed based on matching indices or labels, simplifying data manipulation and computation.

- **Vectorized Operations**: Both Series and DataFrames support vectorized operations, which means that operations are applied to the entire Series or DataFrame, rather than individual elements. This allows for efficient and optimized computation on large datasets.

- **Data Transformation and Manipulation**: Series and DataFrames offer a wide range of functions and methods for data transformation and manipulation. They provide functionalities such as filtering, sorting, merging, joining, grouping, aggregation, and more, making it convenient to perform complex data operations.

- **Integration with Other Libraries**: Both Series and DataFrames integrate well with other libraries commonly used in data analysis and visualization, such as matplotlib, seaborn, and scikit-learn. This allows for seamless integration of data processing, analysis, and visualization tasks.

- **Flexibility and Versatility**: Both Series and DataFrames are flexible and versatile data structures, capable of handling various data types, including numerical, categorical, and textual data. They provide a convenient and consistent interface to work with diverse datasets.

While Series represent a one-dimensional labeled array, DataFrames extend this concept to a two-dimensional structure, where multiple Series objects are combined to form a tabular data structure. The similarities between Series and DataFrames facilitate their usage together, enabling powerful data manipulation and analysis capabilities in Python.

Exploring a DataFrame

Exploring a DataFrame involves gaining insights into its structure, data types, and summary statistics. Pandas provides several methods that facilitate this exploration. Let's dive into each of these methods and their applications:

Using `head()`, `tail()`, and `sample()` to view a subset of a DataFrame:

Similar to Series, DataFrames also provide methods for quickly previewing the data contained within them. These methods allow you to get an overview of the DataFrame's structure, column names, and a subset of the data. Although these methods are similar to their counterparts in Series, they operate on the entire DataFrame rather than a single column.

We will be using housing dataset to quickly examine the structure, content, and distribution of the data.

- **`head()`**: The **`head()`** method allows you to view the first few rows of a DataFrame. By default, it displays the first five rows.

The syntax is as follows:

```
dataframe.head(n=5)
```

```
df = pd.read_csv("housing.csv")
df.head()
```

Output:

	Suburb	Address	Rooms	Type	Price	Method	SellerG	Date	Distance	Postcode	...	Bathroom	Car	Landsize	BuildingArea	YearBuilt
0	Abbotsford	85 Turner St	2	h	1480000.0	S	Biggin	3/12/2016	2.5	3067.0	...	1.0	1.0	202.0	NaN	NaN
1	Abbotsford	25 Bloomburg St	2	h	1035000.0	S	Biggin	4/02/2016	2.5	3067.0	...	1.0	0.0	156.0	79.0	1900.0
2	Abbotsford	5 Charles St	3	h	1465000.0	SP	Biggin	4/03/2017	2.5	3067.0	...	2.0	0.0	134.0	150.0	1900.0
3	Abbotsford	40 Federation La	3	h	850000.0	PI	Biggin	4/03/2017	2.5	3067.0	...	2.0	1.0	94.0	NaN	NaN
4	Abbotsford	55a Park St	4	h	1600000.0	VB	Nelson	4/06/2016	2.5	3067.0	...	1.0	2.0	120.0	142.0	2014.0

5 rows × 21 columns

Figure 3.4: Displaying first five rows

In the preceding code, **df.head()** returns the first five rows of the DataFrame **df**.

You can also specify a custom number of rows to retrieve using the **head()** function. Here's an example that shows how to use a custom value.

In the following code snippet, **df.head(3)** returns the first three rows of the DataFrame **df**. You can change the argument to any desired number of rows.

```
df.head(3)
```

Output:

	Suburb	Address	Rooms	Type	Price	Method	SellerG	Date	Distance	Postcode	...	Bathroom	Car	Landsize	BuildingArea	YearBuilt
0	Abbotsford	85 Turner St	2	h	1480000.0	S	Biggin	3/12/2016	2.5	3067.0	...	1.0	1.0	202.0	NaN	NaN
1	Abbotsford	25 Bloomburg St	2	h	1035000.0	S	Biggin	4/02/2016	2.5	3067.0	...	1.0	0.0	156.0	79.0	1900.0
2	Abbotsford	5 Charles St	3	h	1465000.0	SP	Biggin	4/03/2017	2.5	3067.0	...	2.0	0.0	134.0	150.0	1900.0

3 rows × 21 columns

Figure 3.5: Displaying first three rows

The **head()** function is useful when you want to quickly inspect the initial records of a DataFrame or Series. It provides a convenient way to get an overview of the data and its column names.

- **tail()**: Similar to **head()**, the **tail()** function retrieves the last few rows of a DataFrame or Series. It helps you understand the bottom records of your dataset. By default, it returns the last five rows, but you can customize the number of rows to display.

The syntax is as follows:

```
dataframe.tail(n=5)
```

In the following code snippet, observe **df.tail()** returns the last five rows of the DataFrame **df**.

```
df.tail()
```

Output:

	Suburb	Address	Rooms	Type	Price	Method	SellerG	Date	Distance	Postcode	...	Bathroom	Car	Landsize	BuildingArea
13575	Wheelers Hill	12 Strada Cr	4	h	1245000.0	S	Barry	26/08/2017	16.7	3150.0	...	2.0	2.0	652.0	NaN
13576	Williamstown	77 Merrett Dr	3	h	1031000.0	SP	Williams	26/08/2017	6.8	3016.0	...	2.0	2.0	333.0	133.0
13577	Williamstown	83 Power St	3	h	1170000.0	S	Raine	26/08/2017	6.8	3016.0	...	2.0	4.0	436.0	NaN
13578	Williamstown	96 Verdon St	4	h	2500000.0	PI	Sweeney	26/08/2017	6.8	3016.0	...	1.0	5.0	866.0	157.0
13579	Yarraville	6 Agnes St	4	h	1285000.0	SP	Village	26/08/2017	6.3	3013.0	...	1.0	1.0	362.0	112.0

5 rows × 21 columns

Figure 3.6: *Displaying the last five rows*

Just like the **head()** function, the **tail()** function in Pandas also allows you to fetch a specific number of rows from the end of a DataFrame. This feature is useful when you want to view a desired subset of records from the bottom portion of your data.

By specifying a custom value for the n parameter in the **tail()** function, you can control the number of rows to retrieve. This flexibility enables you to explore the dataset according to your specific requirements.

In the following code snippet, **df.tail(3)** returns the last three rows of the DataFrame **df**. You can modify the argument to any desired number of rows.

```
df.tail(3)
```

Output:

	Suburb	Address	Rooms	Type	Price	Method	SellerG	Date	Distance	Postcode	...	Bathroom	Car	Landsize	BuildingArea
13577	Williamstown	83 Power St	3	h	1170000.0	S	Raine	26/08/2017	6.8	3016.0	...	2.0	4.0	436.0	NaN
13578	Williamstown	96 Verdon St	4	h	2500000.0	PI	Sweeney	26/08/2017	6.8	3016.0	...	1.0	5.0	866.0	157.0
13579	Yarraville	6 Agnes St	4	h	1285000.0	SP	Village	26/08/2017	6.3	3013.0	...	1.0	1.0	362.0	112.0

3 rows × 21 columns

Figure 3.7: *Displaying the last three rows*

- **sample():** The **sample()** function retrieves a random subset of rows from a DataFrame, providing a way to explore the dataset's variability. It allows us to

gain insights into random records and understand the overall data distribution.
The syntax for using `sample()` is as follows:

```
dataframe.sample(n=5, random_state=None)
```

Here, dataframe represents the DataFrame name, **n** specifies the number of rows to fetch, and **`random_state`** is an optional parameter to set a specific random state for reproducibility.

```
# Display a random subset of 6 rows
df.sample(6)
```

Output:

	Suburb	Address	Rooms	Type	Price	Method	SellerG	Date	Distance	Postcode	...	Bathroom	Car	Landsize	BuildingArea
7281	West Footscray	121 Suffolk St	3	h	878000.0	S	Village	30/07/2016	8.2	3012.0	...	1.0	1.0	397.0	127.0
1585	Camberwell	2/3 Tyrone St	2	h	620000.0	VB	Jellis	13/08/2016	7.8	3124.0	...	1.0	1.0	122.0	NaN
7828	Fawkner	3 Brian St	3	h	660000.0	S	Brad	8/04/2017	12.4	3060.0	...	1.0	2.0	585.0	88.0
12646	Beaumaris	19 Bolton St	5	h	3778000.0	S	Buxton	16/09/2017	17.3	3193.0	...	4.0	4.0	1254.0	465.0
2113	Collingwood	8/79 Oxford St	3	u	1500000.0	S	Jellis	22/08/2016	1.6	3066.0	...	2.0	2.0	0.0	159.0
7291	Albion	12 Coolamon St	2	h	600000.0	SP	Barry	22/05/2016	13.9	3020.0	...	1.0	1.0	534.0	90.0

6 rows × 21 columns

Figure 3.8: Displaying random rows

In the preceding example, **`df.sample(6)`** returns a random subset of six rows from the DataFrame **df**. The rows returned can vary each time you run the code due to the random nature of the sampling.

The **`random_state`** parameter can be used to set a specific seed for the random number generator, ensuring reproducibility if the same random state is provided.

Selecting Columns and Rows of a DataFrame

Selecting columns and rows of a DataFrame is a fundamental operation in data analysis using Pandas. It refers to the process of extracting specific portions of data from a DataFrame based on desired criteria, such as column names, row labels, or specific conditions. This allows us to focus on the relevant data for their analysis, visualization, and modeling tasks.

- **Selecting Columns in a DataFrame:** The process of selecting columns refers to the extraction of specific variables or attributes from the DataFrame. Columns represent the vertical entities in the DataFrame, and each column typically represents a different aspect of the data. By selecting columns, you can focus your analysis on specific attributes or variables of interest, allowing for targeted data exploration and analysis. Pandas provides several ways to select columns based on your requirements.

- **Single Column Selection:** Single column selection in a DataFrame refers to the process of extracting a specific column from the DataFrame. This can be done using either the square bracket notation or the dot notation in pandas.

Let's consider the same housing DataFrame we used earlier.

- **Square Bracket Notation:** Using square brackets, you can access a single column by specifying its name as a string within the brackets, such as `df['column_name']`.

```
# Selecting a single column using square brackets
df = pd.read_csv("housing.csv")
df['Rooms']
```

Output:

```
0        2
1        2
2        3
3        3
4        4
        ..
13575    4
13576    3
13577    3
13578    4
13579    4
Name: Rooms, Length: 13580, dtype: int64
```

Figure 3.9: Extract single column using square bracket notation

The expression `df['Rooms']` returns a pandas Series object, which is a one-dimensional labeled array that contains the values from the `'Rooms'` column of the DataFrame.

- **Dot Notation:** Pandas also provides the dot notation, where you can directly access a single column using the DataFrame object followed by a dot and the column name, such as `df.column_name`.

```
df.Rooms
```

Output:

```
0        2
1        2
2        3
3        3
4        4
        ..
13575    4
13576    3
13577    3
13578    4
13579    4
Name: Rooms, Length: 13580, dtype: int64
```

Figure 3.10: Extract single column using dot notation

df.Rooms uses the dot notation to access the column named **'Rooms'** directly from the DataFrame **df** and returns a pandas Series object that represents the values from the **'Rooms'** column.

- **Multiple Column Selection:** Multiple column selection refers to the process of extracting more than one column from a DataFrame. It allows you to focus on a specific subset of columns for analysis or further operations.

To select multiple columns, pass a list of column names within the square brackets.

Let's say we want to select the 'Rooms', 'Price', and 'Landsize' columns from the DataFrame **df**. To select these columns from the DataFrame, we utilize the square bracket notation **df[columns_of_interest]** where **columns_of_interest** contains a list of columns and the resulting dataframe is stored in **selected_columns**.

```
columns_of_interest = ['Rooms', 'Price','Landsize']
selected_columns = df[columns_of_interest]
selected_columns
```

Output:

	Rooms	Price	Landsize
0	2	1480000.0	202.0
1	2	1035000.0	156.0
2	3	1465000.0	134.0
3	3	850000.0	94.0
4	4	1600000.0	120.0
...	...	...	...
13575	4	1245000.0	652.0
13576	3	1031000.0	333.0
13577	3	1170000.0	436.0
13578	4	2500000.0	866.0
13579	4	1285000.0	362.0

13580 rows × 3 columns

Figure 3.11: Selecting multiple columns

We can note that executing **selected_columns** displays the DataFrame, which contains only the **'Rooms'**, **'Price'**, and **'Landsize'** columns. This allows us to focus on these specific columns for further analysis or any other data processing tasks, rather than working with the entire dataset.

- **Selecting Columns by Data Type:** Sometimes, it is useful to select columns based on their data types. Pandas provides the **select_dtypes()** method to accomplish this. For example, to select only the numeric columns from df, you can use the following code:

```
df.select_dtypes(include='number')


numeric_columns = df.select_dtypes(include='number')
numeric_columns
```

Output:

	Rooms	Price	Distance	Postcode	Bedroom2	Bathroom	Car	Landsize	BuildingArea	YearBuilt	Lattitude	Longtitude	Propertycount
0	2	1480000.0	2.5	3067.0	2.0	1.0	1.0	202.0	NaN	NaN	-37.79960	144.99840	4019.0
1	2	1035000.0	2.5	3067.0	2.0	1.0	0.0	156.0	79.0	1900.0	-37.80790	144.99340	4019.0
2	3	1465000.0	2.5	3067.0	3.0	2.0	0.0	134.0	150.0	1900.0	-37.80930	144.99440	4019.0
3	3	850000.0	2.5	3067.0	3.0	2.0	1.0	94.0	NaN	NaN	-37.79690	144.99690	4019.0
4	4	1600000.0	2.5	3067.0	3.0	1.0	2.0	120.0	142.0	2014.0	-37.80720	144.99410	4019.0
...	...	...	...	...	...	...	...	...	...	...	...	...	...
13575	4	1245000.0	16.7	3150.0	4.0	2.0	2.0	652.0	NaN	1981.0	-37.90562	145.16761	7392.0
13576	3	1031000.0	6.8	3016.0	3.0	2.0	2.0	333.0	133.0	1995.0	-37.85927	144.87904	6380.0
13577	3	1170000.0	6.8	3016.0	3.0	2.0	4.0	436.0	NaN	1997.0	-37.85274	144.88738	6380.0
13578	4	2500000.0	6.8	3016.0	4.0	1.0	5.0	866.0	157.0	1920.0	-37.85908	144.89299	6380.0
13579	4	1285000.0	6.3	3013.0	4.0	1.0	1.0	362.0	112.0	1920.0	-37.81188	144.88449	6543.0

13580 rows × 13 columns

Figure 3.12: Selecting multiple columns with datatype as int and float

Similarly, you can select categorical columns using **include='object'**

```
cat_columns = df.select_dtypes(include='object')
cat_columns
```

Output:

	Suburb	Address	Type	Method	SellerG	Date	CouncilArea	Regionname
0	Abbotsford	85 Turner St	h	S	Biggin	3/12/2016	Yarra	Northern Metropolitan
1	Abbotsford	25 Bloomburg St	h	S	Biggin	4/02/2016	Yarra	Northern Metropolitan
2	Abbotsford	5 Charles St	h	SP	Biggin	4/03/2017	Yarra	Northern Metropolitan
3	Abbotsford	40 Federation La	h	PI	Biggin	4/03/2017	Yarra	Northern Metropolitan
4	Abbotsford	55a Park St	h	VB	Nelson	4/06/2016	Yarra	Northern Metropolitan
...	...	...	...	...	...	...	...	...
13575	Wheelers Hill	12 Strada Cr	h	S	Barry	26/08/2017	NaN	South-Eastern Metropolitan
13576	Williamstown	77 Merrett Dr	h	SP	Williams	26/08/2017	NaN	Western Metropolitan
13577	Williamstown	83 Power St	h	S	Raine	26/08/2017	NaN	Western Metropolitan
13578	Williamstown	96 Verdon St	h	PI	Sweeney	26/08/2017	NaN	Western Metropolitan
13579	Yarraville	6 Agnes St	h	SP	Village	26/08/2017	NaN	Western Metropolitan

13580 rows × 8 columns

Figure 3.13: Selecting multiple columns with datatype as object

- **Selecting rows in a DataFrame**: Selecting rows in a DataFrame refers to the process of extracting specific rows from a tabular data structure called a DataFrame.

Similar to selecting columns from a dataframe, there are several ways to select rows.

- **Selecting Rows using Slicing**: In Pandas, slicing allows you to select a subset of the rows from the DataFrame. This operation is performed using Python's standard slicing syntax.

We can see that the data frame consists of 13580 rows and let's see how we can fetch rows using slicing.

```
df.shape
```

Output:

```
df.shape

(13580, 21)
```

Figure 3.14: *DataFrame Shape*

When you slice a DataFrame, you specify the indices of the starting and stopping points of the slice. The resulting slice includes the starting index and excludes the stopping index, following the standard Python list slicing convention.

To select the second and third rows, you would use the following slice:

```
df[1:3]
```

Output:

	Suburb	Address	Rooms	Type	Price	Method	SellerG	Date	Distance	Postcode	...	Bathroom	Car	Landsize	BuildingArea	YearBuilt
1	Abbotsford	25 Bloomburg St	2	h	1035000.0	S	Biggin	4/02/2016	2.5	3067.0	...	1.0	0.0	156.0	79.0	1900.0
2	Abbotsford	5 Charles St	3	h	1465000.0	SP	Biggin	4/03/2017	2.5	3067.0	...	2.0	0.0	134.0	150.0	1900.0

2 rows × 21 columns

Figure 3.15: *Filtering rows using slicing*

The **df[1:3]** code is the slicing operation. This means "*give me the elements from index 1 up to 2, but not including, index 3*".

If you want to select all rows from a certain index to the end, you can leave out the second index. For example, to select all rows from index **13575** onwards, you could use:

```
df[13575:]
```

Output:

```
df[13575:]
```

	Suburb	Address	Rooms	Type	Price	Method	SellerG	Date	Distance	Postcode	...	Bathroom	Car	Landsize	BuildingArea
13575	Wheelers Hill	12 Strada Cr	4	h	1245000.0	S	Barry	26/08/2017	16.7	3150.0	...	2.0	2.0	652.0	NaN
13576	Williamstown	77 Merrett Dr	3	h	1031000.0	SP	Williams	26/08/2017	6.8	3016.0	...	2.0	2.0	333.0	133.0
13577	Williamstown	83 Power St	3	h	1170000.0	S	Raine	26/08/2017	6.8	3016.0	...	2.0	4.0	436.0	NaN
13578	Williamstown	96 Verdon St	4	h	2500000.0	PI	Sweeney	26/08/2017	6.8	3016.0	...	1.0	5.0	866.0	157.0
13579	Yarraville	6 Agnes St	4	h	1285000.0	SP	Village	26/08/2017	6.3	3013.0	...	1.0	1.0	362.0	112.0

5 rows × 21 columns

Figure 3.16: *Filtering rows using slicing from certain index to end*

Conversely, if you want to select all rows from the start-up to a certain index, you can leave out the first index. For example, to select all rows up to (but not including) index 5, you could use:

df[:5]

Output:

```
df[:5]
```

	Suburb	Address	Rooms	Type	Price	Method	SellerG	Date	Distance	Postcode	...	Bathroom	Car	Landsize	BuildingArea	YearBuilt
0	Abbotsford	85 Turner St	2	h	1480000.0	S	Biggin	3/12/2016	2.5	3067.0	...	1.0	1.0	202.0	NaN	NaN
1	Abbotsford	25 Bloomburg St	2	h	1035000.0	S	Biggin	4/02/2016	2.5	3067.0	...	1.0	0.0	156.0	79.0	1900.0
2	Abbotsford	5 Charles St	3	h	1465000.0	SP	Biggin	4/03/2017	2.5	3067.0	...	2.0	0.0	134.0	150.0	1900.0
3	Abbotsford	40 Federation La	3	h	850000.0	PI	Biggin	4/03/2017	2.5	3067.0	...	2.0	1.0	94.0	NaN	NaN
4	Abbotsford	55a Park St	4	h	1600000.0	VB	Nelson	4/06/2016	2.5	3067.0	...	1.0	2.0	120.0	142.0	2014.0

5 rows × 21 columns

Figure 3.17: *Filtering rows using slicing from start to index 4*

loc[] and iloc[] Functions

loc and **iloc** are two pivotal functions in pandas that facilitate data selection from a DataFrame. Although they seem similar, their fundamental difference lies in their indexing style:

The loc Method

loc is a label-based data selection method which means that we have to pass the name of the row or column which we want to select. This method includes the last element of the range.

Syntax:

```
df.loc[row_label, column_label]
```

To better comprehend these functions, let's delve into some Python code. We'll first create a simple DataFrame.

```
data = {
    'fruit': ['apple', 'banana', 'cherry', 'date'],
    'color': ['red', 'yellow', 'red', 'brown'],
    'weight': [120, 150, 45, 60]
}


df = pd.DataFrame(data, index = ['fruit1', 'fruit2', 'fruit3',
'fruit4'])
df
```

Output:

	fruit	color	weight
fruit1	apple	red	120
fruit2	banana	yellow	150
fruit3	cherry	red	45
fruit4	date	brown	60

Figure 3.18: Creating new dataframe

*Using **loc** Select a Single Row by Index Label: Using **loc**, you can select a single row from a DataFrame based on its index label. In the provided example, the DataFrame **df** is created using the given data dictionary and custom index labels **'fruit1'**, **'fruit2'**, **'fruit3'**, and **'fruit4'**.*

The syntax for selecting a single row using loc is as follows:

```
single_row = df.loc[row_label]
```

where:

- **df**: The DataFrame you want to extract the row from.
- **row_label**: The index label of the row you want to select.

If we want to select the row with the index label **'fruit1'** from the DataFrame **df**, we can use loc as follows:

```
df.loc['fruit1']
```

Output:

```
fruit      apple
color        red
weight       120
Name: fruit1, dtype: object
```

Figure 3.19: *Selecting single row by using loc*

The **loc** indexer returns a Pandas Series object containing the values of the selected row, where the index label is shown on the left, and the corresponding values are on the right. In this case, the row with index label **'fruit1'** is returned as a Series. The Series retains the column names as its index, allowing you to access the values using column labels as well. For example, **single_row['fruit']** will give **'apple'**, **single_row['color']** will give **'red'**, and **single_row['weight']** will give 120.

Selecting a single column: To select a single column from a DataFrame using **loc** in Pandas, we can specify the column label within the loc accessor.

The syntax for selecting a single column using loc is as follows:

single_column = df.loc[:, 'column_label']

where:

- **df**: The DataFrame you want to extract the column from.
- **column_label**: The label of the column you want to select.

df.loc[:, 'fruit']

Output:

```
fruit1      apple
fruit2     banana
fruit3     cherry
fruit4       date
Name: fruit, dtype: object
```

Figure 3.20: *Selecting single column by using loc*

The preceding code fetches all rows (indicated by ':') for the **'fruit'** column. The ':' tells pandas to select all rows and the loc indexer returns a Pandas Series object containing the values of the selected column, where the index consists of the row labels. In this case, the **'fruit'** column is returned as a Series, and the row labels (**'fruit1'**, **'fruit2'**, **'fruit3'**, **'fruit4'**) are displayed on the left, while the corresponding values (**'apple'**, **'banana'**, **'cherry'**, **'date'**) are displayed on the right.

Selecting multiple rows and columns: To select multiple rows and columns from a DataFrame using loc in Pandas, you can pass lists of row labels and column labels within the **loc** accessor.

The syntax for selecting multiple rows and columns is as follows:

```
selected_data = df.loc[['row_label1', 'row_label2'], ['column_label1',
'column_label2']]
```

where:

- **df**: The DataFrame you want to extract the data from.
- **['row_label1', 'row_label2']**: A list containing the row labels you want to select.
- **['column_label1', 'column_label2']**: A list containing the column labels you want to select.

In this specific example, we are telling pandas to select rows with labels **'fruit1'** and **'fruit3'**, and for those rows, select the columns with labels **'fruit'** and **'color'**. The output will be a DataFrame that only contains the selected rows and columns.

```
df.loc[['fruit1', 'fruit3'], ['fruit', 'color']]
```

Output:

	fruit	color
fruit1	apple	red
fruit3	cherry	red

Figure 3.21: Selecting a single column by using loc

The `iloc` Method

iloc in pandas is used to select rows and columns by number, in the order that they appear in the DataFrame. You can imagine that each row and each column has a number, starting from 0 and incrementing by 1 for each additional row/column -- **iloc** uses these numbers to access the data.

In other words, **iloc** is an index-based selection method, meaning we have to pass integer index in the method to select specific rows/columns. Unlike **loc**, **iloc** does not consider the DataFrame's index labels for selection; it only uses integer locations.

Syntax:

```
df.iloc[row_index, column_index]
```

Select a single row: When it comes to selecting a single row from a DataFrame using **iloc**, you can retrieve a specific row based on its numerical position (**index**).

The syntax for selecting a single row using iloc is as follows:

```
single_row = df.iloc[row_index]
```

where:

- **df**: The DataFrame you want to extract the row from.
- **row_index:** The integer index of the row you want to select.

For example, suppose we have the following DataFrame **df**:

Output:

```
df

          fruit   color  weight
fruit1    apple     red     120
fruit2   banana  yellow     150
fruit3   cherry     red      45
fruit4     date   brown      60
```

Figure 3.22: Dataframe

```
# Select the first row
```

```
df.iloc[0]
```

Output:

```
fruit       apple
color         red
weight        120
Name: fruit1, dtype: object
```

Figure 3.23: Selecting single row by using iloc

df.iloc[0] selects the first row of the DataFrame. It's important to note that Python uses zero-based indexing, so 0 refers to the first element in the sequence (whether it's a list, a DataFrame, or another data structure). In the context of a DataFrame, **iloc[0]** will return all the column values of the first row.

Select multiple rows: When it comes to selecting multiple rows from a DataFrame, you can retrieve a range or specific indices of rows based on their numerical positions.

The syntax for selecting multiple rows using iloc is:

```
df.iloc[start_index:end_index]]
```

where:

- **start_index** is the index of the first row you want to select (inclusive)
- **end_index** is the index of the last row you want to select (exclusive).

For example, if you want to select the second and third rows of a DataFrame **df**, you can use:

```
df.iloc[1:3]
```

Output:

	fruit	color	weight
fruit2	banana	yellow	150
fruit3	cherry	red	45

Figure 3.24: Selecting multiple rows by using iloc

This code will return a new DataFrame containing the rows with indices 1 and 2. Note that the end index, 3, is exclusive, so the second row is included while the third row is excluded.

You can also pass a list of specific indices to select multiple non-consecutive rows. For instance, to select the first and last row, you would use:

```
# Select the first and last row - Multiple rows
df.iloc[[0, 3]]
```

Output:

	fruit	color	weight
fruit1	apple	red	120
fruit4	date	brown	60

Figure 3.25: Selecting rows using specific indices

This will return a new DataFrame that includes only the rows with indices 0 and 3.

Select a single column: To select a single column from a DataFrame using **iloc**, you can specify the column index position. This is useful when you want to access a column based on its numerical location within the DataFrame.

The syntax for selecting a single column using iloc is:

```
df.iloc[:, column_index]
```

where:

- **df** is your DataFrame,
- **:** denotes selecting all rows
- **column_index** represents the numerical index of the column you want to select.

  ```
  df.iloc[:,1]
  ```

Output:

```
fruit1       red
fruit2    yellow
fruit3       red
fruit4     brown
Name: color, dtype: object
```

Figure 3.26: Selecting single column

So, when we execute **df.iloc[:, 1]**, it selects the entire '**color**' column from the DataFrame **df**. The resulting output will be a pandas Series object that contains the values from the **'color'** column.

Select multiple columns: To select multiple columns from a DataFrame, you can specify a list of column indices.

The syntax for selecting multiple columns using iloc is as follows:

```
df.iloc[:, [col_index1, col_index2, ...]]
```

where:

- **[col_index1, col_index2, ...]** is a list of column indices you want to select.

  ```
  df.iloc[:, [1, 2]]
  ```

Output:

	color	weight
fruit1	red	120
fruit2	yellow	150
fruit3	red	45

Figure 3.27: Selecting multiple columns

The **df.iloc[:, [1, 2]]** expression selects all rows (:) and the columns at indices **1** and **2** from the DataFrame. The resulting output is a new DataFrame that contains only the selected columns, in our case its color and weight.

To select a range of columns using **iloc**, you can utilize column slicing. Here's how you can define and use column slicing with **iloc**:

The syntax for selecting a range of columns using iloc is as follows:

```
df.iloc[:, start_index:end_index]
```

```
#Multiple Columns using Column Slicing
df.iloc[:, 0:2]
```

Output:

	fruit	color
fruit1	apple	red
fruit2	banana	yellow
fruit3	cherry	red
fruit4	date	brown

Figure 3.28: Selecting multiple columns using column slicing

The **df.iloc[:, 0:2]** expression will retrieve all rows (:) and the columns from index **0** to **2** (columns **'fruit'** and **'color'**) from the DataFrame. The resulting output will be a new DataFrame containing only the selected columns.

Note that column indices start at 0, so index 1 corresponds to the second column, and index 2 is exclusive, representing the fourth column.

Selecting multiple rows and columns using iloc: To select multiple rows and columns from a DataFrame using **iloc** in pandas, you can combine row and column indexing. Here's how you can define and use **iloc** to select multiple rows and columns:

The syntax for selecting multiple rows and columns using iloc is as follows:

df.iloc[row_indices, column_indices]

where:

- **df** represents your DataFrame
- **row_indices** is a list of row indices you want to select
- **column_indices** is a list of column indices you want to select.

Let's see this with an example.

df.iloc[[1, 3], [0, 2]]

Output:

	fruit	weight
fruit2	banana	150
fruit4	date	60

Figure 3.29: Selecting multiple rows and columns

The **df.iloc[[1, 3], [0, 2]]** expression retrieved the rows at indices **1** and **3** and the columns at indices **0** and **2** from the DataFrame. The resulting output is a new DataFrame that contains only the selected rows and columns.

Adding and Removing Columns in a DataFrame

Adding and removing columns in a DataFrame are essential data manipulation operations and they allow users to modify the DataFrame's structure by adding new columns or removing existing ones. In this section, we will explore the process of adding and removing columns in a pandas DataFrame.

- **Adding Columns:** Adding columns to a DataFrame is a crucial step in data manipulation and analysis. It allows us to include additional information or calculated features based on existing data. Let's explore the methods for adding columns in a pandas DataFrame.

- **Adding a Single Column:** To add a single column, we can use the assignment operator (=) to assign a new series or array to a column label in the DataFrame. The length of the new data must match the length of the existing DataFrame. Here's an example:

```
# Create a DataFrame
data = {
    'fruit': ['apple', 'banana', 'cherry', 'date'],
    'color': ['red', 'yellow', 'red', 'brown'],
    'weight': [120, 150, 45, 60]
}

df = pd.DataFrame(data)
# Adding a single column
new_column = [10, 20, 30, 40]
df['price'] = new_column
df
```

Output:

	fruit	color	weight	price
0	apple	red	120	10
1	banana	yellow	150	20
2	cherry	red	45	30
3	date	brown	60	40

Figure 3.30: Adding a single column

The code snippet **new_column = [10, 20, 30, 40]** and **df['price'] = new_column** demonstrates how to add a single column to a pandas DataFrame.

In the first line, we create a new list called **new_column** that contains four elements: **10, 20, 30,** and **40.** This list represents the data that we want to add as a new column in the DataFrame.

In the second line, we assign the values from **new_column** to a new column named **'price'** in the DataFrame **df.** By using the square brackets **([ ])** and providing the column label (**'price'**) on the left side of the assignment operator (**=**), we instruct pandas to create a new column with the specified label and populate it with the values from **new_column.**

The output clearly displays the original columns (**'fruit', 'color', 'weight'**) along with the newly added column (**'price'**).

- **Adding Multiple Columns:** To add multiple columns simultaneously, we can use the **pd.concat()** function to concatenate the existing DataFrame with the new columns. We pass a list of series or arrays, and the resulting DataFrame will include the new columns.

```
# Adding multiple columns
new_columns = pd.DataFrame({'taste': ['sweet', 'sweet', 'sour',
'sweet'], 'season': ['winter', 'summer', 'spring', 'autumn']})

df = pd.concat([df, new_columns], axis=1)
df
```

Output:

	fruit	color	weight	price	taste	season
0	apple	red	120	10	sweet	winter
1	banana	yellow	150	20	sweet	summer
2	cherry	red	45	30	sour	spring
3	date	brown	60	40	sweet	autumn

Figure 3.31: Adding multiple columns

The preceding code illustrates how to add multiple columns to a pandas DataFrame. In the first line, we create a new DataFrame called **new_columns** using the **pd.DataFrame()** constructor. The **{'taste': ['sweet', 'sweet', 'sour', 'sweet'], 'season': ['winter', 'summer', 'spring', 'autumn']}** dictionary represents the data for the new columns we want to add. Each key-value pair in the dictionary corresponds to a column label ('taste' and 'season') and the respective values for each row.

In the second line, we use the **pd.concat()** function to concatenate the existing DataFrame **df** with the new DataFrame **new_columns**. By specifying **axis=1**, we ensure that the concatenation is performed along the columns.

After executing the code, we assign the concatenated DataFrame back to **df**. The resulting DataFrame will include the original columns (**'fruit'**, **'color'**, **'weight'**, **'price'**) as well as the newly added columns (**'taste'** and **'season'**).

- **Removing Columns:** Removing unnecessary or redundant columns from a DataFrame can enhance data clarity and analysis efficiency. Let's explore the methods available for removing columns.

- **Removing a Single Column:** To remove a single column, we can use the **drop()** method and specify the column label along with axis=1 to indicate that we are dropping a column.

Here's the syntax:

```
df.drop('column_name', axis=1, inplace=True)

df.drop('price', axis=1, inplace=True)

df
```

Output:

	fruit	color	weight	taste	season
0	apple	red	120	sweet	winter
1	banana	yellow	150	sweet	summer
2	cherry	red	45	sour	spring
3	date	brown	60	sweet	autumn

Figure 3.32: *Removing single column*

The **drop()** method in pandas allows us to remove specified columns or rows from a DataFrame. In this case, we specify **'price'** as the label of the column we want to drop. The **axis=1** parameter indicates that we want to drop a column, as **axis=1** refers to columns.

By setting **inplace=True,** we modify the DataFrame df directly, meaning the changes are applied to the DataFrame itself instead of returning a new DataFrame.

In the updated DataFrame, the **'price'** column is no longer present, and the remaining columns (**'fruit'**, **'color'**, **'weight'**, **'taste'**, **'season'**) remain unchanged.

- **Removing Multiple Columns:** To remove multiple columns from a pandas DataFrame, you can pass a list of column labels to the **drop()** method along with **axis=1**. Here's the Python code to remove the season and **'taste'** columns from the DataFrame:

```
df.drop(['season', 'taste'], axis=1, inplace=True)

df.drop(['season', 'taste'], axis=1, inplace=True)

df
```

Output:

	fruit	color	weight
0	apple	red	120
1	banana	yellow	150
2	cherry	red	45
3	date	brown	60

Figure 3.33: Removing multiple columns

In this updated DataFrame, both the **'season'** and **'taste'** columns are no longer present, and the remaining columns (**'fruit'**, **'color'**, **'weight'**) remain unchanged. The **drop()** method, along with the **axis=1** parameter and **inplace=True**, offers a convenient approach to remove multiple columns from a pandas DataFrame.

Adding and Removing Rows in a DataFrame

Adding and removing rows in a DataFrame allow us to modify the structure and content of a DataFrame by incorporating new data or removing existing rows. In this section, we will explore the methods available to add and remove rows in a DataFrame.

- **Adding a Single Row:** To add a single row, you typically create a new row as a pandas Series or dictionary object containing the values for each column. Then, you assign the new row to a specific index in the DataFrame using the **loc** method. This approach allows you to add a single observation to your DataFrame.

In the following snippet, a dictionary data is defined, containing keys representing the column names (**'fruit'**, **'color'**, **'weight'**) and corresponding lists as values, representing the data for each column. The dictionary is then passed to **pd.DataFrame()** to create a DataFrame **df** with the provided data.

```
# Create a DataFrame
data = {
    'fruit': ['apple', 'banana', 'cherry'],
    'color': ['red', 'yellow', 'red'],
    'weight': [120, 150, 45]
}

df = pd.DataFrame(data)
df
```

Output:

	fruit	color	weight
0	apple	red	120
1	banana	yellow	150
2	cherry	red	45

Figure 3.34: *Dataframe*

A new row is created as a pandas Series object called **new_row**. The values **['kiwi', 'green', 80]** represent the data for the new row, and **df.columns** is used to set the index of the new row to match the column names of the DataFrame **df**.

Using the loc method, **len(df)** is used as the index label to specify the location for the new row. By assigning **new_row** to **df.loc[len(df)]**, the new row is appended to the DataFrame **df**.

```
# Add a single row
new_row = pd.Series(['kiwi', 'green', 80], index=df.columns)
df.loc[len(df)] = new_row
```

We can see that the new row **['kiwi', 'green', 80]** is added to the DataFrame **df**, resulting in an updated DataFrame with the additional row.

```
df
```

Output:

	fruit	color	weight
0	apple	red	120
1	banana	yellow	150
2	cherry	red	45
3	kiwi	green	80

Figure 3.35: *Dataframe with additional row*

- **Adding Multiple Rows:** To add multiple rows to a DataFrame, we can use the **concat** function to concatenate the existing DataFrame with a new DataFrame containing the additional rows.

Here's an example:

```
# Add multiple rows
new_rows = pd.DataFrame([['grapes', 'green', 100], ['mango', 'yellow', 120]], columns=df.columns)
df = pd.concat([df, new_rows], ignore_index=True)
```

Here, a new DataFrame **new_rows** is created using the **pd.DataFrame()** constructor. It consists of a list of lists, where each inner list represents a row of data. The column names for the new DataFrame are specified as **df.columns** to ensure alignment with the existing DataFrame **df**. Each inner list contains the values for the respective columns, representing the data for each row to be added.

The **pd.concat()** function is used to concatenate df with **new_rows**, effectively adding the new rows to the existing DataFrame. By setting **ignore_index=True**, a new index is generated for the resulting DataFrame, ensuring a continuous index without any duplicates. We can see from following snippet, new rows at index 4 and 5 are created.

```
df
```

Output:

	fruit	color	weight
0	apple	red	120
1	banana	yellow	150
2	cherry	red	45
3	kiwi	green	80
4	grapes	green	100
5	mango	yellow	120

Figure 3.36: Dataframe with multiple rows added

- **Removing rows:** Removing rows in a DataFrame involves eliminating specific observations or data points from the DataFrame. It allows you to filter out irrelevant or redundant data to focus on the relevant information. There are different methods to remove rows from a DataFrame.

- **Removing a Single Row:** Removing a single row from a DataFrame can be achieved using the **drop()** method. This method allows you to specify the index label or row label of the row you want to remove.

Here's the general syntax:

```
df.drop(index, inplace=True)
```

Here, a DataFrame called **df** is created using the provided data dictionary. The data dictionary contains three columns (**'fruit'**, **'color'**, **'weight'**) and the corresponding values for each column.

```
# Create a DataFrame
data = {
    'fruit': ['apple', 'banana', 'cherry', 'kiwi'],
    'color': ['red', 'yellow', 'red', 'green'],
    'weight': [120, 150, 45, 80]
}


df = pd.DataFrame(data)
df
```

Output:

	fruit	color	weight
0	apple	red	120
1	banana	yellow	150
2	cherry	red	45
3	kiwi	green	80

Figure 3.37: *Create dataframe*

The **drop()** method is applied to the DataFrame **df** to remove a single row. By specifying **index=2**, we indicate that the row at index 2 (the third row) should be removed. Setting **inplace=True** ensures that the modification is applied directly to the DataFrame **df**.

```
# Removing a Single Row
df.drop(index=2, inplace=True)
```

We can observe that the row at index 2, representing the fruit **'cherry'**, color **'red'**, and weight **45**, is removed from the DataFrame **df**. The resulting DataFrame **df** reflects the removal of the specified row, with the remaining rows preserved and the index labels adjusted accordingly.

Output:

	fruit	color	weight
0	apple	red	120
1	banana	yellow	150
3	kiwi	green	80

Figure 3.38: *Updated dataframe with single row deleted*

- **Removing Multiple Rows:** To remove multiple rows from a DataFrame, you can pass a list of index labels or row labels to the **drop()** method.

Here's the general syntax:

```
df.drop(index_list, inplace=True)
```

First, we create a DataFrame called df using the provided data dictionary. The dictionary contains three columns **('fruit', 'color', 'weight')** and their respective values.

```
data = {
    'fruit': ['apple', 'banana', 'cherry', 'kiwi', 'mango'],
    'color': ['red', 'yellow', 'red', 'green', 'yellow'],
    'weight': [120, 150, 45, 80, 120]
}


df = pd.DataFrame(data)
df
```

Output:

	fruit	color	weight
0	apple	red	120
1	banana	yellow	150
2	cherry	red	45
3	kiwi	green	80
4	mango	yellow	120

Figure 3.39: *Dataframe*

To remove multiple rows, we create a list **rows_to_remove** that contains the indices of the rows we want to remove. In this example, we specify indices **1** and **3** to be removed.

By using the **drop()** method with **index=rows_to_remove**, we indicate the rows to be removed from the DataFrame **df**. Setting **inplace=True** modifies the DataFrame directly.

```
# Removing Multiple Rows
rows_to_remove = [1, 3]
df.drop(index=rows_to_remove, inplace=True)
```

We can see from the following snippet, the rows at indices 1 and 3 are removed from the DataFrame **df**. The resulting DataFrame **df** reflects the removal of the specified rows, with the remaining rows preserved.

```
df
```

Output:

```
df

     fruit   color   weight

0    apple     red      120

2    cherry    red       45

4    mango  yellow      120
```

Figure 3.40: Updated dataframe with multiple rows

Renaming Columns in a DataFrame

Renaming columns in a DataFrame is a common task in data analysis and manipulation. It allows us to modify column names to improve clarity, consistency, or align them with specific requirements. In this section, we will explore various methods available in pandas to rename columns in a DataFrame.

Why Rename Columns?

Column names play a crucial role in a DataFrame as they provide meaningful labels for the data stored within. Renaming columns in a DataFrame is important for several reasons, and understanding their significance can greatly enhance the data analysis process. Here are the key reasons why renaming columns is essential:

- **Clarity and Readability**: Renaming columns allows us to provide clear and descriptive names that accurately represent the data they contain. Meaningful column names make it easier to understand the content of a DataFrame, especially when working with complex datasets. Clear column names enable efficient communication and collaboration among data analysts, ensuring everyone interprets the data consistently.

- **Consistency and Standardization**: Renaming columns helps establish consistent naming conventions throughout the DataFrame. By adhering to a standardized naming scheme, it becomes easier to organize and compare data across different datasets or columns. Consistent column names also facilitate data integration and merging, particularly when combining multiple DataFrames or performing database operations.

- **Data Analysis and Exploration**: Renaming columns can greatly impact the efficiency of data analysis. Intuitive and informative column names streamline the exploration and manipulation of data. It becomes easier to select, filter, aggregate, or perform calculations on specific columns, enhancing the overall analytical workflow. Well-named columns save time by eliminating the need for excessive documentation or additional data preprocessing steps.

- **Data Visualization and Reporting**: Clear column names contribute to effective data visualization and reporting. When creating charts, graphs, or dashboards, descriptive column names make it easier for stakeholders to understand the visualized data. Additionally, when generating reports or sharing data insights, well-named columns improve the readability and interpretation of the presented information.

Renaming a single column: Renaming a single column in a DataFrame is a simple task using the **rename()** method in pandas. Let's explore the syntax, provide a Python code example, and discuss the role of each parameter:

Syntax of the rename() method for renaming a single column:

```
df.rename(columns={'current_name': 'new_name'}, inplace=True)
```

- **df**: The DataFrame in which you want to rename the column.

- **columns**: A dictionary-like object that maps the current column name to the new column name.

- **'current_name'**: The current name of the column you want to rename.

- **'new_name'**: The new name you want to assign to the column.

- **inplace=True**: It modifies the DataFrame in-place.

In the following code example, a DataFrame named df is created with two columns: **'fruit'** and **'color'**. The goal is to rename the **'color'** column to '**fruit_color**'.

```
# Create a DataFrame
data = {'fruit': ['apple', 'banana', 'cherry'], 'color': ['red', 'yel-
low', 'red']}
df = pd.DataFrame(data)
df
```

Output:

	fruit	color
0	apple	red
1	banana	yellow
2	cherry	red

Figure 3.41: Dataframe created

To achieve this, the **rename()** method is used on the DataFrame **df**. Within the **rename()** method, the columns parameter is specified as a dictionary. The key-value pair **'color': 'fruit_color'** is used, where **'color'** represents the current name of the column, and '**fruit_color**' represents the desired new name.

By setting **inplace=True**, the DataFrame **df** is modified directly, ensuring that the changes are applied to the DataFrame itself.

```
# Rename the 'color' column to 'fruit_color'
df.rename(columns={'color': 'fruit_color'}, inplace=True)
```

We can observe, the column originally named **'color'** is now renamed as **'fruit_color'**, reflecting the change made using the **rename()** method.

```
df
```

Output:

	fruit	fruit_color
0	apple	red
1	banana	yellow
2	cherry	red

Figure 3.42: Dataframe with single column name updated

Renaming multiple columns: Renaming multiple columns in a DataFrame using the **rename()** method allows you to modify the names of multiple columns simultaneously. Let's dive into the syntax, provide a Python code example and explain the role of each parameter.

Syntax of the rename() method for renaming multiple columns:

```
df.rename(columns={'current_name1': 'new_name1', 'current_name2': 'new_name2'}, inplace=True)
```

- **df**: The DataFrame in which you want to rename the columns.
- **columns**: A dictionary-like object that maps the current column names to the new column names.

- **'current_name1'**, **'current_name2'**: The current names of the columns you want to rename.

- **'new_name1'**, **'new_name2'**: The new names you want to assign to the columns.

- **inplace=True**: Modifies the DataFrame in-place.

In the following code example, a DataFrame named **df** is created using the given data dictionary. The goal is to rename the **'fruit'** column to **'fruit_name'** and the **'color'** column to **'fruit_color'**.

```
# Create a DataFrame
data = {'fruit': ['apple', 'banana', 'cherry'], 'color': ['red', 'yel-
low', 'red']}
df = pd.DataFrame(data)


df
```

Output:

	fruit	color
0	apple	red
1	banana	yellow
2	cherry	red

Figure 3.43: Dataframe

To rename multiple columns, the **rename()** method is used, passing a dictionary to the columns parameter. In this example, we want to rename the **'fruit'** column to **'fruit_name'** and the **'color'** column to **'fruit_color'**. The dictionary maps the current column names to the desired new names.

By setting **inplace=True**, the DataFrame df is modified directly, and the columns are renamed accordingly.

As a result, the column originally named **'fruit'** is now renamed as **'fruit_name'**, and the column originally named **'color'** is now renamed as **'fruit_color'**, reflecting the changes made using the **rename()** method.

```
# Rename the 'fruit' and 'color' columns
df.rename(columns={'fruit': 'fruit_name', 'color': 'fruit_color'}, in-
place=True)
df
```

Output:

	fruit_name	fruit_color
0	apple	red
1	banana	yellow
2	cherry	red

Figure 3.44: Dataframe with multiple column names updated

Reordering Columns in a DataFrame

Reordering columns in a DataFrame refers to changing the sequence or order of the columns. It allows you to rearrange the columns to better suit your analysis needs, improve readability, or align with specific requirements. In pandas, there are multiple approaches to reordering columns in a DataFrame.

Reordering Columns Using Indexing

Reordering columns using indexing refers to the process of changing the sequence or order of columns within a DataFrame by explicitly selecting and arranging them based on their labels. It provides a simple and direct approach to rearrange the columns according to specific requirements.

To reorder columns using indexing, you need to create a new DataFrame by indexing the existing DataFrame with a list of column names in the desired order. By passing the list of column names within the square brackets, you select and rearrange the columns accordingly. The new DataFrame reflects the changes made by reordering the columns.

Let's consider a DataFrame with columns **'fruit'**, **'color'**, and **'weight'**, and we want to reorder the columns such that **'color'** comes before **'weight'**.

```
# Create a sample DataFrame
data = {'fruit': ['apple', 'banana', 'cherry'],
        'color': ['red', 'yellow', 'red'],
        'weight': [120, 150, 45]}
df = pd.DataFrame(data)
df
```

Output:

	fruit	color	weight
0	apple	red	120
1	banana	yellow	150
2	cherry	red	45

Figure 3.45: Dataframe

By specifying **df[['color', 'weight', 'fruit']]**, we select the columns **'color'**, **'weight'**, and **'fruit'** in that order. The DataFrame is then updated to reflect this new column order. The reassignment of the indexed DataFrame to df ensures that the changes are preserved.

```
# Reordering columns using indexing
df = df[['color', 'weight', 'fruit']]
df
```

Output:

	color	weight	fruit
0	red	120	apple
1	yellow	150	banana
2	red	45	cherry

Figure 3.46: *Columns reordering using indexing*

we can verify the changes and observe the updated DataFrame will now have the columns in the order: **'color'**, **'weight'**, and **'fruit'**.

Reordering Columns Using The reindex() Method

The **reindex()** method is a pandas function that returns a new DataFrame with the specified column order. It allows you to redefine the index labels, column labels, or both. By passing a new list of column names to the columns parameter of the **reindex()** method, you can reorder the columns in the resulting DataFrame.

Let's consider the same example used earlier, that is, DataFrame with columns **'fruit'**, **'color'**, and **'weight'**, and we want to reorder the columns so that **'color'** comes before **'fruit'** and **'weight'**:

```
data = {'fruit': ['apple', 'banana', 'cherry'],
        'color': ['red', 'yellow', 'red'],
        'weight': [120, 150, 45]}
df = pd.DataFrame(data)
df
```

Output:

	fruit	color	weight
0	apple	red	120
1	banana	yellow	150
2	cherry	red	45

Figure 3.47: *Dataframe*

Let us reorder the columns in a DataFrame **df** by using the **reindex()** method. The **reindex()** method allows us to create a new DataFrame with the columns arranged in a specific order.

In this case, we define a list called **new_order** that specifies the desired column order as **['color', 'fruit', 'weight']**. By passing this list to the columns parameter of the **reindex()** method, we create a new DataFrame where the columns are rearranged accordingly.

The new DataFrame have the columns in the order specified by the **new_order** list.

```
# Reordering columns using reindex()
new_order = ['color', 'fruit', 'weight']
df = df.reindex(columns=new_order)
df
```

Output:

	color	fruit	weight
0	red	apple	120
1	yellow	banana	150
2	red	cherry	45

Figure 3.48: *Columns reordering using reindex*

Reordering Columns Using The `loc[]` Indexer

Reordering columns using the **loc[]** indexer involves selecting and rearranging columns in a DataFrame based on their labels or names. The **loc[]** indexer allows us to access and manipulate specific rows and columns by label-based indexing. By specifying the desired order of column labels within the **loc[]** indexer, we can effectively reorder the columns in the DataFrame.

We start with a DataFrame df containing columns, **'fruit'**, **'color'**, and **'weight'** then we are reordering the columns in a DataFrame **df** using the **loc[]** indexer.

The **loc[]** indexer allows us to access and manipulate specific rows and columns in a

DataFrame using label-based indexing. In this case, we are using it to select all rows (:) and rearrange the columns in the specified order **['color', 'fruit', 'weight']**.

By passing **[:, ['color', 'fruit', 'weight']]** to the **loc[]** indexer, we are selecting all rows **(:)** and specifying the desired order of columns. The resulting DataFrame will have the columns arranged as **'color'**, **'fruit'**, and **'weight'**.

```
# Reordering columns using the loc[] indexer
df = df.loc[:, ['color', 'fruit', 'weight']]
df
```

Output:

	color	fruit	weight
0	red	apple	120
1	yellow	banana	150
2	red	cherry	45

Figure 3.49: Columns reordering using loc

Reordering Columns Using The `Iloc[]` Indexer

Reordering columns using the **iloc[]** indexer involves selecting and rearranging columns in a DataFrame based on their integer positions. The **iloc[]** indexer allows us to access and manipulate specific rows and columns using integer-based indexing. By specifying the desired order of column positions within the **iloc[]** indexer, we can effectively reorder the columns in the DataFrame.

Reordering the columns using the **iloc[]** indexer is similar to the **loc[]** indexer, but instead of label-based indexing, we use integer positions. We can use either a single integer position or a list of integer positions to select the desired columns.

In the following code, we use the **iloc[]** indexer on the DataFrame **df** and specify **[:, [1, 0, 2]]**. The : before the comma denotes that we want to select all rows. Inside the square brackets, we provide a list **[1, 0, 2]** to indicate the desired order of the columns based on their positions. In this case, the column at position 1 (**'color'**) will come before the column at position 0 (**'fruit'**), followed by the column at position 2 (**'weight'**).

Assigning the reordered DataFrame back to **df** ensures that the changes are preserved.

```
# Reordering columns using the iloc[] indexer
df = df.iloc[:, [1, 0, 2]]
df
```

	color	fruit	weight
0	red	apple	120
1	yellow	banana	150
2	red	cherry	45

Figure 3.50: Columns reordering using iloc

Data Filtering Using Boolean Expressions

Data filtering is an essential technique in data analysis that allows us to extract specific subsets of data based on certain conditions. In Pandas, boolean expressions provide a flexible and efficient way to filter rows in a DataFrame.

In this section, we will explore the art of filtering rows in a DataFrame using boolean expressions with Pandas. We will dive deep into the concepts and see practical code examples to enhance our understanding with the tools to efficiently filter data in our analysis.

Understanding Boolean Expressions

Boolean expressions involve comparisons and logical operations that result in either True or False values. They are commonly used to evaluate conditions and make decisions based on the outcomes. Let's delve into the components of boolean expressions and explore some examples.

1. **Boolean Values**: Boolean values are the fundamental building blocks of boolean expressions. They can take two possible values: **True** or **False**. These values are used to represent the truth or falsity of a condition.

```
x = True
y = False

print(x)
print(y)
```

Output:

```
True
False
```

Figure 3.51: Boolean values

2. **Comparison Operators**: Comparison operators are used to compare values and evaluate conditions. They return a boolean value based on the comparison result. Here are the commonly used comparison operators:

- Equality (==): Checks if two values are equal.
- Inequality (!=): Checks if two values are not equal.
- Greater than (>): Checks if the left operand is greater than the right operand.
- Less than (<): Checks if the left operand is less than the right operand.
- Greater than or equal to (>=): Checks if the left operand is greater than or equal to the right operand.
- Less than or equal to (<=): Checks if the left operand is less than or equal to the right operand.

```
x = 5
y = 10


print(x == y)
print(x != y)
print(x > y)
print(x < y)
print(x >= y)
print(x <= y)
```

Output:

```
False
True
False
True
False
True
```

Figure 3.52: Comparison operator

3. **Logical Operators:** Logical operators are used to combine boolean values or expressions and perform logical operations. They include the following operators:

- Logical AND (**and**): Returns **True** if both operands are **True**.
- Logical OR (**or**): Returns **True** if at least one of the operands is **True**.
- Logical NOT (**not**): Returns the opposite of the operand's boolean value.

```
x = True
y = False


print(x and y)
```

```
print(x or y)
print(not x)
```

Output:

```
False
True
False
```

Figure 3.53: *Logical operators*

4. **Boolean Expressions:** Boolean expressions are formed by combining comparison and logical operators to evaluate complex conditions. They can be used to control program flow or filter data based on specific criteria.

```
x = 5
y = 10
z = 7


# Boolean expression using comparison and logical operators
result = (x < y) and (z > y or x == z)


print(result)
```

Output:

```
False
```

Figure 3.54: *Boolean expression using comparison and logical operators*

In the following example, the boolean expression **x < y** evaluates to True, and the expression (**z > y** or x **== z**) evaluates to True as well. Finally, the expression (**x < y**) and (**z > y** or x **== z**) evaluates to True because both sub-expressions are True.

Understanding boolean expressions is essential for filtering rows in a DataFrame based on specific conditions. In the subsequent sections, we will explore how to utilize boolean expressions effectively to filter data using Pandas.

Boolean Indexing

Boolean indexing is a powerful technique in Pandas that allows us to filter rows in a DataFrame based on boolean expressions. It involves using boolean arrays or boolean Series to select specific rows that satisfy certain conditions. Let's explore this concept in detail with some Python code examples.

Consider the following DataFrame:

```
data = {
    'Name': ['John', 'Alice', 'Bob', 'Emily', 'Michael'],
    'Age': [30, 25, 35, 27, 32],
    'Department': ['HR', 'IT', 'IT', 'HR', 'Finance'],
    'Salary': [50000, 60000, 55000, 45000, 70000]
}
```

```
df = pd.DataFrame(data)
df
```

Output:

	Name	Age	Department	Salary
0	John	30	HR	50000
1	Alice	25	IT	60000
2	Bob	35	IT	55000
3	Emily	27	HR	45000
4	Michael	32	Finance	70000

Figure 3.55: Dataframe

Now, let's use boolean indexing to filter rows based on certain conditions.

- **Filtering Rows Based on a Single Condition:** We can filter rows based on a single condition by creating a boolean expression that evaluates to either True or False for each row. For example, let's filter rows where the age is greater than 30:

  ```
  filtered_df = df[df['Age'] > 30]
  filtered_df
  ```

Output:

	Name	Age	Department	Salary
2	Bob	35	IT	55000
4	Michael	32	Finance	70000

Figure 3.56: Filtering rows on a single condition

In this example, the expression **df['Age'] > 30** generates a boolean series of true and false values, indicating whether each row satisfies the condition. Using this boolean

Series as an index in the DataFrame **(df[boolean_series])** returns only the rows where the corresponding values are True.

- **Filtering Rows Based on Multiple Conditions:** We can also filter rows based on multiple conditions by combining boolean expressions using logical operators like **&** (and) and **|** (or). For example, let's filter rows where the age is greater than 30 and the department is 'IT':

```
filtered_df = df[(df['Age'] > 30) & (df['Department'] == 'IT')]
filtered_df
```

Output:

	Name	Age	Department	Salary
2	Bob	35	IT	55000

Figure 3.57: *Filtering rows on multiple conditions*

In this example, we create two separate boolean expressions: **(df['Age'] > 30)** and **(df['Department'] == 'IT')**. By combining these expressions using the **&** operator, we filter the DataFrame to include only the rows that satisfy both conditions.

- **Filtering Rows Based on String Matching:** Boolean indexing also allows us to filter rows based on string matching. We can use string methods and boolean expressions to achieve this. For example, let's filter rows where the department starts with 'H':

```
filtered_df = df[df['Department'].str.startswith('H')]
filtered_df
```

Output:

	Name	Age	Department	Salary
0	John	30	HR	50000
3	Emily	27	HR	45000

Figure 3.58: *Filtering rows based on string matching*

In this example, we use the **str.startswith()** method to create a boolean Series that indicates whether each department value starts with 'H'. By using this boolean Series for indexing, we obtain the rows where the condition is True.

- **Filtering Rows Based on Membership:** Filtering rows based on membership allows us to select rows where a specific value is present in a list or another column. Pandas provides the **isin()** method, which is particularly useful for this type of filtering.

```
filtered_df = df[df['Department'].isin(['HR', 'Finance'])]
filtered_df
```

Output:

	Name	Age	Department	Salary
0	John	30	HR	50000
3	Emily	27	HR	45000
4	Michael	32	Finance	70000

Figure 3.59: Filtering rows based on membership

In this example, **df['Department'].isin(['HR', 'Finance'])** creates a boolean Series that checks if each value in the **'Department'** column is present in the provided list. Using this boolean Series for indexing, we obtain the rows where the condition is True.

- **Filtering Rows Based on Null or Non-Null Values:** Filtering rows based on null or non-null values is crucial when dealing with missing data. Pandas provides the **isnull()** and **notnull()** methods to handle these cases.

Example 1: Filtering Rows Based on Null Values

Suppose we want to filter rows where the **'Salary'** column has null values. We can achieve this using the **isnull()** method:

```
filtered_df = df[df['Salary'].isnull()]
filtered_df
```

Name	Age	Department	Salary

Figure 3.60: Filtering rows based on null values

In this example, **df['Salary'].isnull()** creates a boolean Series that evaluates to True for rows where the **'Salary'** column has null values. Since no rows satisfy this condition, an empty DataFrame is returned.

Example 2: Filtering Rows Based on Non-Null Values

Now let's filter rows where the **'Salary'** column has non-null values. We can accomplish this using the **notnull()** method:

```
filtered_df = df[df['Salary'].notnull()]
```

```
filtered_df
```

Output:

	Name	Age	Department	Salary
0	John	30	HR	50000
1	Alice	25	IT	60000
2	Bob	35	IT	55000
3	Emily	27	HR	45000
4	Michael	32	Finance	70000

Figure 3.61: *Filtering rows based on non-null values*

The line in code **filtered_df = df[df['Salary'].notnull()]** creates a new DataFrame, **filtered_df**, by filtering the rows of the original DataFrame, **df**, based on the condition that the **'Salary'** column has non-null values. It achieves this by using boolean indexing with the expression **df['Salary'].notnull()**, which evaluates to True for rows where the **'Salary'** value is not null and False for rows with null values. As a result, **filtered_df** contains only the rows from **df** where the **'Salary'** column has valid values, allowing you to focus on the relevant data for further analysis or computations while excluding any rows with missing salary information.

Arithmetic Operations on DataFrames

Performing arithmetic operations on DataFrames is a common task when working with data. Whether it's calculating simple sums, computing averages, or applying more complex mathematical operations, pandas provides a range of methods to handle these tasks efficiently.

Arithmetic operations on DataFrames are similar to the ones we saw in Series. Since each column in a DataFrame is essentially a Series, performing arithmetic operations on DataFrames is done in a column-wise manner. Pandas aligns the data based on the column and row labels, making it easy to perform element-wise operations between DataFrames and constants or between two DataFrames.

Creating a DataFrame

Let's start by creating a simple DataFrame to demonstrate various arithmetic operations.

```
data = {
    'A': [1, 2, 3, 4, 5],
    'B': [10, 20, 30, 40, 50],
    'C': [100, 200, 300, 400, 500]
}
```

```
df = pd.DataFrame(data)
df
```

Output:

	A	B	C
0	1	10	100
1	2	20	200
2	3	30	300
3	4	40	400
4	5	50	500

Figure 3.62: *Dataframe*

Our DataFrame df now contains three columns - A, B, and C. Now, let's demonstrate some arithmetic operations on this DataFrame:

Addition (+): In Pandas, the addition operation (+) is used to perform element-wise addition between two DataFrames or between a DataFrame and a scalar value. It allows users to combine or modify data in a flexible manner, resulting in a new DataFrame with the calculated values.

Scalar Addition: When you add a scalar value to a DataFrame, that value is added to each element in the DataFrame. For example, if you add 10 to a DataFrame, each element in the DataFrame will increase by 10.

```
# Adding a scalar to the DataFrame
df_add_scalar = df + 10
df_add_scalar
```

Output:

	A	B	C
0	11	20	110
1	12	30	210
2	13	40	310
3	14	50	410
4	15	60	510

Figure 3.63: *Scalar addition*

Here we are adding the scalar value 10 to the DataFrame **df**. Each element in the original DataFrame **df** is increased by 10 to obtain the corresponding elements in the resulting DataFrame df_add_scalar.

For example, in the resulting DataFrame, the element in the first row and first column, which was 1 in the original DataFrame, becomes 11 (1 + 10). Similarly, the element in the second row and third column, which was 10 in the original DataFrame, becomes 20 (10 + 10).

The output demonstrates how scalar addition works in DataFrame arithmetic. The scalar value 10 is applied element-wise to each element in the DataFrame, resulting in a new DataFrame with updated values, which are ten units higher than the original values.

DataFrame Addition: When you add two DataFrames together, the corresponding elements from each DataFrame are added together. This is an element-wise addition and requires both DataFrames to have the same shape (same number of rows and columns).

```
# Adding two DataFrames element-wise
df_add_df = df + df
df_add_df
```

Output:

	A	B	C
0	2	20	200
1	4	40	400
2	6	60	600
3	8	80	800
4	10	100	1000

Figure 3.64: Adding two dataframes

Here we are adding the DataFrame **df** to itself. In this operation each element in the original DataFrame **df** is added to its corresponding element from the same DataFrame, leading to each value being doubled in the resulting DataFrame **df_add_df**.

For example, in the resulting DataFrame, the element in the first row and first column is 2 (1 + 1). Similarly, the element in the second row and third column is 20 (10 + 10).

The output demonstrates how DataFrame addition works. The corresponding elements from two identical DataFrames are added together element-wise, resulting in a new DataFrame with values that are twice the original values.

Subtraction (-): In Pandas, the subtraction operation (-) is used to perform element-wise subtraction between two DataFrames or between a DataFrame and a scalar value.

Scalar Subtraction: When you subtract a scalar value from a DataFrame, that value is subtracted from each element in the DataFrame. For example, if you subtract **5** from a DataFrame, each element in the DataFrame will decrease by **5**.

```
# Subtracting a scalar from the DataFrame
df_subtract_scalar = df - 5
df_subtract_scalar
```

Output:

Figure 3.65: *Scalar subtraction*

We are subtracting the scalar value 5 from the DataFrame **df**. Each element in the original DataFrame **df** is decreased by 5 to obtain the corresponding elements in the resulting DataFrame **df_subtract_scalar**.

For example, in the resulting DataFrame, the element in the first row and first column, which was 1 in the original DataFrame, becomes -4 (1 - 5). Similarly, the element in the second row and third column, which was 10 in the original DataFrame, becomes 5 (10 - 5).

This operation demonstrates how scalar subtraction works in DataFrame arithmetic. The scalar value 5 is applied element-wise to each element in the DataFrame, resulting in a new DataFrame with updated values, which are five units lower than the original values.

DataFrame Subtraction: When you subtract one DataFrame from another, the corresponding elements from the second DataFrame are subtracted from the elements of the first DataFrame. This is an element-wise subtraction and requires both DataFrames to have the same shape.

```
# Subtracting two DataFrames element-wise
df_subtract_df = df - df
df_subtract_df
```

Output:

	A	B	C
0	0	0	0
1	0	0	0
2	0	0	0
3	0	0	0
4	0	0	0

Figure 3.66: Subtracting two dataframes

In this operation, the corresponding elements from each DataFrame are subtracted from each other element-wise leading to all elements being zero in the resulting DataFrame **df_subtract_df**.

Multiplication (*): Multiplication operation (*) is used to perform element-wise multiplication between two DataFrames or between a DataFrame and a scalar value resulting in a new DataFrame with the calculated values.

Scalar Multiplication: When you multiply a DataFrame by a scalar value, each element in the DataFrame is multiplied by that scalar. For example, if you multiply the DataFrame by 2, each element will be doubled.

```
# Multiplying the DataFrame by a scalar
df_multiply_scalar = df * 2
df_multiply_scalar
```

Output:

	A	B	C
0	2	20	200
1	4	40	400
2	6	60	600
3	8	80	800
4	10	100	1000

Figure 3.67: Scalar multiplication

In Scalar Multiplication, each element in the original DataFrame **df** is multiplied by 2 to obtain the corresponding elements in the resulting DataFrame **df_multiply_scalar**.

For example, in the resulting DataFrame, the element in the first row and first column, which was 1 in the original DataFrame, becomes 2 (1 * 2). Similarly, the element in the second row and third column, which was 10 in the original DataFrame, becomes 20 (10 * 2).

DataFrame Multiplication: When you multiply two DataFrames together, the corresponding elements from each DataFrame are multiplied together. This is an element-wise multiplication and requires both DataFrames to have the same shape.

```
# Element-wise multiplication of two DataFrames
df_multiply_df = df * df
df_multiply_df
```

Output:

	A	B	C
0	1	100	10000
1	4	400	40000
2	9	900	90000
3	16	1600	160000
4	25	2500	250000

Figure 3.68: Multiply two dataframes

In this operation, the corresponding elements from each DataFrame are multiplied together element-wise resulting in a new DataFrame with values that are the square of the original values.

For example, in the resulting DataFrame, the element in the first row and second column is 25 (5 * 5). Similarly, the element in the second row and third column is 100 (10 * 10).

Division (/): Pandas employs the division operation (/) to carry out element-wise division either between two DataFrames or between a DataFrame and a scalar value. This functionality enables users to seamlessly combine or manipulate data, leading to the creation of a new DataFrame that contains the results of the division.

Scalar Division: When you divide a DataFrame by a scalar value, each element in the DataFrame is divided by that scalar. For example, if you divide the DataFrame by 3, each element will be divided by 3.

```
# Dividing the DataFrame by a scalar
df_divide_scalar = df / 3
df_divide_scalar
```

Output:

	A	B	C
0	0.333333	3.333333	33.333333
1	0.666667	6.666667	66.666667
2	1.000000	10.000000	100.000000
3	1.333333	13.333333	133.333333
4	1.666667	16.666667	166.666667

Figure 3.69: *Scalar division*

This operation demonstrates how scalar division works in DataFrame arithmetic. The scalar value 3 is applied element-wise to each element in the DataFrame, resulting in a new DataFrame with updated values, which are approximately one-third of the original values.

For example, in the resulting DataFrame, the element in the first row and first column, which was 1 in the original DataFrame, becomes approximately 0.3333 (1/3). Similarly, the element in the second row and third column, which was 10 in the original DataFrame, becomes approximately 3.3333 (10/3).

DataFrame Division: When you divide one DataFrame by another, the corresponding elements from the first DataFrame are divided by the elements of the second DataFrame. This is an element-wise division and requires both DataFrames to have the same shape.

```
# Element-wise division of two DataFrames
df_divide_df = df / df
df_divide_df
```

Output:

	A	B	C
0	1.0	1.0	1.0
1	1.0	1.0	1.0
2	1.0	1.0	1.0
3	1.0	1.0	1.0
4	1.0	1.0	1.0

Figure 3.70: *Dataframes division*

In this operation, the corresponding elements from two identical DataFrames are divided element-wise, resulting in a new DataFrame with all elements equal to 1.0. This is because dividing a DataFrame by itself effectively cancels out the division, leaving all values unchanged.

Conclusion

In this chapter, we explored the fundamental concepts of Pandas DataFrames, a versatile two-dimensional labeled data structure capable of holding various data types. We covered a wide range of topics, starting from creating DataFrames using dictionaries and NumPy ndarrays. Understanding the similarities and differences between Series and DataFrames provided valuable insights into their functionality. We learned how to select specific columns, rows, and subsets of data, and how to view DataFrame sections using `head()`, `tail()`, and `sample()`. The chapter also encompassed techniques for adding and removing columns and rows, as well as renaming and reordering columns to suit our needs. Using `loc[]` and `iloc[]`, we mastered the art of data selection based on labels and integer positions. Additionally, we explored filtering data using boolean expressions and `isin()` to extract relevant information. Performing arithmetic operations on DataFrames showcased the power of element-wise computations.

In the next chapter, we shift our focus to the crucial aspect of data cleaning, an indispensable step in the data analysis process. We delve into the significance of data cleaning and its impact on data quality. By the end of this chapter, readers will be equipped with essential skills to clean and prepare datasets, ensuring more accurate and reliable analyses for their data-driven endeavors.

Exercise Questions

1. Create a DataFrame named df with the following data using a dictionary and display its content:

Name	Age	Score
Alice	25	85
Bob	22	90
Claire	27	78

2. Given a NumPy ndarray data with shape (**3**, **4**), create a DataFrame named **df_data** with column names '**A**', '**B**', '**C**', and '**D**', and display the first 2 rows using `head()`

3. Add a new column named **'Gender'** to the DataFrame **df** with values ['**F**', '**M**', '**F**'], respectively.

4. Reorder the columns in the DataFrame **df** in the order: **'Name'**, **'Test_Score'**, **'Age'**, **'Gender'**.

5. Filter the rows in the DataFrame **df** where the **'Age'** is greater than **25** and '**Test_Score**' is greater than or equal to **80**.

CHAPTER 4
Data Cleaning with Pandas

In this chapter, we will explore data cleaning with Pandas, a crucial step in the data analysis process. We will learn to identify and handle missing data using functions like `isna()`, `isnull()`, `notnull()`, `dropna()`, `fillna()`, and `interpolate()`. Additionally, we will discover how to address duplicate data using `duplicated()` and `drop_duplicates()`. Through case studies and best practices, we will gain practical insights into improving data quality, ensuring accurate and reliable analysis results. Mastering data cleaning techniques will equip us with the skills to prepare datasets effectively for meaningful data analysis and informed decision-making.

Structure

In this chapter, we will discuss the following topics:

- Overview of Data Cleaning and Its Importance in Data Analysis
- Identifying and Handling Missing Data
  - Learn to use the `isna()`, `isnull()`, and `notnull()` functions to identify missing data in Pandas
  - Learn to use the `dropna()`, `fillna()`, and `interpolate()` functions to handle missing data in Pandas
- Handling Duplicates
  - Learn to use the `duplicated()`, `drop_duplicates()` functions to handle duplicate data in Pandas

Overview of Data Cleaning

Data cleaning, also known as data cleansing or data scrubbing, is the process of identifying and correcting errors, inconsistencies, and inaccuracies in a dataset. It involves various techniques and methodologies to ensure that the data is accurate, reliable, and suitable for analysis. Data cleaning is a crucial step in the data analysis workflow because the quality of the insights and conclusions drawn from data analysis heavily relies on the quality of the underlying data.

The raw data collected from various sources may contain errors due to human entry mistakes, system errors, or data transmission issues. Additionally, data may have missing values, duplicate entries, or inconsistencies that can skew the analysis results if not addressed properly. Data cleaning aims to rectify these issues and produce a clean and trustworthy dataset that can be used for more accurate and meaningful analysis.

Importance of Data Cleaning in Data Analysis

Data cleaning is of utmost importance in the data analysis process for several reasons:

- **Improved Accuracy:** Cleaning the data ensures that errors and inconsistencies are corrected, leading to more accurate and reliable analysis results. High-quality data is fundamental for making informed business decisions and drawing meaningful insights.

- **Reliable Insights:** Data analysis often involves making inferences and conclusions based on patterns and trends observed in the data. Cleaning the data helps in reducing biases and errors, providing more credible and trustworthy insights.

- **Enhanced Decision-Making:** Decision-making based on flawed or unclean data can lead to incorrect conclusions and suboptimal choices. Clean data increases the chances of making informed decisions that align with the actual state of affairs.

- **Efficient Processing:** Data cleaning streamlines the data processing pipeline by removing unnecessary noise and irrelevant information. This results in faster and more efficient analysis, as analysts can focus on relevant data.

- **Better Data Integration:** When working with multiple datasets from different sources, data cleaning ensures that the data can be effectively integrated, reducing conflicts and discrepancies.

Common Data Cleaning Challenges

Data cleaning can be a complex and time-consuming task, and various challenges are encountered during the process. Some of the common data cleaning challenges include:

- **Missing Data:** Datasets may have missing values for various reasons, and handling them appropriately is crucial. The presence of missing data can impact analysis results if not addressed properly.

- **Duplicate Entries:** Duplicated data entries can skew analysis and lead to incorrect conclusions. Identifying and removing duplicates is essential to maintain data integrity.

- **Inconsistent Data:** Inconsistent data occurs when the same information is represented differently in different parts of the dataset. This can arise due to data entry errors or varying data standards.

- **Outliers:** Outliers are data points that deviate significantly from the rest of the data. They can distort analysis results, and determining whether to keep or remove outliers is a critical decision in data cleaning.

- **Data Validation:** Ensuring the accuracy and validity of the data is a challenging task. Verifying data against predefined rules or constraints is essential to detect errors and discrepancies.

- **Handling Large Datasets:** Cleaning large datasets can be resource-intensive, requiring efficient algorithms and techniques to process and clean the data effectively.

Identifying and Handling Missing Data

Understanding Missing Data

Missing data refers to the absence of values in certain fields or columns of a dataset. It can occur due to various reasons, such as data not being collected, data corruption during storage or transmission, or human errors in data entry. Dealing with missing data is essential to avoid biased or inaccurate analysis results. In this section, we will explore how to identify missing data in a dataset and apply appropriate techniques to handle it using Pandas.

"NaN" (Not a Number) in Python (NumPy and Pandas): In Python, the most common representation for missing or undefined numerical values is "**NaN**," which stands for "*Not a Number*." This is typically used in numerical arrays or data structures like NumPy arrays or Pandas DataFrames. The NumPy and Pandas libraries use "**NaN**" as a special floating-point value to represent missing data.

`isna()`, `isnull()`, and `notnull()` Functions to Identify Missing Data in Pandas

`isna()` and `isnull()` are two Pandas functions that serve the same purpose of detecting missing values in a DataFrame or Series. They are interchangeable and return Boolean masks that indicate whether each element in the DataFrame or Series is missing (**NaN** or **None**) or not.

`isna()` Function

`isna()` function is used to detect missing values (**NaN** or **None**) in a DataFrame or Series. It returns a Boolean mask of the same shape as the input object, where each element is True if the corresponding element in the DataFrame or Series is missing and False if the element is not missing. The **isna()** function is essentially a utility method to check for missing data in a structured and convenient way.

Syntax:

```
DataFrame.isna()
```

```
Series.isna()
```

Parameters: None

Returns:

A DataFrame or Series of Boolean values, where each element is True if the corresponding element is missing (**NaN** or **None**) and False if it is not missing.

Let's create a DataFrame df containing some missing values represented by **NaN**. The DataFrame **df** contains three columns: '**A**', '**B**', and '**C**'. Columns '**A**' and '**B**' have missing values, represented by **NaN**.

```
import pandas as pd
import numpy as np


# Create a DataFrame with missing values
data = {
    'A': [1, 2, np.nan, 4, None],
    'B': [None, 6, 7, 8, np.nan],
    'C': [10, 20, 30, 40, 50]
}


df = pd.DataFrame(data)


df
```

Output:

	A	B	C
0	1.0	NaN	10
1	2.0	6.0	20
2	NaN	7.0	30
3	4.0	8.0	40
4	NaN	NaN	50

Figure 4.1: *Creating a DataFrame*

Now, let's use the **isna()** function to detect missing values in the DataFrame:

```
# Use isna() to detect missing values in the DataFrame
```

```
missing_data = df.isna()
missing_data
```

	A	B	C
0	False	True	False
1	False	False	False
2	True	False	False
3	False	False	False
4	True	True	False

Figure 4.2: *Check missing values using isna()*

The **isna()** function generates a Boolean DataFrame of the same shape as the original DataFrame df, where each element is True if the corresponding element in df is missing (i.e., **NaN** or **None**) and False if the element is not missing.

Let's interpret the results for each column:

- In column 'A', the third and fifth rows are missing (**True**) as they contain **NaN**, while the other rows have valid values (**False**).

- In column 'B', the first and fifth rows are missing (**True**) as they contain None and **NaN**, respectively, while the second, third, and fourth rows have valid values (**False**).

- Column 'C' has no missing values, so all elements in the 'C' column are False.

isnull() Function

The **isnull()** function in Pandas is utilized to identify missing values (**NaN** or **None**) within a DataFrame or Series. It generates a Boolean mask of the same shape as the original object, where each element is set to True if the corresponding element in the DataFrame or Series is missing, and False if the element contains valid data. Notably, the **isnull()** function serves as a convenient approach for detecting missing data and is equivalent to using the **isna()** function, both yielding the same results.

Syntax:

```
DataFrame.isnull()
Series.isnull()
```

Parameters: None

Returns:

A DataFrame or Series of Boolean values, where each element is **True** if the corresponding element is missing (**NaN** or **None**) and False if it is not missing.

Let's utilize the DataFrame that was previously created, containing missing values, and proceed to employ the **isnull()** function to identify these missing values within the DataFrame.

```
# Use isnull() to detect missing values in the DataFrame
missing_data = df.isnull()
missing_data
```

Output:

Figure 4.3: Check missing values using isnull()

The **isnull()** function applied to the DataFrame returns a Boolean mask called **missing_data**, indicating True for the positions where the corresponding values are missing and False where the values are present.

Similar to the interpretation using **isna()**, the **isnull()** function helps us quickly identify the positions of missing values in the DataFrame. By understanding the locations of missing data, we can efficiently implement appropriate data cleaning and analysis strategies to ensure accurate and reliable outcomes in our data-driven tasks.

notnull() Function

The **notnull()** function is used to identify non-missing values in a DataFrame or Series. It returns a Boolean mask of the same shape as the input object, where each element is True if the corresponding element in the DataFrame or Series is not missing and False if the element is missing (**NaN** or **None**).

Let's demonstrate the usage of the **notnull()** function with an example:

Use **notnull()** to detect non-missing values in the DataFrame

not_missing_data = df.notnull()

not_missing_data

Output:

	A	B	C
0	True	False	True
1	True	True	True
2	False	True	True
3	True	True	True
4	False	False	True

Figure 4.4: Check missing values using notnull()

not_missing_data = df.notnull() is a line of code that uses the **notnull()** function to detect non-missing values in the DataFrame **df**. It creates a new DataFrame called **not_missing_data**, which is a Boolean mask having the same shape as the original DataFrame **df**. In this mask, each element is **True** if the corresponding element in the DataFrame **df** is not missing (that is, contains valid data), and **False** if the element is missing.

- **Column 'A':** The Boolean mask indicates that the first, second, and fourth rows are marked as **True**, which means they contain non-missing values in the 'A' column. The third and fifth rows are marked as False, indicating missing values in the 'A' column.

- **Column 'B':** The Boolean mask marks the second, third, and fourth rows as **True**, indicating non-missing values in the 'B' column. The first and fifth rows are marked as False, indicating missing values in the 'B' column.

- **Column 'C':** The Boolean mask shows that all elements in the 'C' column are marked as **True**, indicating no missing values in this column.

By using the **notnull()** function, we can easily identify the locations of non-missing values in the DataFrame. This information is valuable for data cleaning, analysis, and decision-making processes, as it allows us to focus on the available data and handle the missing data appropriately, depending on the requirements of the analysis.

Using dropna(): Removing Rows with Missing Values

The **dropna()** function in Pandas is used to remove rows with missing values from a DataFrame. By default, it removes any row containing at least one missing value.

This function helps in eliminating incomplete or unreliable data, which may adversely affect data analysis.

Syntax:

`DataFrame.dropna(axis=0, how='any', inplace=False)`

- **axis:** Specifies the axis along which to drop rows. By default, it is set to 0, meaning rows are dropped.
- **how:** Determines the criteria for dropping rows. It can take values **'any'** (default) or **'all'**. **'any'** drops rows containing any missing value, while **'all'** drops rows with all missing values.
- **inplace:** If **True**, it modifies the DataFrame in place and returns **None**. If **False** (default), it returns a new DataFrame with the rows dropped.

In the preceding example, we have created a DataFrame **df** with missing values represented by **NaN** and **None**.

```
# Create a DataFrame with missing values
data = {
    'A': [1, 2, np.nan, 4, None],
    'B': [None, 6, 7, 8, np.nan],
    'C': [10, 20, 30, 40, 50]
}


df = pd.DataFrame(data)


print("Original DataFrame:")
print(df)
```

Output:

```
Original DataFrame:
       A    B   C
0    1.0  NaN  10
1    2.0  6.0  20
2    NaN  7.0  30
3    4.0  8.0  40
4    NaN  NaN  50
```

Figure 4.5: DataFrame with missing values

In the given code snippet, the **dropna()** function is used to remove rows with missing values from the DataFrame **df**. The dropna() function is a convenient method in Pandas that helps to eliminate rows containing any **NaN** or **None** values, ensuring a cleaner and more reliable dataset for data analysis.

```
# Using dropna() to remove rows with missing values
df_dropped = df.dropna()
print("\nDataFrame after dropping rows with missing values:")
print(df_dropped)
```

```
DataFrame after dropping rows with missing values:
     A    B   C
1  2.0  6.0  20
3  4.0  8.0  40
```

Figure 4.6: *Drop rows with missing values*

When the **dropna()** function is applied to the DataFrame **df**, it removes rows that have missing values. By default, it removes any row that contains at least one missing value (i.e., **NaN** or **None**). The resulting DataFrame **df_dropped** contains only the rows with complete data, where missing values have been removed.

This operation is particularly useful when dealing with datasets containing missing data, as it allows us to focus on meaningful and complete data for analysis. The DataFrame **df_dropped** provides a cleaned version of the original DataFrame, with rows that have missing values removed.

It is important to note that the **dropna()** function does not modify the original DataFrame **df** by default. If you want to modify df in place, you can pass **inplace=True** as an argument to the **dropna()** function. Otherwise, a new DataFrame with the rows removed will be returned.

Using dropna() with a Subset of Columns

When using **dropna()** with a subset of columns, you can remove rows that have missing values in only specific columns, leaving the other columns intact. This can be helpful when you want to focus on certain columns for analysis and handle missing data in those columns differently from others.

In this example, we have a DataFrame df with missing values represented by **NaN** and **None**. We use the **dropna()** function with the subset parameter to specify that we only want to consider columns '**A**' and '**B**' for removing rows with missing values.

```
# Create a DataFrame with missing values
data = {
    'A': [1, 2, np.nan, 4, None],
    'B': [None, 6, 7, 8, np.nan],
```

```
    'C': [10, 20, 30, 40, 50]
}
```

```
df = pd.DataFrame(data)
```

```
print("Original DataFrame:")
print(df)
```

Output:

```
Original DataFrame:
     A    B   C
0  1.0  NaN  10
1  2.0  6.0  20
2  NaN  7.0  30
3  4.0  8.0  40
4  NaN  NaN  50
```

Figure 4.7: DataFrame with missing values

When **df.dropna(subset=['A', 'B'])** is executed, the function removes rows that have missing values in columns '**A**' or '**B**', but it leaves the rows with missing values in column '**C**' unchanged. The resulting **DataFrame df_dropped_subset** contains only the rows with complete data in columns '**A**' and '**B**'.

```
# Using dropna() to remove rows with missing values in column 'A' and 'B'
df_dropped_subset = df.dropna(subset=['A', 'B'])
```

```
print("\nDataFrame after dropping rows with missing values in column
'A' and 'B':")
print(df_dropped_subset)
```

Output:

```
DataFrame after dropping rows with missing values in column 'A' and 'B':
     A    B   C
1  2.0  6.0  20
3  4.0  8.0  40
```

Figure 4.8: Drop selected rows with missing values

As seen in the output, rows 0 and 2, which have missing values in columns '**A**' and '**B**', have been removed, while rows 1 and 3 with complete data in those columns are retained. The row with index 4 is also removed since it has missing values in both columns '**A**' and '**B**'.

Using **dropna()** with a subset of columns enables us to handle missing data in a targeted manner, focusing on specific columns while preserving the integrity of other columns in the DataFrame for further analysis or processing.

Fillna() function

The **fillna()** function in Pandas is used to fill missing values (**NaN** or **None**) in a DataFrame or Series with specified values or interpolation methods. It provides several ways to handle missing data, depending on the nature of the data and the analysis requirements. Let's explore different examples of using **fillna()** with various data types and strategies for filling missing values.

Numeric Data - Filling with Constant Value

When dealing with missing numeric data in a dataset, one approach is to fill those missing values with a constant value. This means that all the missing cells will be replaced by the same fixed value. The choice of the constant value depends on the context and the nature of the data. Some common choices include 0, -1, or a specific value that is known to be outside the range of the valid data.

The advantage of filling missing values with a constant is that it does not introduce any bias in the data. However, it is essential to be cautious when using this method, as it might affect the statistical properties and relationships between variables.

Let's demonstrate filling missing numeric data with a constant value using the **fillna()** function in pandas with an example.

In this example, we have a pandas DataFrame df with two columns '**A**' and '**B**', where '**A**' contains some missing values represented as **None**, and '**B**' also contains missing values.

```
# Sample data with missing values
data = {'A': [1, 2, None, 4, 5],
        'B': [None, 10, 20, None, 50]}
df = pd.DataFrame(data)


print("Original DataFrame:")
print(df)
```

Output:

```
Original DataFrame:
     A     B
0  1.0   NaN
1  2.0  10.0
2  NaN  20.0
3  4.0   NaN
4  5.0  50.0
```

***Figure 4.9**: Sample DataFrame with missing values*

The **fillna()** function is applied to the DataFrame df, and all the missing values **(NaN)** in the DataFrame are replaced with the constant value 0.

```
# Fill missing values in the DataFrame with a constant value, e.g., 0
constant_filled_df = df.fillna(0)


print("\nDataFrame with Missing Values Filled by Constant (0):")
print(constant_filled_df)
```

Output:

```
DataFrame with Missing Values Filled by Constant (0):
     A     B
0   1.0   0.0
1   2.0  10.0
2   0.0  20.0
3   4.0   0.0
4   5.0  50.0
```

Figure 4.10: Filling missing values with a constant value

The resulting **DataFrame constant_filled_df** contains the same shape as the original DataFrame, but with the missing values replaced by 0. This method ensures that the missing values are no longer present in the DataFrame, making it suitable for certain types of analyses and computations.

It's important to note that filling missing values with a constant has its implications. For numeric data, filling with a constant like 0 can potentially introduce biases in statistical analyses, especially if 0 has a specific meaning in the context of the data. Therefore, it's essential to carefully consider the implications of filling missing values with a constant and to choose an appropriate constant value based on the nature of the data and the requirements of the analysis. Additionally, other methods like filling with the mean, median, or interpolation might be more suitable depending on the dataset and the analysis being performed.

Numeric Data - Filling with Mean or Median

When dealing with missing numeric data, an alternative approach is to fill those missing values with the mean or median of the non-missing values in the same column. This method is useful when the missing values are assumed to have a central tendency similar to the existing data points in that column. By using the mean or median, we aim to minimize the impact of missing data on the overall statistical properties of the dataset.

Using the mean is suitable when the data distribution is approximately symmetric, without significant outliers. On the other hand, if the data distribution is skewed or contains outliers, the median might be a more robust choice for filling missing values.

Let's demonstrate filling missing numeric data with the mean and median using the **fillna()** function in pandas with an example. We will be using the same DataFrame used in the preceding example.

Filling Missing Values in Column 'A' with the Mean of Non-Missing Values

In the code snippet displayed in *Figure 4.11*, we use the **fillna()** method to fill the missing values in column '**A**' of the DataFrame df with the mean of the non-missing values present in the same column. The **df['A'].mean()** calculates the mean of all non-missing values in column '**A**', and then the **fillna()** method fills the missing values in '**A**' with this computed mean. This method ensures that the missing values in column '**A**' are replaced by a value that represents the average of the existing data points in that column. It helps maintain the central tendency of the data and ensures that the overall statistical properties are preserved.

```
# Fill missing values in column 'A' with the mean of non-missing values
in column 'A'

mean_filled_df_A = df.copy()

mean_filled_df_A['A'] = df['A'].fillna(df['A'].mean())
```

In the DataFrame **mean_filled_df_A**, the missing value in column '**A**' at index 2 has been filled with the mean of the non-missing values in the same column, which is approximately 3.0. The rest of the values in column '**A**' remain unchanged.

```
print("\nDataFrame with Missing Values Filled by Mean:")

print(mean_filled_df_A)
```

```
DataFrame with Missing Values Filled by Mean:
     A     B
0   1.0   NaN
1   2.0  10.0
2   3.0  20.0
3   4.0   NaN
4   5.0  50.0
```

Figure 4.11: Column A missing values filled with mean

Filling Missing Values in Column 'B' with the Median of Non-Missing Values

We use the **fillna()** method to fill the missing values in column '**B**' of the DataFrame df with the median of the non-missing values in the same column. The **df['B'].median()** calculates the median of all non-missing values in column '**B**', and then the **fillna()** method fills the missing values in '**B**' with this computed median. Filling with the median is a robust approach, especially when the data distribution is skewed or contains outliers, as the median is less sensitive to extreme values. By using the median, we aim to mitigate the impact of outliers on the imputation process, providing a more robust estimation for the missing values in column '**B**'.

```
# Fill missing values in column 'B' with the median of non-missing
values in column 'B'
median_filled_df_B = df.copy()
median_filled_df_B['B'] = df['B'].fillna(df['B'].median())
```

```
DataFrame with Missing Values Filled by Median:
     A     B
0   1.0  20.0
1   2.0  10.0
2   NaN  20.0
3   4.0  20.0
4   5.0  50.0
```

Figure 4.12: Filling missing values with median

In the DataFrame **median_filled_df_B**, the missing values in column '**B**' have been filled with the median of the non-missing values in the same column, which is 20.0. The median value provides a robust estimation for filling the missing values as it is less sensitive to extreme values or outliers in the data. After filling with the median, the DataFrame retains the other values in column '**B**' as they were.

Categorical Data – Filling with a Specific Category and Mode

When dealing with missing categorical data, one common approach is to fill the missing values with a specific category or label. This method is suitable when the missing values are assumed to represent a distinct category that is different from the existing categories in the dataset. By filling missing values with a specific category, we avoid introducing bias into the data and maintain the categorical nature of the variable.

When dealing with missing categorical data, there are two common approaches for filling the missing values: filling with a specific category and filling with the mode.

Filling with a Specific Category

This method involves filling the missing categorical values with a predetermined category or label that represents the absence of a valid category. It is suitable when the missing values are assumed to have a distinct meaning from the existing categories in the dataset. Common choices for a specific category include labels like "**Unknown**," "**Not Applicable**," "**Other**," or any other value that clearly indicates the absence of a valid category. By using a specific category, we ensure that the missing values are treated distinctly in subsequent analyses and avoid introducing biases into the data.

In this example, we have a pandas DataFrame **df** with a column **'Country'** representing a list of countries, where some country names are missing and are represented as None.

```
# Sample data with missing country name
data = {'Country': ['USA', 'Canada', None, 'Germany', None, 'India']}
df = pd.DataFrame(data)


print("Original DataFrame:")
print(df)
```

Output:

```
Original DataFrame:
    Country
0       USA
1    Canada
2      None
3   Germany
4      None
5     India
```

Figure 4.13: DataFrame with categorical column

We then use the **fillna('Unknown')** method to fill all the missing country names in the **'Country'** column with the label **'Unknown'**. The resulting DataFrame **specific_filled_df** contains the **'Country'** column with missing country names replaced by the specific category **'Unknown'**.

```
# Fill missing country names with a specific category 'Unknown'
specific_filled_df = df['Country'].fillna('Unknown')


print("\nDataFrame with Missing Country Names Filled by 'Unknown':")
print(specific_filled_df)
```

Output:

```
DataFrame with Missing Country Names Filled by 'Unknown':
0          USA
1       Canada
2      Unknown
3      Germany
4      Unknown
5        India
Name: Country, dtype: object
```

Figure 4.14: Missing value filled with unknown

We can observe from the output, the missing values at index 2 and 4 are now filled with **'Unknown'**, indicating that these entries do not have valid country names. This explicit handling of missing categorical data helps in maintaining the integrity of the data and provides clarity regarding the absence of country information in those entries.

Filling with the Mode

The mode represents the most frequent category in a categorical variable. When using the mode, missing categorical values are filled with the category that appears most frequently in the non-missing values of the same column. This method is suitable when the missing values are believed to be similar to the most common category in the dataset. Filling with the mode helps to retain the overall distribution of categories and ensures that the central tendency of the categorical variable is preserved.

In the following example, we use pandas to fill missing categorical data with the mode and use the same DataFrame as in the previous example.

In the provided code, we calculate the mode of the **'Country'** column using the **mode()** function. The **mode()** function is applied to the **'Country'** column, which returns a pandas Series containing the most frequently occurring country name in the **'Country'** column. In this case, **'Canada'** is the most prevalent country name in the dataset, occurring more frequently than any other country name.

```
# Calculate the mode of the 'Country' column
mode_country = df['Country'].mode()[0]
print("\nMode of 'Country' column:", mode_country)
```

Output:

```
Mode of 'Country' column: Canada
```

Figure 4.15: Finding the mode

In the following code, missing country names in the **'Country'** column have been filled with the mode value, which is **'Canada'**. As a result, all the missing values in the **'Country'** column have been replaced with the mode category, ensuring that the most common country name is used to fill the missing entries.

```
# Fill missing country names with the mode
mode_filled_df = df['Country'].fillna(mode_country)
print("\nDataFrame with Missing Country Names Filled by Mode:")
print(mode_filled_df)
```

Output:

```
DataFrame with Missing Country Names Filled by Mode:
0         USA
1      Canada
2      Canada
3     Germany
4      Canada
5       India
Name: Country, dtype: object
```

Figure 4.16: *Missing value filled with mode*

The resulting **DataFrame mode_filled_df** reflects the changes, and it now contains the **'Country'** column with the missing country names filled by **'Canada'**, preserving the overall distribution of country names in the dataset.

Backfill (Bfill) or Forward Fill (Ffill)

When dealing with missing data, using backfill (**bfill**) or forward fill (**ffill**) are two methods to fill the missing values with the most recent available data (**ffill**) or the next available data (**bfill**), respectively.

Forward Fill (Ffill)

Forward fill (**ffill**) is a method used to fill missing values in a dataset by propagating the last known value forward to fill the gaps. When encountering a missing value, the forward fill method looks for the most recent non-missing value before the missing data point and uses it to fill the missing value. This process continues until all missing values are filled or until another missing value is encountered.

Forward fill is particularly useful when working with time series data or any sequential data where the observations have a natural order. In such cases, filling missing values with the most recent available data is often a reasonable approach, as it helps maintain the temporal continuity of the dataset.

```
data = {
    'A': [1, 2, None, 4, None, 6],
    'B': [3, None, 7, None, 11, 13]
}

df = pd.DataFrame(data)
print("Original DataFrame:")
print(df)
```

Output:

```
Original DataFrame:
     A     B
0   1.0   3.0
1   2.0   NaN
2   NaN   7.0
3   4.0   NaN
4   NaN  11.0
5   6.0  13.0
```

Figure 4.17: *DataFrame with missing values*

In this example, we have a pandas DataFrame df with two columns '**A**' and '**B**', where both columns contain some missing values (represented as **None** in Python).

We use the **ffill()** method to perform forward fill on the DataFrame, filling the missing values in each column with the most recent non-missing value observed before the missing data point. The resulting DataFrame **forward_filled_df** contains the missing values filled using forward fill.

```
# Fill missing values using forward fill (ffill)

forward_filled_df = df.ffill()

print("\nDataFrame with Missing Values Filled by Forward Fill (Ffill):")

print(forward_filled_df)
```

Output:

```
DataFrame with Missing Values Filled by Forward Fill (Ffill):
     A     B
0   1.0   NaN
1   1.0  10.0
2   3.0  10.0
3   3.0  30.0
4   5.0  50.0
```

Figure 4.18: *Filling Missing Value with ffill*

In the output, you can see that the missing values in each column '**A**' and '**B**' have been filled with the most recent non-missing values. For example, the missing value in index 1 of column '**A**' has been filled with the value 1.0, which is the most recent non-missing value before index 1. Similarly, the missing value in index 2 of column '**B**' has been filled with the value 10.0, which is the most recent non-missing value before index 2.

The forward-filled DataFrame remains unchanged in index 0 of column '**B**', and it still contains a missing value (**NaN**). This is because there is no previous non-missing value to propagate forward for the missing value at index 0.

In situations where the first row of a column contains missing values, forward fill cannot be applied to fill those missing values since there is no previous data to use for filling.

Backward Fill (Bfill)

Backward fill (**bfill**) is a method used to fill missing values in a dataset by propagating the next known value backward to fill the gaps. It is particularly useful in time series data or any sequential data where the observations have a natural order. The backward fill method fills the missing value with the next available data point in the column. This process continues until all missing values are filled or until another missing value is encountered.

In the following code, we have a pandas DataFrame df with missing values (NaN) in some cells of columns A and B. We use the **bfill()** method to perform backward fill on the DataFrame. The **bfill()** method propagates the next known value backward to fill the missing values in each column.

```
# Fill missing values using backward fill (bfill)
backward_filled_df = df.bfill()


print("Original DataFrame:")
print(df)


print("\nDataFrame with Missing Values Filled by Backward Fill (Bfill):")
print(backward_filled_df)
```

Output:

```
Original DataFrame:
     A     B
0  1.0   NaN
1  NaN  10.0
2  3.0   NaN
3  NaN  30.0
4  5.0  50.0

DataFrame with Missing Values Filled by Backward Fill (Bfill):
     A     B
0  1.0  10.0
1  3.0  10.0
2  3.0  30.0
3  5.0  30.0
4  5.0  50.0
```

Figure 4.19: *Filling Missing Value with bfill*

From the output, we can observe the following:

- At index 0 of column 'A', the value **1.0** remains unchanged, as it is not a missing value **(NaN)**.

- At index **0** of column '**B**', the missing value (originally **NaN**) is filled with the value **10.0**, which is the next non-missing value after index 0 in column '**B**'.

- At index **1** of column '**A**', the missing value (originally **NaN**) is filled with the value **3.0**, which is the next non-missing value after index 1 in column '**A**'.

- At index **2** of column '**B**', the missing value (originally **NaN**) is filled with the value **30.0**, which is the next non-missing value after index 2 in column '**B**'.

- At index **3** of column '**A**', the missing value (originally **NaN**) is filled with the value **5.0**, which is the next non-missing value after index 3 in column '**A**'.

The **bfill()** method propagates the available values backward to fill missing values, resulting in a DataFrame with missing values replaced by the next available data points in their respective columns.

Interpolation for Handling Missing Data

Interpolation is a technique used to estimate missing values in a dataset based on the existing data points. It is particularly useful for handling missing data in time series or sequential data, where missing values can occur due to various reasons such as sensor failures or data collection gaps. Interpolation methods calculate the missing values by considering the values of neighboring data points, making an educated guess of what the missing values might be.

One common interpolation method is linear interpolation, where missing values are estimated based on a straight line connecting two neighboring data points. Another method is cubic interpolation, which uses a cubic polynomial to fit the data points and provides a smoother estimate of the missing values.

Let's demonstrate how to use linear interpolation to fill missing values in a pandas DataFrame.

Suppose we have the following DataFrame with missing values:

```
# Sample data with missing values
data = pd.DataFrame({'A': [1, 2, np.nan, 4, np.nan], 'B': [5, np.nan, 7, 8, 9]})
data
```

Output:

	A	B
0	1.0	5.0
1	2.0	NaN
2	NaN	7.0
3	4.0	8.0
4	NaN	9.0

Figure 4.20: *DataFrame with missing values*

We can use the **interpolate()** function to fill the missing values in each column using linear interpolation.

Linear interpolation

Linear interpolation is a simple and widely used method for estimating values between two known data points. It works on the assumption that the relationship between data points is linear, meaning that the change between consecutive data points is constant. The linear interpolation process involves drawing a straight line between two adjacent data points and estimating values along that line to fill in missing data.

```
# Linear interpolation
data_linear_interpolated = data.interpolate(method='linear')

print("Linear Interpolation:")
print(data_linear_interpolated)
```

Output:

```
Linear Interpolation:
     A    B
0  1.0  5.0
1  2.0  6.0
2  3.0  7.0
3  4.0  8.0
4  4.0  9.0
```

Figure 4.21: *Filling missing values with Linear Interpolate*

For the missing value in **column B** at index **1**, pandas performs linear interpolation between the data points (**1.0**, **5.0**) and (**4.0**, **8.0**) to estimate the value as **6.0**.

For the missing value in column A at index 2, pandas performs linear interpolation between the data points (**2.0**, **6.0**) and (**4.0**, **8.0**) to estimate the value as **3.0**.

The other missing value in column **A** at index **4** is filled with the value **4.0** because there is no other data point to perform the interpolation.

Time-Based Interpolation

Time-based interpolation is a specialized type of interpolation used for time-series data, where the missing values are estimated based on the time index of the data points. In pandas, we can perform time-based interpolation using the **DataFrame.interpolate()** method with the **method='time'** parameter. This method takes into account the time index and performs interpolation accordingly.

Let's create a sample time-series DataFrame with missing values and then perform time-based interpolation on it using pandas.

```
# Sample time-series data with missing values
time_index = pd.date_range(start='2023-01-01', periods=5, freq='D')
time_series_data = pd.Series([10, np.nan, 30, np.nan, 50], index=time_index)


print("Time-Series Data with Missing Values:")
print(time_series_data)
```

```
Time-Series Data with Missing Values:
2023-01-01    10.0
2023-01-02     NaN
2023-01-03    30.0
2023-01-04     NaN
2023-01-05    50.0
Freq: D, dtype: float64
```

Figure 4.22: TimeSeries DataFrame with missing values

Now, let's perform time-based interpolation on this time-series data using the **DataFrame.interpolate()** method with **method='time'**.

```
# Time-based interpolation
time_series_interpolated = time_series_data.interpolate(method='time')


print("\nTime-Based Interpolated Data:")
print(time_series_interpolated)
```

Output:

```
Time-Based Interpolated Data:
2023-01-01    10.0
2023-01-02    20.0
2023-01-03    30.0
2023-01-04    40.0
2023-01-05    50.0
Freq: D, dtype: float64
```

Figure 4.23: Time-based interpolation

In the time-series data, we have two missing values at timestamps '**2023-01-02**' and '**2023-01-04**'. When we performed time-based interpolation, pandas filled in the missing values based on the time distance between available data points.

For the missing value at '**2023-01-02**', pandas performed time-based interpolation between the available data points '**2023-01-01**' (**10.0**) and '**2023-01-03**' (**30.0**) and estimated the value as **20.0**.

For the missing value at '**2023-01-04**', pandas performed time-based interpolation between the available data points '**2023-01-03**' (**30.0**) and '**2023-01-05**' (**50.0**) and estimated the value as **40.0**.

The time-based interpolated data now provides a continuous time-series representation with the missing values estimated based on the timestamps.

Handling Duplicates

Duplicates in data refer to identical or nearly identical records that appear more than once in a dataset. These duplicates can lead to skewed analysis, inaccurate statistics, and biased results. Therefore, it is essential to identify and remove duplicate data from datasets to ensure data integrity and reliability of analyses. In this section, we will explore how to identify and remove duplicates using Python and its popular data manipulation library, pandas.

Understanding Duplicates in Data

Before diving into the code, it's essential to understand what duplicate data means. Duplicate data occurs when two or more records in a dataset have the same values in all or most of their columns. These duplicates can be either exact duplicates or very similar records with slight variations.

`duplicated()`: Detecting Duplicated Rows

In pandas, the **duplicated()** function is used to identify duplicate rows in a DataFrame. It helps us to find out which rows are duplicates and which rows are unique based on the values in one or more columns. The function returns a Boolean Series where each element corresponds to a row in the DataFrame. The value is True for rows that are duplicates and False for non-duplicate rows.

The default behavior of **duplicated()** is to mark all duplicates after the first occurrence as True, which means the first occurrence is considered non-duplicate. You can customize this behavior using the keep parameter.

Syntax:

```
DataFrame.duplicated(subset=None, keep='first')
```

Parameters:

- **subset:** A column label or sequence of labels that uniquely identifies rows for duplicate consideration. If subset is not specified, the function considers all columns for detecting duplicates.
- **keep:** Determines which duplicates (if any) to mark as True.
- **'first' (default):** Mark duplicates except for the first occurrence.
- **'last':** Mark duplicates except for the last occurrence.
- **False:** Mark all duplicates as True.
- **Returns:** A Boolean Series where each element indicates whether the corresponding row is a duplicate (**True**) or not (**False**).

Let's illustrate the use of **duplicated()** with a simple example.

In this example, we created a DataFrame **df** with some duplicate rows based on the **'ID'** column.

```
# Sample data with duplicates
data = {
    'ID': [1, 2, 3, 4, 1, 5, 2],
    'Name': ['Alice', 'Bob', 'Charlie', 'David', 'Alice', 'Eve', 'Bob'],
    'Age': [25, 30, 22, 28, 25, 29, 30]
}


df = pd.DataFrame(data)


df
```

	ID	Name	Age
0	1	Alice	25
1	2	Bob	30
2	3	Charlie	22
3	4	David	28
4	1	Alice	25
5	5	Eve	29
6	2	Bob	30

Figure 4.24: DataFrame created with duplicate rows

When we call **df.duplicated()**, it returns a Boolean Series where the rows with duplicate records are marked as **True**, and the rest are marked as **False**. Rows 4 and 6 have duplicate records based on the **'ID'** column, so they are marked as True in the output.

```
# Using duplicated() to detect duplicate rows
duplicates = df.duplicated()
print(duplicates)
```

Output:

```
0    False
1    False
2    False
3    False
4     True
5    False
6     True
dtype: bool
```

Figure 4.25: *Boolean Series with duplicate records*

By default, **duplicated()** used the entire row to detect duplicates. If you want to specify a subset of columns to check for duplicates, you can use the **subset** parameter. For example, if you only want to consider the **'ID'** and **'Name'** columns for detecting duplicates.

```
duplicates_subset = df.duplicated(subset=['ID', 'Name'])
print(duplicates_subset)
```

Output:

```
0    False
1    False
2    False
3    False
4     True
5    False
6     True
dtype: bool
```

Figure 4.26: *Finding duplicate records in ID and Name columns*

In this case, the function checks for duplicates only in the **'ID'** and **'Name'** columns, and the result remains the same as before.

Using drop_duplicates(): Removing Duplicated Rows

The **drop_duplicates()** function identifies and removes duplicate rows from the DataFrame, keeping only the first occurrence of each duplicated row by default. This means that the first occurrence of a set of duplicates is considered non-duplicate, and subsequent duplicates are removed.

Syntax:

DataFrame.drop_duplicates(subset=None, keep='first', inplace=False)

Parameters:

- **subset:** A column label or sequence of labels that uniquely identifies rows for duplicate consideration. If subset is not specified, the function considers all columns for detecting duplicates.
- **keep:** Determines which duplicates (if any) to keep.
- **'first' (default):** Keep the first occurrence and remove subsequent duplicates.
- **'last':** Keep the last occurrence and remove previous duplicates.
- **False:** Remove all occurrences of duplicates.
- **inplace:** If True, modifies the DataFrame in place and returns **None**. If **False** (default), returns a new DataFrame with duplicates removed.
- **Returns:** If inplace is **False** (default), the function returns a new DataFrame with duplicates removed. If **inplace** is **True**, the function returns None, and the original DataFrame is modified in place.

Example

Let's illustrate the use of **drop_duplicates()** with a simple example.

In this example, we will use same DataFrame df as in the previous example with duplicate rows based on the **'ID'** column. When we call **df.drop_duplicates()**, it removes the duplicate rows and keeps only the first occurrence of each duplicated row, resulting in a new DataFrame called **df_no_duplicates**.

The rows with **index 4** and **6** in the original DataFrame were duplicates based on the **'ID'** column. After using **drop_duplicates()**, these duplicates were removed, and the new DataFrame **df_no_duplicates** contains only the unique records.

```
# Using drop_duplicates() to remove duplicate rows

df_no_duplicates = df.drop_duplicates()

print(df_no_duplicates)
```

Output:

```
     ID    Name  Age
0    1    Alice   25
1    2      Bob   30
2    3  Charlie   22
3    4    David   28
5    5      Eve   29
```

Figure 4.27: *Dropping duplicates*

Conclusion

In this chapter, we covered the importance of data cleaning in data analysis. We learned how to identify and handle missing data using functions like **isna()**, **isnull()**, **notnull()**, **dropna()**, **fillna()**, and **interpolate()** in Pandas. Additionally, we explored methods for detecting and managing duplicate data using **duplicated()** and **drop_duplicates()**. Data cleaning is a critical step to ensure data integrity and accuracy, providing a solid foundation for meaningful and reliable data analysis.

In the upcoming chapter, we will focus on the data filtering capabilities of Pandas. Data filtering allows us to extract specific subsets of data from a DataFrame based on various conditions or criteria. We will explore how to filter data based on column values, using logical operators. Furthermore, we will learn how to handle null or missing values during the filtering process, ensuring a comprehensive data analysis and accurate insights.

Exercise Questions

1. Given a DataFrame, how can you identify missing data using Pandas? Explain the difference between **isna()**, **isnull()**, and **notnull()** functions.

2. You have a DataFrame with missing values, and you want to remove rows containing any missing data. Which Pandas function should you use, and how can you apply it?

3. Suppose you have a DataFrame with missing values, and you want to fill those missing values with a specific value or method. Which Pandas function can you use to achieve this, and what are some common techniques for filling missing data?

4. You have a DataFrame with duplicate records, and you want to keep only the first occurrence of each duplicated row. Which function in Pandas should you use to remove duplicates while preserving the first occurrence?

5. Suppose you want to drop rows containing missing data only in specific columns of a DataFrame. How can you achieve this using the subset parameter in the **dropna()** function?

## CHAPTER 5

Data Filtering with Pandas

Welcome to *Chapter* 5 of our data manipulation journey with Pandas! In this chapter, we will explore the powerful capabilities of Pandas for data filtering. Data filtering is a fundamental technique in data analysis that allows us to extract specific subsets of data from a DataFrame based on predefined conditions. By focusing on relevant subsets of data, we can derive valuable insights and make informed decisions from complex datasets.

Throughout this chapter, we will embark on the core of data filtering, understanding how to filter rows and columns based on different conditions using logical operators, and numerical comparisons.

Structure

In this chapter, we will discuss the following topics:

- Definition of Data Filtering and its Importance in Data Analysis
- Overview of Pandas and its Capabilities for Data Filtering
- Filtering a DataFrame Based on a Specific Column or Set of Columns
- Filtering by Equality, Inequality, and Logical Operators
- Filtering by Numeric Methods
- Filtering by Where Condition
- Filtering by Date and Time Methods
- Filtering Null or Missing Values

Data Filtering and its Importance in Data Analysis

In the context of data analysis, datasets often contain a vast amount of information, including irrelevant or redundant data. Data filtering serves as a fundamental data preprocessing step to refine and tailor the dataset to suit the requirements of the analysis or investigation at hand. By applying filters, analysts can zoom in on the data that is pertinent to their specific research question, which streamlines the analysis process and improves the accuracy of results.

Data filtering is typically conducted on tabular data structures like DataFrames, where rows represent observations, and columns represent variables. Analysts can filter rows or columns based on various conditions, such as numerical comparisons, string matching, date ranges, or combinations of multiple conditions. The filtering process can be performed using logical operators like equality, inequality, AND, OR, NOT, as well as specialized filtering methods provided by data manipulation libraries, such as Pandas in Python.

Importance of Data Filtering in Data Analysis

- **Reducing Data Size:** Datasets can often be vast, containing a large number of rows and columns. By filtering the data, unnecessary or less relevant information can be excluded, resulting in a smaller and more manageable dataset. This makes data analysis more efficient and reduces computational overhead.

- **Extracting Relevant Information:** Filtering enables analysts to extract subsets of data that are most relevant to the research question or analysis objectives. It allows them to zoom in on specific aspects of the data, making it easier to identify patterns, trends, and insights.

- **Preparing Data for Analysis:** Data filtering helps in preparing the data for further analysis. By removing irrelevant or incorrect data points, analysts can ensure data accuracy and quality, which is crucial for making informed decisions based on reliable information.

- **Identifying Anomalies and Outliers:** Filtering can be used to identify and investigate outliers or anomalous data points. These extreme values might be errors or contain valuable information, and filtering allows analysts to isolate and examine them separately.

- **Facilitating Time Series Analysis:** In time series data, filtering based on specific dates or times is essential for studying temporal patterns, trends, and seasonality. It helps in understanding how data changes over time and assists in forecasting future behavior.

- **Enabling Comparative Analysis:** Data filtering allows for comparisons between different groups or subsets of the data. For example, one can compare the performance of different products, regions, or demographics by filtering the data based on these categories.

- **Enhancing Visualization:** Filtering the data before visualization can lead to more informative and concise visual representations. By focusing on specific segments of the data, visualizations can convey the intended message more effectively.

Pandas Capabilities for Data Filtering

Pandas provides powerful data manipulation and analysis tools. It is widely used in data science and data analysis projects due to its ease of use, versatility, and efficient handling of structured data. Pandas offers various data structures, but the primary one is the DataFrame, which is heavily used for data filtering and manipulation tasks.

Pandas' key capabilities for data filtering include:

- **Conditional Indexing:** Pandas enables you to filter rows based on specific conditions applied to column values. This is achieved by creating boolean masks that indicate whether a certain condition is met for each row.

- **Logical Operators:** We can combine conditions using logical operators like **&** (and) and **|** (or) to create complex filtering criteria, allowing us to extract data subsets that meet intricate requirements.

- **Numeric Filtering:** Pandas supports filtering rows based on numeric conditions, such as filtering rows with values greater than, less than, or within a certain range.

- **Date and Time Filtering:** With Pandas' datetime functionalities, you can filter data based on date and time conditions. This is particularly useful when dealing with time-series data.

- **Filtering by Null Values:** Pandas provides methods to filter rows or columns with missing values (`NaN`) or non-missing values, allowing you to handle incomplete data effectively.

- **Querying with `.query()`:** Pandas offers the `.query()` method, allowing you to write SQL-like queries to filter data based on specific conditions.

By harnessing these capabilities, Pandas equips data analysts and scientists with a comprehensive toolkit for extracting relevant subsets of data from large and complex datasets, streamlining the analysis process and enabling informed decision-making.

Filtering a DataFrame Based on a Specific Column or Set of Columns

In *Chapter 3, Pandas DataFrame*, we learned about column-wise filtering where we select specific columns from a DataFrame. Now, in this chapter, we are revisiting this concept to further understand how to manipulate and extract data.

Filtering a DataFrame based on a specific column or set of columns labels means selecting and extracting a subset of data from the DataFrame, where only the specified columns are included. The process involves applying conditions or selections to the column labels to retain the desired columns and create a new DataFrame or Pandas Series with the filtered data.

Filtering with a single column in a DataFrame refers to the process of selecting and extracting data from a specific column, resulting in a Pandas Series containing the values from that column. The process involves using the DataFrame indexing operator (**[]**) with the label of the column you want to keep.

To demonstrate filtering with a single column from the Boston Housing Dataset, we will use the **load_boston()** function from the **sklearn.datasets** module.

```
import pandas as pd
from sklearn.datasets import load_boston


# Load the Boston Housing Dataset
boston = load_boston()


# Create a DataFrame from the dataset
df = pd.DataFrame(boston.data, columns=boston.feature_names)
# Add the target column (median house prices) to the DataFrame
df['MEDV'] = boston.target


# Display the first few rows of the DataFrame
print(df.head())
```

Output:

```
      CRIM    ZN  INDUS  CHAS    NOX     RM   AGE     DIS  RAD    TAX \
0  0.00632  18.0   2.31   0.0  0.538  6.575  65.2  4.0900  1.0  296.0
1  0.02731   0.0   7.07   0.0  0.469  6.421  78.9  4.9671  2.0  242.0
2  0.02729   0.0   7.07   0.0  0.469  7.185  61.1  4.9671  2.0  242.0
3  0.03237   0.0   2.18   0.0  0.458  6.998  45.8  6.0622  3.0  222.0
4  0.06905   0.0   2.18   0.0  0.458  7.147  54.2  6.0622  3.0  222.0

   PTRATIO       B  LSTAT  MEDV
0     15.3  396.90   4.98  24.0
1     17.8  396.90   9.14  21.6
2     17.8  392.83   4.03  34.7
3     18.7  394.63   2.94  33.4
4     18.7  396.90   5.33  36.2
```

Figure 5.1: Load Boston housing dataset

In the preceding code, we loaded the Boston Housing Dataset using the **load_boston()** function, created a DataFrame **df** from the dataset, and displayed the first few rows of the DataFrame.

Now, let's filter a single column, such as **'CRIM' (per capita crime rate by town)**, from the DataFrame:

```
filtered_single_column = df['CRIM']
```

```
# Display the filtered_single_column
print(filtered_single_column.head())
```

Output:

```
0    0.00632
1    0.02731
2    0.02729
3    0.03237
4    0.06905
Name: CRIM, dtype: float64
```

Figure 5.2: Filter single column

The **filtered_single_column** will contain a Pandas Series that contains all the values from the **'CRIM'** column of the DataFrame **df**. The Series will have the same index as the original DataFrame, so each value in the Series corresponds to a specific row in the DataFrame.

Filtering using multiple columns involves selecting and extracting specific columns from a DataFrame. This allows you to focus on a subset of columns that are of interest for your analysis:

```
# Filtering using multiple columns 'CRIM' and 'ZN'
```

```
filtered_columns = df[['CRIM', 'ZN']]
print(filtered_columns.head())
```

Output:

```
      CRIM    ZN
0  0.00632  18.0
1  0.02731   0.0
2  0.02729   0.0
3  0.03237   0.0
4  0.06905   0.0
```

Figure 5.3: Filter multiple columns

In the line **filtered_columns = df[['CRIM', 'ZN']]**, you are filtering a DataFrame named df to create a new DataFrame named **filtered_columns**. This new DataFrame includes only the columns labeled **'CRIM'** and **'ZN'** from the original DataFrame. The double square brackets are used to enclose the list of column labels you want to retain, effectively selecting and extracting these specific columns. This operation allows to narrow down the data to a subset of columns of interest, making it easier to analyze, visualize, or manipulate relevant information within the dataset.

Filtering using multiple columns is helpful when we want to work with a specific subset of attributes from your dataset. This can make our analysis more focused and concise, as we are dealing with a reduced set of information that is directly relevant to our research or exploration.

Filtering by Equality, Inequality, and Logical Operators

Filtering by equality, inequality, and logical operators involves the process of selecting and extracting particular rows from a DataFrame based on specified conditions that involve comparisons between the values of different columns.

Filtering by equality involves selecting and extracting rows from a DataFrame where a specific column's value matches a given value. This is useful when we want to isolate rows with a particular attribute or characteristic.

Suppose we want to filter the dataset to include only rows where the **'CHAS' (Charles River dummy variable)** value is equal to 1.

Let's see how to achieve this:

filtered_by_chas = df[df['CHAS'] == 1]

print(filtered_by_chas.head())

Output:

```
        CRIM    ZN  INDUS  CHAS    NOX     RM    AGE     DIS  RAD    TAX \
142  3.32105   0.0  19.58   1.0  0.871  5.403  100.0  1.3216  5.0  403.0
152  1.12658   0.0  19.58   1.0  0.871  5.012   88.0  1.6102  5.0  403.0
154  1.41385   0.0  19.58   1.0  0.871  6.129   96.0  1.7494  5.0  403.0
155  3.53501   0.0  19.58   1.0  0.871  6.152   82.6  1.7455  5.0  403.0
160  1.27346   0.0  19.58   1.0  0.605  6.250   92.6  1.7984  5.0  403.0

     PTRATIO       B  LSTAT  MEDV
142     14.7  396.90  26.82  13.4
152     14.7  343.28  12.12  15.3
154     14.7  321.02  15.12  17.0
155     14.7   88.01  15.02  15.6
160     14.7  338.92   5.50  27.0
```

Figure 5.4: Filtering by equality

The expression **df['CHAS'] == 1** generates a boolean Series where each element indicates whether the corresponding row in the **'CHAS'** column is equal to 1 or not. By employing this boolean Series as an indexing mechanism within the outer square brackets, the DataFrame is selectively filtered to preserve only the rows where the condition holds True, signifying instances where the **'CHAS'** value equals 1. This process effectively creates a new DataFrame that exclusively contains rows satisfying the specified condition, allowing for focused analysis of data segments possessing the desired attribute.

Filtering by inequality involves selecting and extracting rows from a DataFrame where a specific column's value satisfies a given condition, such as being greater than, less than, greater than or equal to, or less than or equal to a certain value. This is useful for isolating data points that fall within a particular range or meet specific criteria.

- **Greater Than (>) Filtering** involves selecting rows from a DataFrame where a specific column's value is greater than a given value. This filtering condition is used to isolate rows with values that exceed a specified threshold.

```
# Filter rows where 'RM' (average number of rooms per dwelling)
is greater than 6


filtered_greater_than = df[df['RM'] > 6]

print(filtered_greater_than.head())
```

Output:

```
      CRIM    ZN  INDUS  CHAS    NOX     RM   AGE     DIS  RAD    TAX  \
0  0.00632  18.0   2.31   0.0  0.538  6.575  65.2  4.0900  1.0  296.0
1  0.02731   0.0   7.07   0.0  0.469  6.421  78.9  4.9671  2.0  242.0
2  0.02729   0.0   7.07   0.0  0.469  7.185  61.1  4.9671  2.0  242.0
3  0.03237   0.0   2.18   0.0  0.458  6.998  45.8  6.0622  3.0  222.0
4  0.06905   0.0   2.18   0.0  0.458  7.147  54.2  6.0622  3.0  222.0

   PTRATIO       B  LSTAT  MEDV
0     15.3  396.90   4.98  24.0
1     17.8  396.90   9.14  21.6
2     17.8  392.83   4.03  34.7
3     18.7  394.63   2.94  33.4
4     18.7  396.90   5.33  36.2
```

Figure 5.5: *Filtering using greater than*

The condition **df['RM'] > 6** creates a boolean Series where each element indicates whether the corresponding row's 'RM' value (average number of rooms per dwelling) is greater than 6.

The resulting DataFrame **filtered_greater_than** thus contains those rows from the original DataFrame where houses have more than 6 rooms on average.

- **Less Than (<) Filtering** involves selecting rows from a DataFrame where a specific column's value is less than a given value.

  ```
  # Filter rows where 'TAX' (full-value property-tax rate per
  $10,000) is less than 300
  ```

  ```
  filtered_less_than = df[df['TAX'] < 300]
  print(filtered_less_than.head())
  ```

Output:

```
      CRIM    ZN  INDUS  CHAS    NOX     RM   AGE     DIS  RAD    TAX  \
0  0.00632  18.0   2.31   0.0  0.538  6.575  65.2  4.0900  1.0  296.0
1  0.02731   0.0   7.07   0.0  0.469  6.421  78.9  4.9671  2.0  242.0
2  0.02729   0.0   7.07   0.0  0.469  7.185  61.1  4.9671  2.0  242.0
3  0.03237   0.0   2.18   0.0  0.458  6.998  45.8  6.0622  3.0  222.0
4  0.06905   0.0   2.18   0.0  0.458  7.147  54.2  6.0622  3.0  222.0

   PTRATIO       B  LSTAT  MEDV
0     15.3  396.90   4.98  24.0
1     17.8  396.90   9.14  21.6
2     17.8  392.83   4.03  34.7
3     18.7  394.63   2.94  33.4
4     18.7  396.90   5.33  36.2
```

Figure 5.6: *Filtering using lesser than*

In the preceding code, we filter the DataFrame to include only rows where the **'TAX'** value (full-value property-tax rate per $10,000) is **less than 300.** This generates a subset of houses with property tax rates lower than 300, which can be useful for targeted tax analysis.

- **Greater Than or Equal To (>=) Filtering** involves selecting rows from a DataFrame where a specific column's value is greater than or equal to a given value. This filtering condition is used to isolate rows with values that are at or above a specified threshold. It's valuable for focusing on data points that exhibit a certain level of magnitude or quality, providing insights into instances that meet or exceed the designated value for a particular attribute.

For example, you might use it to filter for products with ratings of 4 stars or higher, or houses with prices equal to or greater than a certain amount. This filtering approach helps narrow down the data to instances that meet a specific quality or performance standard.

```
# Filter rows where 'NOX' (nitric oxides concentration) is greater than
or equal to 0.5
```

```
filtered_greater_equal = df[df['NOX'] >= 0.5]
print(filtered_greater_equal.head())
```

Output:

```
        CRIM    ZN  INDUS  CHAS    NOX     RM    AGE     DIS  RAD    TAX  \
0    0.00632  18.0   2.31   0.0  0.538  6.575   65.2  4.0900  1.0  296.0
6    0.08829  12.5   7.87   0.0  0.524  6.012   66.6  5.5605  5.0  311.0
7    0.14455  12.5   7.87   0.0  0.524  6.172   96.1  5.9505  5.0  311.0
8    0.21124  12.5   7.87   0.0  0.524  5.631  100.0  6.0821  5.0  311.0
9    0.17004  12.5   7.87   0.0  0.524  6.004   85.9  6.5921  5.0  311.0

     PTRATIO       B  LSTAT  MEDV
0       15.3  396.90   4.98  24.0
6       15.2  395.60  12.43  22.9
7       15.2  396.90  19.15  27.1
8       15.2  386.63  29.93  16.5
9       15.2  386.71  17.10  18.9
```

Figure 5.7: Filtering using greater than or equal to

The code **filtered_greater_equal = df[df['NOX'] >= 0.5]** performs filtering on the DataFrame df using the condition that the **'NOX'** column values (representing nitric oxides concentration) are **greater than or equal to 0.5**.

This generates a subset of houses with higher levels of nitric oxide concentration, facilitating analysis of air pollution impacts on property values.

- **Less Than or Equal To (<=) Filtering** involves selecting rows from a DataFrame where a specific column's value is less than or equal to a given value.

For example, you might use it to filter for products with prices of $50 or less, or individuals with ages equal to or below a certain limit. This filtering technique helps narrow down the data to instances that meet a specific standard or requirement.

```
# Filter rows where 'DIS' (weighted distances to five Boston employment
centers) is less than or equal to 2.0

filtered_less_equal = df[df['DIS'] <= 2.0]

print(filtered_less_equal.head())
```

Output:

```
         CRIM   ZN  INDUS  CHAS    NOX     RM   AGE     DIS  RAD    TAX  \
123   0.15038  0.0  25.65   0.0  0.581  5.856  97.0  1.9444  2.0  188.0
125   0.16902  0.0  25.65   0.0  0.581  5.986  88.4  1.9929  2.0  188.0
126   0.38735  0.0  25.65   0.0  0.581  5.613  95.6  1.7572  2.0  188.0
127   0.25915  0.0  21.89   0.0  0.624  5.693  96.0  1.7883  4.0  437.0
128   0.32543  0.0  21.89   0.0  0.624  6.431  98.8  1.8125  4.0  437.0

      PTRATIO       B  LSTAT  MEDV
123      19.1  370.31  25.41  17.3
125      19.1  385.02  14.81  21.4
126      19.1  359.29  27.26  15.7
127      21.2  392.11  17.19  16.2
128      21.2  396.90  15.39  18.0
```

Figure 5.8: Filtering using less than or equal to

In this code, we filter the DataFrame to include only rows where the **'DIS'** value (weighted distances to employment centers) is **less than or equal to 2.0**.

This generates a subset of houses located close to employment centers, facilitating analysis of transportation accessibility in relation to property values.

Logical Operators are used to combine or modify conditions in programming, allowing us to create more complex conditions for filtering, branching, and decision-making. Python provides three main logical operators: and, or, and not.

Let us see an example for each logical operator.

- **Logical AND (and):** The logical AND operator is a binary operator that is used to combine two or more conditions. It returns True only if all of its operands are True. If any of the operands is False, the operator returns False. In other words, the logical AND operator evaluates to True if and only if all the conditions it connects are satisfied.

Let's say we have two conditions, A and B. When you use the logical AND operator between these two conditions (A and B), the resulting combined condition will be **True** only if both condition A and condition B are True. If either condition A or condition B (or both) is **False**, the combined condition will evaluate to False.

Keeping the preceding idea in mind, let us filter houses from the Boston Housing Dataset that have more than 6 rooms (**'RM' > 6**) and are located near an employment center (**'DIS' <= 2.0**). We can achieve this using the logical AND operator:

```
# Filter houses with more than 6 rooms and located near an employment
center
```

```
filtered_and = df[(df['RM'] > 6) & (df['DIS'] <= 2.0)]
print(filtered_and.head())
```

Output:

```
        CRIM   ZN  INDUS  CHAS    NOX    RM    AGE     DIS  RAD    TAX  \
128  0.32543  0.0  21.89   0.0  0.624  6.431   98.8  1.8125  4.0  437.0
137  0.35233  0.0  21.89   0.0  0.624  6.454   98.4  1.8498  4.0  437.0
139  0.54452  0.0  21.89   0.0  0.624  6.151   97.9  1.6687  4.0  437.0
140  0.29090  0.0  21.89   0.0  0.624  6.174   93.6  1.6119  4.0  437.0
145  2.37934  0.0  19.58   0.0  0.871  6.130  100.0  1.4191  5.0  403.0

     PTRATIO       B  LSTAT  MEDV
128     21.2  396.90  15.39  18.0
137     21.2  394.08  14.59  17.1
139     21.2  396.90  18.46  17.8
140     21.2  388.08  24.16  14.0
145     14.7  172.91  27.80  13.8
```

Figure 5.9: Filtering using logical AND

In this code, the expression **(df['RM'] > 6) & (df['DIS'] <= 2.0)** uses the logical AND operator (**&**) to combine two conditions. The resulting DataFrame **filtered_and** will contain only houses that satisfy both conditions simultaneously: having more than 6 rooms and being located near an employment center.

- **Logical OR (or):** The logical OR operator is a binary operator used to combine two or more conditions. It returns **True** if at least one of its operands is **True**. If all of its operands are False, the operator returns **False**. In essence, the logical OR operator evaluates to **True** if any of the conditions it connects are satisfied.

Again, we have two conditions, **A** and **B**. When we use the logical **OR** operator between these two conditions (**A** or **B**), the resulting combined condition will be **True** if either condition **A** or condition **B** (or both) is **True**. It will evaluate to False only if both conditions **A** and **B** are **False**.

Suppose we want to filter houses from the Boston Housing Dataset that either have more than 6 rooms (**'RM' > 6**) or are located near an employment center (**'DIS' <= 2.0**). You can achieve this using the logical **OR** operator:

```
# Filter houses with more than 6 rooms or located near an employment center


filtered_or = df[(df['RM'] > 6) | (df['DIS'] <= 2.0)]

print(filtered_or.head())
```

Output:

```
      CRIM    ZN  INDUS  CHAS    NOX     RM   AGE     DIS  RAD    TAX  \
0  0.00632  18.0   2.31   0.0  0.538  6.575  65.2  4.0900  1.0  296.0
1  0.02731   0.0   7.07   0.0  0.469  6.421  78.9  4.9671  2.0  242.0
2  0.02729   0.0   7.07   0.0  0.469  7.185  61.1  4.9671  2.0  242.0
3  0.03237   0.0   2.18   0.0  0.458  6.998  45.8  6.0622  3.0  222.0
4  0.06905   0.0   2.18   0.0  0.458  7.147  54.2  6.0622  3.0  222.0

   PTRATIO       B  LSTAT  MEDV
0     15.3  396.90   4.98  24.0
1     17.8  396.90   9.14  21.6
2     17.8  392.83   4.03  34.7
3     18.7  394.63   2.94  33.4
4     18.7  396.90   5.33  36.2
```

Figure 5.10: Filtering using logical OR

In this code, the expression **(df['RM'] > 6) | (df['DIS'] <= 2.0)** uses the logical OR operator (**|**) to combine two conditions. The resulting DataFrame **filtered_or** will contain houses that satisfy either of the conditions: having more than 6 rooms or being located near an employment center.

- **Logical NOT (not):** The logical NOT operator is a unary operator used to negate a single condition. It returns True if its operand is False, and vice versa. In other words, the logical NOT operator negates the truth value of the condition it operates on.

Assume we have a condition A. When you use the logical NOT operator before this condition (**not** A), the resulting condition will be True if condition A is False, and it will be False if condition A is True.

Suppose you want to filter houses from the Boston Housing Dataset that do not have more than 6 rooms (**'RM' <= 6**). You can achieve this using the logical NOT operator:

```
# Filter houses that do not have more than 6 rooms


filtered_not = df[~(df['RM'] > 6)]

print(filtered_not.head())
```

Output:

```
      CRIM    ZN  INDUS  CHAS    NOX     RM    AGE     DIS  RAD    TAX  \
8   0.21124  12.5   7.87   0.0  0.524  5.631  100.0  6.0821  5.0  311.0
12  0.09378  12.5   7.87   0.0  0.524  5.889   39.0  5.4509  5.0  311.0
13  0.62976   0.0   8.14   0.0  0.538  5.949   61.8  4.7075  4.0  307.0
15  0.62739   0.0   8.14   0.0  0.538  5.834   56.5  4.4986  4.0  307.0
16  1.05393   0.0   8.14   0.0  0.538  5.935   29.3  4.4986  4.0  307.0

    PTRATIO       B  LSTAT  MEDV
8      15.2  386.63  29.93  16.5
12     15.2  390.50  15.71  21.7
13     21.0  396.90   8.26  20.4
15     21.0  395.62   8.47  19.9
16     21.0  386.85   6.58  23.1
```

Figure 5.11: *Filtering using logical NOT*

In this code, the expression **~(df['RM'] > 6)** uses the logical NOT operator **(~)** to negate the condition. The resulting DataFrame **filtered_not** will contain houses that do not have more than 6 rooms.

Filtering by Numeric Methods

Filtering by numeric methods involves utilizing various numerical conditions, operations, and functions to selectively extract rows from a DataFrame based on numeric attributes. These methods enable you to focus on specific subsets of data that meet certain numerical criteria, such as values within a particular range, certain conditions, or specific mathematical transformations. Here are some commonly used numeric filtering method.

query() Method: The **query()** method in pandas is used to filter data from a DataFrame using a string expression. This expression can involve column names from the DataFrame, comparison operators (>, <, >=, <=, ==, !=), and logical operators (and, or, not). The **query()** method provides a more readable and concise way to filter data compared to traditional boolean indexing.

```
filtered_query = df.query('RM > 6 and MEDV > 25')

print(filtered_query.head())
```

Output:

```
        CRIM     ZN  INDUS  CHAS    NOX     RM   AGE     DIS  RAD    TAX  \
2    0.02729    0.0   7.07   0.0  0.469  7.185  61.1  4.9671  2.0  242.0
3    0.03237    0.0   2.18   0.0  0.458  6.998  45.8  6.0622  3.0  222.0
4    0.06905    0.0   2.18   0.0  0.458  7.147  54.2  6.0622  3.0  222.0
5    0.02985    0.0   2.18   0.0  0.458  6.430  58.7  6.0622  3.0  222.0
7    0.14455   12.5   7.87   0.0  0.524  6.172  96.1  5.9505  5.0  311.0

     PTRATIO       B  LSTAT  MEDV
2       17.8  392.83   4.03  34.7
3       18.7  394.63   2.94  33.4
4       18.7  396.90   5.33  36.2
5       18.7  394.12   5.21  28.7
7       15.2  396.90  19.15  27.1
```

Figure 5.12: *Filtering using query*

In this example, we use the **query()** method to filter the DataFrame **df**. The expression **'RM > 6 and MEDV > 25'** specifies that we want to retain rows where the **'RM'** column (average number of rooms per dwelling) is greater than 6 and the **'MEDV'** column (median value of owner-occupied homes) is greater than 25. The resulting **filtered_query** DataFrame contains rows that satisfy both conditions.

Using **query()** can improve code readability, especially when dealing with complex conditions involving multiple columns and operators.

between() Method: The **between()** method in pandas is used to filter data from a DataFrame based on values that fall within a specified range for a given column. It takes two arguments: the lower bound and the upper bound of the desired range. It applies the filtering condition to a specified column and returns a boolean Series indicating whether each row's value in that column falls within the specified range. This boolean Series can then be used for boolean indexing to extract the desired subset of data.

```
filtered_between = df[df['TAX'].between(200, 400)]

print(filtered_between.head())
```

Output:

```
        CRIM     ZN  INDUS  CHAS    NOX     RM   AGE     DIS  RAD    TAX  \
0    0.00632   18.0   2.31   0.0  0.538  6.575  65.2  4.0900  1.0  296.0
1    0.02731    0.0   7.07   0.0  0.469  6.421  78.9  4.9671  2.0  242.0
2    0.02729    0.0   7.07   0.0  0.469  7.185  61.1  4.9671  2.0  242.0
3    0.03237    0.0   2.18   0.0  0.458  6.998  45.8  6.0622  3.0  222.0
4    0.06905    0.0   2.18   0.0  0.458  7.147  54.2  6.0622  3.0  222.0

     PTRATIO       B  LSTAT  MEDV
0       15.3  396.90   4.98  24.0
1       17.8  396.90   9.14  21.6
2       17.8  392.83   4.03  34.7
3       18.7  394.63   2.94  33.4
4       18.7  396.90   5.33  36.2
```

Figure 5.13: *Filtering using between*

In this example, we use the **between()** method to filter the DataFrame **df**. The condition **df['TAX'].between(200, 400)** checks whether the values in the 'TAX' column (property tax rates) are **between 200 and 400**. The resulting **filtered_between** DataFrame contains rows where the property tax rates are within this specified range.

isin() Method: The **isin()** method in pandas is used to filter data from a DataFrame based on whether values in a specified column are present in a given list, tuple, or array.

The **isin()** method takes a single argument, which is the list, tuple, or array containing the values you want to check for. It applies the filtering condition to a specified column and returns a boolean Series indicating whether each row's value in that column is present in the provided list.

```
age_values = [65.2, 90.0]
filtered_isin_age = df[df['AGE'].isin(age_values)]
print(filtered_isin_age.head())
```

Output:

```
        CRIM    ZN  INDUS  CHAS    NOX     RM   AGE     DIS   RAD    TAX  \
0    0.00632  18.0   2.31   0.0  0.538  6.575  65.2  4.0900   1.0  296.0
104  0.13960   0.0   8.56   0.0  0.520  6.167  90.0  2.4210   5.0  384.0
119  0.14476   0.0  10.01   0.0  0.547  5.731  65.2  2.7592   6.0  432.0
460  4.81213   0.0  18.10   0.0  0.713  6.701  90.0  2.5975  24.0  666.0

     PTRATIO       B  LSTAT  MEDV
0       15.3  396.90   4.98  24.0
104     20.9  392.69  12.33  20.1
119     17.8  391.50  13.61  19.3
460     20.2  255.23  16.42  16.4
```

Figure 5.14: *Filtering using isin*

In this example, we're using the **isin()** method to filter the DataFrame df based on the **'AGE'** column (proportion of owner-occupied units built prior to 1940). The condition **df['AGE'].isin(age_values)** checks whether the values in the **'AGE'** column match any of the values in the **age_values** list (which contains **65.2** and **90.0**). The resulting **filtered_isin_age** DataFrame contains rows where the **'AGE'** values match either **65.2** or **90.0**.

Filtering by Where Condition

Filtering by the **where()** condition in pandas involves creating a mask based on a specific condition and applying it to a DataFrame to retain rows that meet the condition while replacing non-matching rows with **NaN** values. This method maintains the original shape of the DataFrame and is commonly used for conditional masking and element-wise operations.

```
filtered_where = df.where(df['RM'] > 7)
```

```
print(filtered_where.head())
```

Output:

```
    CRIM   ZN  INDUS  CHAS    NOX     RM   AGE     DIS  RAD    TAX  PTRATIO  \
0    NaN  NaN    NaN   NaN    NaN    NaN   NaN     NaN  NaN    NaN      NaN
1    NaN  NaN    NaN   NaN    NaN    NaN   NaN     NaN  NaN    NaN      NaN
2  0.02729  0.0   7.07   0.0  0.469  7.185  61.1  4.9671  2.0  242.0     17.8
3    NaN  NaN    NaN   NaN    NaN    NaN   NaN     NaN  NaN    NaN      NaN
4  0.06905  0.0   2.18   0.0  0.458  7.147  54.2  6.0622  3.0  222.0     18.7

        B  LSTAT   MEDV
0     NaN    NaN    NaN
1     NaN    NaN    NaN
2  392.83   4.03   34.7
3     NaN    NaN    NaN
4  396.90   5.33   36.2
```

Figure 5.15: Filtering using Where condition

In this example, we are using the same Housing Dataset and the **.where()** method to filter the DataFrame based on the **'RM'** column (average number of rooms per dwelling) where the condition **df['RM'] > 7** is met. The resulting **filtered_where** DataFrame retains rows where the number of rooms per dwelling is greater than 7 and replaces non-matching rows with **NaN** values.

Remember that the **where()** method retains the original shape of the DataFrame and replaces non-matching rows with **NaN** values. If you want to remove the rows where the condition is not met, you can use the **.dropna()** method after applying **.where()**:

```
filtered_where = df.where(df['RM'] > 6).dropna()
```

Filtering by Date and Time Methods

Filtering by date and time methods in pandas involves using various techniques to extract specific subsets of data from a DataFrame based on date and time attributes. These methods are especially useful when dealing with time-series data, allowing you to focus on specific time intervals, dates, or temporal conditions for analysis.

Date and Time Indexing: Date and time indexing in pandas involves setting a datetime column as the index of a DataFrame. This allows for easy and efficient filtering and slicing of data based on date and time attributes. When the datetime column is set as the index, you can directly specify date ranges to extract specific subsets of data.

Let's create a DataFrame with a datetime column as the index and demonstrate how date and time indexing works:

```
# Create a sample DataFrame with datetime index


date_rng = pd.date_range(start='2023-01-01', end='2023-01-10', freq='D')
values = range(len(date_rng))
```

```
df = pd.DataFrame({'value': values}, index=date_rng)


print("Original DataFrame:")
print(df)
```

Output:

```
Original DataFrame:
            value
2023-01-01    0
2023-01-02    1
2023-01-03    2
2023-01-04    3
2023-01-05    4
2023-01-06    5
2023-01-07    6
2023-01-08    7
2023-01-09    8
2023-01-10    9
```

Figure 5.16: Create a DataFrame with dates as index

In the preceding code, a sample DataFrame named **df** is created using pandas. The DataFrame consists of a datetime index generated using the **pd.date_range()** function, which creates a sequence of dates ranging from January 1st, 2023, to January 10th, 2023, with a frequency of one day ('**D**'). The DataFrame contains a single column named **'value'** with incremental values corresponding to the date index.

```
filtered_date_index = df['2023-01-03':'2023-01-07']
print("Filtered DataFrame using Date Indexing:")
print(filtered_date_index)
```

Output:

```
Filtered DataFrame using Date Indexing:
            value
2023-01-03    2
2023-01-04    3
2023-01-05    4
2023-01-06    5
2023-01-07    6
```

Figure 5.17: Filtering with Datetime index

We can observe in the preceding code, the DataFrame df is being filtered using date indexing. By using the syntax **df['2023-01-03':'2023-01-07']**, we are extracting a subset of the original DataFrame that includes rows corresponding to the dates from January 3rd, 2023, to January 7th, 2023, inclusive. This technique leverages the datetime index to conveniently select data within a specific date range, enabling streamlined analysis and visualization for the chosen time.

loc[] with Date and Time Filtering: The **loc[]** indexer in pandas is a powerful way to select subsets of data from a DataFrame using labels. It can also be used with boolean conditions to filter data based on date and time attributes.

The **loc[]** indexer can be combined with Boolean conditions to filter data based on specific date or time ranges.

```
filtered_loc = df.loc[df.index >= '2023-01-05']

print(filtered_loc)
```

Output:

```
            value
2023-01-05    4
2023-01-06    5
2023-01-07    6
2023-01-08    7
2023-01-09    8
2023-01-10    9
```

Figure 5.18: *Filtering using loc*

In this example, the **loc[]** indexer is used to filter the DataFrame df based on a date condition. The condition **df.index >= '2023-01-05'** selects rows where the index (which is a datetime index) is greater than or equal to '2023-01-05'. The result is a DataFrame containing only the rows that satisfy the condition.

This method provides a convenient way to retrieve data from a specific date onwards, making it particularly useful for time-series analysis where you want to focus on data beyond a certain date.

query() Method with Date Filtering: The **query()** method in pandas allows us to filter a DataFrame using a string expression that includes date and time conditions. This method is useful for quickly selecting subsets of data based on specific date ranges.

```
filtered_query = df.query('index >= "2023-01-06"')

print(filtered_query)
```

Output:

```
            value
2023-01-06    5
2023-01-07    6
2023-01-08    7
2023-01-09    8
2023-01-10    9
```

Figure 5.19: *Filtering date using query*

In this example, the **query()** method is employed to filter the DataFrame df based on a date condition. The query string **'index >= "2023-01-06"'** specifies that we want to select rows where the index (which is a datetime index) is greater than or equal to **'2023-01-06'**. The result is a DataFrame containing only the rows that satisfy the specified condition.

Using **.query()** can help streamline our code by allowing you to write conditions in a more concise and expressive way, making it easier to select data based on date and time attributes.

between_time() Method: The **between_time()** method in pandas is used to filter data based on a specific time interval within a day. This method is particularly useful when you want to extract data that falls within a specific time range, regardless of the date.

Let's create a sample DataFrame by generating a sequence of datetime values using **pd.date_range()**. The sequence begins at '**2023-01-01 08:00**' and spans 24 hours with an hourly frequency ('H'). These datetime values represent timestamps for each hour.

```
date_rng = pd.date_range(start='2023-01-01 08:00', periods=10, freq='H')
values = range(len(date_rng))
df = pd.DataFrame({'value': values}, index=date_rng)
df
```

Output:

	value
2023-01-01 08:00:00	0
2023-01-01 09:00:00	1
2023-01-01 10:00:00	2
2023-01-01 11:00:00	3
2023-01-01 12:00:00	4
2023-01-01 13:00:00	5
2023-01-01 14:00:00	6
2023-01-01 15:00:00	7
2023-01-01 16:00:00	8
2023-01-01 17:00:00	9

Figure 5.20: *Create a DataFrame with datetime Index*

Now let us extract rows from the DataFrame that correspond to a specific time interval within a day.

```
filtered_between_time = df.between_time('10:00', '16:00')
```

```
print(filtered_between_time)
```

Output:

```
                     value
2023-01-01 10:00:00      2
2023-01-01 11:00:00      3
2023-01-01 12:00:00      4
2023-01-01 13:00:00      5
2023-01-01 14:00:00      6
2023-01-01 15:00:00      7
2023-01-01 16:00:00      8
```

***Figure* 5.21**: *Filter data using between_time*

The code filters the DataFrame df to extract rows with time values between '10:00' and '16:00', regardless of the date. The resulting DataFrame **filtered_between_time** contains data within this daily time interval, which is particularly useful for analyzing patterns that recur consistently during those hours across different dates.

Filtering Null or Missing Values

We have already discussed the significance of filtering null or missing values in *Chapter 3, Pandas DataFrame*, but let's revisit the concept briefly. Filtering null or missing values involves the process of selecting and working with rows in a DataFrame that contain these undefined values. In pandas, these values are often represented as **NaN**.

Let's create a DataFrame named **df** to represent student exam scores. The DataFrame contains three columns: **'Name'**, **'Math'**, and **'English'**. The 'Name' column lists the names of five students, while the **'Math'** and **'English'** columns represent their respective exam scores. Notably, some entries in the **'Math'** and **'English'** columns contain missing values represented by **NaN**.

```
# Create a sample DataFrame with student exam scores

data = {'Name': ['Alice', 'Bob', 'Charlie', 'David', 'Eve'],
        'Math': [85, np.nan, 72, 90, 65],
        'English': [90, 78, np.nan, 85, 92]}
df = pd.DataFrame(data)
df
```

Output:

	Name	Math	English
0	Alice	85.0	90.0
1	Bob	NaN	78.0
2	Charlie	72.0	NaN
3	David	90.0	85.0
4	Eve	65.0	92.0

Figure 5.22: Create DataFrame with null values

Using isna() for Filtering: The **isna()** method in pandas generates a boolean mask that indicates whether each cell in a DataFrame contains a missing value (**NaN**) or not. This mask can be used to filter rows or columns based on the presence of missing values.

```
missing_scores_mask = df.isna()
missing_scores_filtered = df[missing_scores_mask.any(axis=1)]


print("Original DataFrame:")
print(df)
print("\nMask for Missing Scores:")
print(missing_scores_mask)
print("\nRows with Missing Scores:")
print(missing_scores_filtered)
```

```
Original DataFrame:
      Name  Math  English
0    Alice  85.0     90.0
1      Bob   NaN     78.0
2  Charlie  72.0      NaN
3    David  90.0     85.0
4      Eve  65.0     92.0

Mask for Missing Scores:
    Name   Math  English
0  False  False    False
1  False   True    False
2  False  False     True
3  False  False    False
4  False  False    False

Rows with Missing Scores:
      Name  Math  English
1      Bob   NaN     78.0
2  Charlie  72.0      NaN
```

Figure 5.23: Filter data using isna

The **isna()** method generates a boolean mask **missing_scores_mask,** where True indicates cells with missing values and False indicates cells with non-missing values. By applying **.any(axis=1)** to the mask, we identify rows where at least one exam score is missing. The result is the **missing_scores_filtered** DataFrame, which contains only the rows with missing scores.

Using notna() for Filtering: The **notna()** method creates a boolean mask where each cell is **True** if the value is not missing (not **NaN**) and False otherwise. This mask can be used to filter rows based on the absence of missing values.

```
# Using .notna() to filter rows without missing scores


non_missing_scores_mask = df.notna()
non_missing_scores_filtered = df[non_missing_scores_mask.all(axis=1)]


print("Original DataFrame:")
print(df)
print("\nMask for Non-Missing Scores:")
print(non_missing_scores_mask)
print("\nRows without Missing Scores:")
print(non_missing_scores_filtered)
```

Output:

```
Original DataFrame:
      Name  Math  English
0    Alice  85.0     90.0
1      Bob   NaN     78.0
2  Charlie  72.0      NaN
3    David  90.0     85.0
4      Eve  65.0     92.0

Mask for Non-Missing Scores:
    Name   Math  English
0   True   True     True
1   True  False     True
2   True   True    False
3   True   True     True
4   True   True     True

Rows without Missing Scores:
    Name  Math  English
0  Alice  85.0     90.0
3  David  90.0     85.0
4    Eve  65.0     92.0
```

Figure 5.24: Filter Data using notna

The **notna()** method generates a boolean mask **non_missing_scores_mask**, where **True** indicates cells with non-missing values and **False** indicates cells with missing values. By applying **all(axis=1)** to the mask, we pinpoint rows where both math and English scores are present. The resultant **non_missing_scores_filtered** DataFrame contains only the rows with complete scores.

Conclusion

In this chapter, we have thoroughly explored the practice of data filtering in Pandas. This chapter illuminated the significance of filtering data to extract targeted subsets that fuel insightful analyses and visualizations. By navigating Pandas' versatile filtering techniques, we have gained proficiency in extracting information based on column values, logical operators, numeric conditions, and date-time methods. Additionally, we have learned how to manage missing values, enhancing our ability to unveil valuable insights within datasets.

In the next chapter, titled *Grouping and Aggregating Data*, we will look into the power of aggregation in Pandas. This chapter explores techniques to group data based on specific criteria and apply functions for summary statistics. We'll uncover the built-in aggregation methods, and user-defined functions, enabling insights from datasets through effective grouping and summarization.

Exercise Questions

1. Filter the given DataFrame to retain only the rows where the **'Age'** column is greater than 30.

2. Filter the DataFrame to include rows where the **'Income'** is greater than 5000 and the **'Age'** is less than 40.

3. Given a DataFrame with a **'Timestamp'** column, filter it to retain rows where the date falls in June.

4. Filter a DataFrame to include rows where the **'Score'** column is not missing (not **NaN**), while also dropping rows with any missing values in other columns.

CHAPTER 6
Grouping and Aggregating Data

In previous chapters, we embarked on a comprehensive journey through the foundations of data manipulation and analysis. We explored into the intricacies of handling Series and DataFrames, mastering the art of structuring and managing data. Along this path, we dedicated our efforts to the pivotal practices of data cleaning, ensuring our datasets were primed for meaningful exploration. Moreover, we harnessed the potency of data filtering to extract pertinent subsets from extensive datasets.

In this chapter, we will dive into the world of data expertise, focusing on aggregation – a lively tool woven into Pandas that makes data analysis more exciting. Aggregation acts as a guide through a huge sea of information, helping us find patterns and learn from heaps of data. We will group data in smart ways and use special tools to understand it better. Imagine opening a treasure chest full of useful information! This chapter is like a treasure map, showing you how to use aggregation to make sense of big sets of data.

By putting similar data together and using clever methods, we can figure out the most important facts about our data. It's like finding the most popular color in a bunch of crayons or the average age of people in a room. As we read on, we will learn different ways to do this, like using specific parts of our data to group it, and then doing special math on each group to get useful numbers. We will also see how to use this on big sets of data that might otherwise be overwhelming. This journey is like exploring a new land, discovering all the tools we have to make our data talk to us. So, let's dive into this adventure and learn how to find the stories hidden in our data!

Structure

In this chapter, we will discuss the following topics:

- Introduction to Groupby and Aggregation
- Group by Using Split-Apply-Combine
- Built-in Aggregation Methods

- Applying Different Functions to DataFrame Columns
- Grouping DataFrame with Index Levels and Columns
- Aggregation with User-Defined Functions
- Iterating Through Groups
- Discretization and Binning

Introduction to Groupby and Aggregation

Groupby and aggregation are core concepts in data analysis, particularly when working with tabular data. These techniques enable you to organize and summarize data in meaningful ways, facilitating insights and patterns discovery from large datasets.

- **Groupby:** Groupby involves the process of splitting data into groups based on one or more criteria. This can be a categorical variable or a combination of variables. Grouping helps create subsets of data that share similar characteristics. Once grouped, you can perform various operations on each group independently.

- **Aggregation:** Aggregation is the process of applying a function to each group and combining the results into a compact form for analysis. Aggregation functions can include sum, average, count, maximum, minimum, and more. These functions help you derive meaningful statistics and summaries from grouped data, revealing trends, patterns, and relationships.

Benefits of Groupby and Aggregation

Groupby and aggregation are essential techniques in data analysis, offering several advantages, including:

- **Data Segmentation:** Grouping data based on specific attributes allows you to create subsets for analysis. This segmentation helps in understanding different aspects of your data and uncovering hidden insights.

- **Summarized Insights:** Aggregation functions such as sum, mean, and count provide summarized views of data subsets. These insights are easier to interpret and communicate compared to raw data.

- **Pattern Recognition:** Grouping data can reveal patterns, trends, and relationships that might not be apparent in the overall dataset. This aids in identifying commonalities and outliers within specific groups.

- **Exploratory Analysis:** Groupby enables targeted exploratory analysis, helping you investigate trends within smaller, more manageable datasets before diving into detailed analysis.

- **Effective Reporting:** Aggregated data is suitable for generating reports and visualizations, simplifying complex information, and supporting data-driven decision-making.

- **Feature Generation:** Aggregating data can lead to the creation of new features, enriching your dataset for machine learning tasks.

- **Efficiency:** Aggregation reduces the volume of data, making computations faster and more efficient, particularly with large datasets.

- **Informed Decisions:** Groupby and aggregation provide insights that guide informed decisions, whether in business strategy, research, or other domains.

Groupby Using Split-Apply-Combine

The concept of *group by using split-apply-combine* is a fundamental technique that empowers data analysts to extract meaningful insights from datasets. This process involves three essential steps: splitting the data into groups based on specific criteria, applying a function to each group, and then combining the results to generate comprehensive insights.

Step 1: Splitting the Data: In this initial phase, the dataset is divided into distinct groups based on specific attributes or criteria. Imagine having a sales dataset with information about products, and sales amounts. To better understand the sales performance by product, we can split the data into groups based on different product categories.

Step 2: Applying a Function: With the data grouped, the next step involves applying a function to each group. This function can be anything that helps us gather insights from the data. For instance, we might want to calculate the average sales for each product category. This involves taking the sales values within each group, summing them up, and then dividing them by the number of sales entries in that category.

Step 3: Combining the Results: After applying the function to each group, we consolidate the results. In our example, the average sales calculated for each product category are brought together to form a comprehensive summary. This summary reveals the performance of different product categories in terms of sales.

Example:

Let's consider a real-world example with a dataset of sales transactions. Suppose we have the following data:

Product	Sales
A	100
B	150

A	200
B	120

Table 6.1: *Sales Data*

Step 1: Splitting the Data: We start by grouping the data based on the **'Product'** column:

Grouped Data:

- Group A: [100, 200]
- Group B: [150, 120]

Step 2: Applying a Function: We apply the mean function to each group:

Average Sales per Group:

- Group A: (100 + 200) / 2 = 150
- Group B: (150 + 120) / 2 = 135

Step 3: Combining the Results: The calculated average sales are combined to provide a Summary:

- Group A: Average Sales = 150
- Group B: Average Sales = 135

We will look into each of these steps comprehensively, accompanied by illustrative examples. The aim is to provide a clear and thorough understanding of each phase.

Splitting an Object into Groups:

Splitting an object into groups is a fundamental technique that involves categorizing data within a dataset into distinct subsets or groups based on specific criteria. This process forms the basis for further analysis and exploration within each subgroup.

Here's the syntax for splitting an object into groups using the **groupby** technique:

```
grouped_data = df.groupby('column_to_group_by')
```

In this syntax:

df is the name of your DataFrame.

grouped_data is the result of the grouping operation, which represents the grouped data.

You can replace **column_to_group_by** with the actual name of the column by which you want to group your data

Let's explore this concept further using various examples from the IMDb movie ratings dataset.

Example 1: Splitting by Genre

Suppose we have the IMDb dataset containing movie ratings, genres, and release years. We want to split the data into groups based on movie genres to analyze how ratings differ across genres.

```
import pandas as pd
```

```
#load the dataset
df = pd.read_csv('imdb.csv')
```

```
# Display the first few rows of the dataset
df.head()
```

Output:

	Series_Title	Released_Year	Runtime	Genre	IMDB_Rating	Director	Star1	No_of_Votes	Gross	Metascore
0	The Shawshank Redemption	1994	142	Drama	9.3	Frank Darabont	Tim Robbins	2343110	28341469.0	80.0
1	The Godfather	1972	175	Crime	9.2	Francis Ford Coppola	Marlon Brando	1620367	134966411.0	100.0
2	The Dark Knight	2008	152	Action	9.0	Christopher Nolan	Christian Bale	2303232	534858444.0	84.0
3	The Godfather: Part II	1974	202	Crime	9.0	Francis Ford Coppola	Al Pacino	1129952	57300000.0	90.0
4	12 Angry Men	1957	96	Crime	9.0	Sidney Lumet	Henry Fonda	689845	4360000.0	96.0

Figure 6.1: *Load IMDB dataset*

In the provided code snippet, the IMDb dataset is loaded using the variable name **'df'** from a CSV file named **'imdb.csv'**. The dataset is then displayed using the **head()** function to show the first few rows of the data.

The IMDb dataset typically contains information about movies, including attributes such as **'Movie'**, **'Genre'**, **'Director'**, **'Year'**, and **'Rating'**. Each row in the dataset represents a movie entry, where columns contain details such as the movie's title, genre, director, release year, and user ratings. This dataset is often used for various analyses and insights into the world of movies, enabling researchers, analysts, and enthusiasts to explore movie trends, ratings, and more.

```
grouped_by_genre = df.groupby('Genre')
```

```
grouped_by_genre
```

Output:

```
# Grouping data by Genre
grouped_by_genre = df.groupby('Genre')

grouped_by_genre

<pandas.core.groupby.generic.DataFrameGroupBy object at 0x00000268C72F8640>
```

Figure 6.2: *Group data by genre*

The **groupby()** function on the DataFrame **'df'** groups the data by the **'Genre'** column. The result is a GroupBy object named **'grouped_by_genre'**, which represents the grouped data.

```
# Displaying the first few rows of each group


for genre, group in grouped_by_genre:
    print(f"Genre: {genre}")
    print(group[['Series_Title', 'IMDB_Rating']].head())
    print()
```

Output:

```
Genre: Action
                                       Series_Title  IMDB_Rating
2                                     The Dark Knight          9.0
5           The Lord of the Rings: The Return of the King          8.9
8                                           Inception          8.8
10   The Lord of the Rings: The Fellowship of the Ring          8.8
13                 The Lord of the Rings: The Two Towers          8.7

Genre: Adventure
               Series_Title  IMDB_Rating
21                Interstellar          8.6
47           Back to the Future          8.5
93        Inglourious Basterds          8.3
110                  Das Boot          8.3
114  2001: A Space Odyssey          8.3

Genre: Animation
                        Series_Title  IMDB_Rating
23        Sen to Chihiro no kamikakushi          8.6
43                      The Lion King          8.5
46                     Hotaru no haka          8.5
56                     Kimi no na wa.          8.4
58   Spider-Man: Into the Spider-Verse          8.4

Genre: Biography
            Series_Title  IMDB_Rating
7        Schindler's List          8.9
15            Goodfellas          8.7
18              Hamilton          8.6
35      The Intouchables          8.5
38            The Pianist          8.5
```

Figure 6.3: Display the grouped data

We can observe from the preceding result, a loop is used to iterate through each group within the previously created **grouped_by_genre** groupBy object. This loop allows us to examine the data within each genre group individually. For each iteration, the variable genre holds the current genre value (for example, **'Action'**, Animation), while the variable group contains the corresponding group of data associated with that genre.

Also, note how movies or series within different genres are organized and presented. This approach aids in visualizing the characteristics and ratings of various media within each genre, contributing to a deeper understanding of how content is distributed and rated across different genres in the IMDb dataset.

Let's see another example and group movies by their directors, displaying the count of movies each director has made.

```
# Grouping movies by director
grouped_by_director = df.groupby('Director')


# Counting the number of movies per director
movie_count_by_director = grouped_by_director.size()


# Displaying the movie counts for each director
print(movie_count_by_director)
```

Output:

```
Director
Aamir Khan              1
Aaron Sorkin            1
Abdellatif Kechiche     1
Abhishek Chaubey        1
Abhishek Kapoor         1
                       ..
Zack Snyder             2
Zaza Urushadze          1
Zoya Akhtar             2
Çagan Irmak             1
Ömer Faruk Sorak        1
Length: 548, dtype: int64
```

Figure 6.4: Grouped movies by director

From the preceding result, we can see we are analyzing the IMDb dataset centered around movie directors. We begin by using the **groupby()** function to group the dataset by the **'Director'** column, effectively creating clusters of movies associated with each director. This forms the basis for our examination.

Next, we employ the **size()** method on the resulting **GroupBy** object, which computes the size (count) of each group. This translates into the number of movies directed by each individual. The outcome is a Pandas Series that links director names to their respective movie counts. By printing this Series, we obtain a clear picture of how prolific each director is in terms of movie production. This analysis reveals insights into the variations in directorial output within the dataset and assists in identifying directors who have made substantial contributions to the film industry.

Built-in Aggregation Methods

Built-in aggregation methods in pandas are pre-defined functions that enable you to carry out standard statistical computations on data grouped based on specific criteria. These methods efficiently calculate summary statistics for each group, simplifying the process of extracting valuable insights from your dataset.

Statistical Calculations

Built-in aggregation methods encompass a range of statistical calculations that offer insights into different aspects of your data. Some common examples include:

- **Mean (mean())**: Computes the average value of a column within each group.
- **Sum (sum())**: Adds up the values of a column within each group, revealing the total.
- **Minimum (min())**: Identifies the smallest value in a column within each group.
- **Maximum (max())**: Finds the largest value in a column within each group.
- **Count (count())**: Counts the number of non-null values in a column within each group.
- **Median (median())**: Calculates the middle value in a column within each group.
- **Standard Deviation (std())**: Measures the dispersion of values in a column within each group.
- **Variance (var())**: Quantifies the variability of values in a column within each group.

Syntax:

```
result = grouped_data['column_to_apply_aggregation'].method()
```

Choose a column (**'column_to_apply_aggregation'**) within the grouped data on which you want to perform aggregation. Replace **'column_to_apply_aggregation'** with the actual column name. After specifying the column, apply a built-in aggregation method using the desired statistical calculation method (for example, **mean()**, **sum()**, **min()**, **max()**, **count()**, and so on).

Let's explore how to apply various aggregation methods to grouped data.

- **Mean:** The `mean()` built-in aggregation method in pandas calculates the average (arithmetic mean) value of the data within each group. It is used to find the central tendency of a numerical column for each group in a grouped dataset.

Suppose we want to calculate the average IMDb rating for each genre. Here's how you can achieve this using the `mean()` aggregation method:

```
# Grouping data by Genre
grouped_data = df.groupby('Genre')


# Calculating average IMDb rating for each genre using mean()
average_rating_by_genre = grouped_data['IMDB_Rating'].mean()


# Display the result
print(average_rating_by_genre)
```

Output:

```
Genre
Action      7.949419
Adventure   7.937500
Animation   7.930488
Biography   7.938636
Comedy      7.901290
Crime       8.016822
Drama       7.957439
Family      7.800000
Fantasy     8.000000
Film-Noir   7.966667
Horror      7.909091
Mystery     7.975000
Thriller    7.800000
Western     8.350000
Name: IMDB_Rating, dtype: float64
```

Figure 6.5: Calculate the average IMDB rating based on Genre

We can see that the resulting **average_rating_by_genre** Series showcases the calculated average ratings for various genres.

For instance, the output reveals that movies in the **'Crime'** genre have an average IMDb rating of approximately **8.02**, while those in the **'Comedy'** genre have an average rating of about **7.90**. This analysis provides insights into the overall viewer satisfaction and perception of different movie genres based on their average IMDb ratings.

- **Sum:** The `sum()` built-in aggregation method in pandas calculates the total sum of the data within each group. It is used to aggregate numerical values by adding them up for each group in a grouped dataset.

Imagine using the movie dataset with columns **'Genre'**, and **'Gross'**. We aim to calculate the total Gross earnings for each genre. Here's how you can achieve this using the **sum()** aggregation method:

```
# Grouping data by Genre
grouped_data = df.groupby('Genre')


# Calculating total gross earnings for each genre using sum()
total_gross_by_genre = grouped_data['Gross'].sum()


# Display the result
print(total_gross_by_genre)
```

Output:

```
Genre
Action       3.263226e+10
Adventure    9.496922e+09
Animation    1.463147e+10
Biography    8.276358e+09
Comedy       1.566387e+10
Crime        8.452632e+09
Drama        3.540997e+10
Family       4.391106e+08
Fantasy      7.827267e+08
Film-Noir    1.259105e+08
Horror       1.034649e+09
Mystery      1.256417e+09
Thriller     1.755074e+07
Western      5.822151e+07
Name: Gross, dtype: float64
```

Figure 6.6: *Calculate the total gross based on genre*

The output presented in the **'total_gross_by_genre'** variable reveals a comprehensive overview of the combined gross earnings for movies categorized under different genres. For instance, it showcases that the **'Action'** genre has accumulated substantial gross earnings of approximately 32.63 billion dollars, while the **'Adventure'** genre accounts for around 9.50 billion dollars in earnings. This breakdown provides valuable insights into the financial success of various genres, allowing us to compare their respective contributions to the total box office earnings.

- **Minimum:** The **min()** built-in aggregation method in pandas calculates the minimum value within each group. It is used to find the smallest value of a numerical column for each group in a grouped dataset.

Consider columns like '**Series_Title**', '**Genre**', '**Released_Year**', and '**IMDB_Rating**'. We want to determine the lowest IMDb rating for movies in each genre. Here's how you can use the **min()** aggregation method for this purpose:

```
# Grouping data by Genre

grouped_data = df.groupby('Genre')


# Finding lowest IMDb rating for each genre using min()

lowest_rating_by_genre = grouped_data['IMDB_Rating'].min()


# Display the result

print(lowest_rating_by_genre)
```

Output:

```
Genre
Action        7.6
Adventure     7.6
Animation     7.6
Biography     7.6
Comedy        7.6
Crime         7.6
Drama         7.6
Family        7.8
Fantasy       7.9
Film-Noir     7.8
Horror        7.6
Mystery       7.6
Thriller      7.8
Western       7.8
Name: IMDB_Rating, dtype: float64
```

Figure 6.7: Calculate the lowest rating based on genre

We can observe the output presented within the '**lowest_rating_by_genre**' variable, which reveals the minimum IMDb rating attributed to movies within each respective genre. Notably, movies categorized under genres such as '**Action**', '**Adventure**', '**Animation**', and others share a uniform lowest IMDb rating of **7.6**.

- **Maximum:** The **max()** method calculates the maximum value within each group. It is employed to identify the highest value of a numerical column for each group in a grouped dataset.

Let's illustrate this with an example and identify the highest number of votes garnered by movies within each genre. The **max()** aggregation method can be effectively applied to achieve this goal. The following example demonstrates how to use the **max()** method in this context:

```
# Grouping data by Genre
grouped_data = df.groupby('Genre')


# Finding highest number of votes for each genre using max()
highest_votes_by_genre = grouped_data['No_of_Votes'].max()


# Display the result
print(highest_votes_by_genre)
```

Output:

```
Genre
Action          2303232
Adventure       1512360
Animation        999790
Biography       1213505
Comedy           939631
Crime           1826188
Drama           2343110
Family           372490
Fantasy           88794
Film-Noir        158731
Horror           787806
Mystery         1129894
Thriller          27733
Western          688390
Name: No_of_Votes, dtype: int64
```

Figure 6.8: *Calculate the max number of votes based on Genre*

The provided output presents a breakdown of the highest number of votes received by movies within various genres, obtained through the utilization of the **max()** aggregation method on the **'No_of_Votes**' column. Each genre is accompanied by its respective maximum vote count. Notably, genres such as **'Action'** and **'Adventure'** exhibit the highest numbers of votes, reaching **2,303,232** and **1,512,360** votes, respectively.

- **Count:** The **count()** method calculates the number of non-null values within each group. It is used to determine the count of valid entries in a specific column for each group in a grouped dataset.

Let's illustrate this with an example where we aim to determine the count of valid IMDb ratings for movies within distinct genres. To achieve this, we can effectively employ the **count()** aggregation method.

```
# Grouping data by Genre
grouped_data = df.groupby('Genre')


# Counting valid IMDb ratings for each genre using count()
valid_ratings_count_by_genre = grouped_data['IMDB_Rating'].count()
```

```
# Display the result
print(valid_ratings_count_by_genre)
```

Output:

```
Genre
Action        172
Adventure      72
Animation      82
Biography      88
Comedy        155
Crime         107
Drama         289
Family          2
Fantasy         2
Film-Noir       3
Horror         11
Mystery        12
Thriller        1
Western         4
Name: IMDB_Rating, dtype: int64
```

Figure 6.9: Counting number of ratings based on genre

The displayed output illustrates the outcome of employing the **count()** aggregation method. Each genre is accompanied by the count of movies within that genre possessing valid IMDb ratings. Notably, genres such as **'Action'**, **'Adventure'**, **'Animation'**, and others exhibit their respective counts of movies with valid ratings. For instance, the **'Action'** genre has **172** movies with available ratings, while the **'Adventure'** genre contains **72**. This insight offers a clear overview of viewer engagement and participation in rating movies across different genres, highlighting the genres that have garnered more ratings from the audience.

- **Median:** The **median()** method calculates the median value within each group. It is utilized to determine the middle value in a sorted list of values for each group in a grouped dataset.

Here's an example that demonstrates the use of the **median()** aggregation method on an IMDb movie dataset, but this time, we'll group the data by the **'Released_Year'** column to calculate the median IMDb rating for movies released in each year:

```
# Grouping data by Released_Year
grouped_data = df.groupby('Released_Year')


# Computing median IMDb rating for movies released in each year using
median()
median_rating_by_year = grouped_data['IMDB_Rating'].median()
```

```
# Display the result
print(median_rating_by_year)
```

Output:

```
Released_Year
1920    8.1
1921    8.3
1922    7.9
1924    8.2
1925    8.1
        ...
2017    7.8
2018    8.0
2019    7.9
2020    8.0
PG      7.6
Name: IMDB_Rating, Length: 100, dtype: float64
```

***Figure 6.10**: Compute median of IMDB ratings for each Genre*

The displayed output represents the result of applying the **median()** aggregation method to an IMDb movie dataset grouped by the **'Released_Year'** column. Each year or label is accompanied by the calculated median IMDb rating for movies released in that specific year. For instance, movies released in **1921** attained a median rating of **8.3**, while those released in 2020 garnered a median rating of **8.0**.

This output offers valuable insights into the distribution of IMDb ratings across different years, providing a sense of the central tendency of movie ratings for each year and category.

- **Standard Deviation:** The **std()** method calculates the standard deviation within each group. It is utilized to measure the dispersion or variability of values within each group in a grouped dataset.

Let's consider an example where we group the IMDb movie dataset by the **'Genre'** column and calculate the standard deviation of IMDb ratings for movies within each genre:

```
# Grouping data by Genre
grouped_data = df.groupby('Genre')
```

```
# Computing standard deviation of IMDb ratings for movies within each
genre using std()
std_deviation_by_genre = grouped_data['IMDB_Rating'].std()
```

```
# Display the result
print(std_deviation_by_genre)
```

Output:

```
Genre
Action      0.304258
Adventure   0.229781
Animation   0.253221
Biography   0.267140
Comedy      0.228771
Crime       0.335477
Drama       0.267229
Family      0.000000
Fantasy     0.141421
Film-Noir   0.152753
Horror      0.311302
Mystery     0.310791
Thriller         NaN
Western     0.420317
Name: IMDB_Rating, dtype: float64
```

Figure 6.11: *Compute standard deviation of IMDB ratings for each genre*

The displayed output shows the result of applying the **std()** aggregation method to the IMDb movie dataset grouped by the **'Genre'** column. Each genre is associated with the calculated standard deviation of IMDb ratings for movies within that specific genre. The values represent the degree of variability or dispersion of IMDb ratings within each genre. For instance:

- The **'Action'** genre has a standard deviation of approximately 0.304, indicating that the IMDb ratings for action movies tend to deviate by around 0.304 from the mean rating within the genre.

- Similarly, for **'Adventure'**, the standard deviation is approximately 0.230, suggesting that IMDb ratings for adventure movies have a spread of around 0.230 from the mean.

- The **'Family'** genre has a standard deviation of 0.000, which suggests that all movies within this genre have the same IMDb rating, resulting in no variability.

Lower standard deviation values indicate that the ratings are clustered closely around the mean, while higher values indicate more spread or variability in the ratings. The output provides insights into how consistent or diverse IMDb ratings are for movies within different genres, helping us understand the distribution of ratings within each genre category.

- **Variance:** The **var()** method calculates the variance within each group. Variance is a statistical measure that quantifies the dispersion or spread of values within a dataset. It indicates how much individual values deviate from the mean value of the dataset.

Let's calculate the variance of IMDb ratings for movies within each genre:

```
# Grouping data by Genre
grouped_data = df.groupby('Genre')
```

```
# Computing variance of IMDb ratings for movies within each genre using
var()

variance_by_genre = grouped_data['IMDB_Rating'].var()
```

```
# Display the result

variance_by_genre
```

Output:

```
Genre
Action       0.092573
Adventure    0.052799
Animation    0.064121
Biography    0.071364
Comedy       0.052336
Crime        0.112545
Drama        0.071411
Family       0.000000
Fantasy      0.020000
Film-Noir    0.023333
Horror       0.096909
Mystery      0.096591
Thriller          NaN
Western      0.176667
Name: IMDB_Rating, dtype: float64
```

Figure 6.12: *Compute variance of IMDB ratings for each Genre*

The output displayed represents the variance of IMDb ratings calculated for movies within each genre using the **var()** aggregation method. Variance is a measure of how much individual IMDb ratings deviate from the mean rating within each genre. Here's an interpretation of the output:

- For the **'Action'** genre, the variance is approximately **0.093**. This indicates that the IMDb ratings for action movies tend to deviate by around **0.093** from the mean rating within the genre.

- In the **'Adventure'** genre, the variance is about **0.053**, suggesting that IMDb ratings for adventure movies have a spread of approximately **0.053** from the mean.

- The **'Family'** genre has a variance of **0.000**, meaning that all movies within this genre have the same IMDb rating, resulting in no variability.

In general, higher variance values imply that IMDb ratings for movies within a genre are more spread out from the mean, indicating greater diversity in viewer opinions. Conversely, lower variance values indicate that ratings are clustered closely around the mean. The output offers insights into the extent of variability in IMDb ratings for movies within different genres, helping us understand the distribution of ratings and viewer opinions within each genre category.

Applying Different Functions to DataFrame Columns

Applying different functions to DataFrame columns refers to the process of calculating various summary statistics or aggregations for specific columns of a pandas DataFrame. This is done using the **agg()** function, which allows you to specify different aggregation functions for different columns. This approach is valuable for quickly extracting multiple insights from your data in a single operation.

For instance, you can compute the mean, sum, maximum, minimum, or other statistics for specific columns, all in one go. This is particularly useful when you want to analyze different aspects of your data across multiple columns simultaneously.

Syntax:

```
result = df.agg({'Column1': 'function1', 'Column2': 'function2', ...})
```

In the syntax, replace **Column1, Column2**, and so on with the names of the DataFrame columns you want to analyze. Similarly, replace **function1, function2**, and so on with the specific aggregation functions you want to apply to each column.

This approach simplifies the process of obtaining various insights from your data, allowing you to efficiently gather a wide range of information without having to apply each aggregation function separately.

Let's explore a couple of examples!

Example 1: Calculating Different Aggregations for IMDb Ratings and No. of Votes

Let's say for IMDb dataset with columns '**IMDB_Rating**' and '**No_of_Votes**', we want to find the mean IMDb rating and the sum of votes for analysis. You can achieve this using the following code:

```
# Applying different aggregation functions to IMDb ratings and No. of Votes
result = df.agg({'IMDB_Rating': 'mean', 'No_of_Votes': 'sum'})
result
```

Output:

```
IMDB_Rating    7.949300e+00
No_of_Votes    2.736929e+08
dtype: float64
```

Figure 6.13: Different aggregations

Example 2: Finding Maximum Gross Earnings and Minimum Metascore

Using the same IMDb dataset as our reference, let's demonstrate applying different functions. For instance, we will identify the highest gross earnings and the lowest Metascore among the films.

```
result = df.agg({'Gross': 'max', 'Metascore': 'min'})
result
```

```
Gross          936662225.0
Metascore             28.0
dtype: float64
```

Figure 6.14: *Calculate maximum gross earnings and minimum metascore*

Grouping DataFrame with Index Levels and Columns

Grouping a DataFrame with index levels and columns involves using one or more columns as the index to form groups while simultaneously performing aggregation operations across specific columns. This provides a more comprehensive way to analyze data by considering multiple levels of organization and summarizing the data accordingly.

Syntax:

```
grouped = df.groupby([index_level_1, index_level_2, ...])[column_1,
column_2, ...].agg(aggregation_functions)
```

Here's what each part of the syntax means:

- **df**: This is the DataFrame you want to perform the grouping on.
- **[index_level_1, index_level_2, ...]**: This is a list of columns that you want to use as index levels for grouping. You can specify one or more columns to form a hierarchical index for grouping.
- **[column_1, column_2, ...]**: This is a list of columns you want to aggregate. These are the columns for which you want to calculate summary statistics.
- **agg(aggregation_functions)**: This part specifies the aggregation functions to apply to the columns you've selected. You can pass a dictionary of column names as keys and aggregation functions as values.

Consider columns like **'Genre'**, **'Released_Year'**, **'IMDB_Rating'**, **and 'No_of_Votes'**. If we want to group the data by both **'Genre'** and **'Released_Year'** while calculating the average IMDb rating and the total number of votes for each group, we can use the following code:

```
# Grouping by 'Genre' and 'Released_Year', and calculating average rat-
ing and total votes
grouped = df.groupby(['Genre', 'Released_Year']).agg({'IMDB_Rating':
'mean', 'No_of_Votes': 'sum'})
```

```
# Display the result
Grouped
```

Output:

Genre	Released_Year	IMDB_Rating	No_of_Votes
	1924	8.2	41985
	1926	8.1	81156
Action	1932	7.8	25312
	1938	7.9	47175
	1948	7.8	65162
...	...	...	...
Thriller	1967	7.8	27733
	1965	8.3	232772
	1966	8.8	688390
Western	1968	8.5	302844
	1976	7.8	65659

434 rows × 2 columns

Figure 6.15: *Calculate average rating and total no. of votes based on Genre and Released year*

The output represents a multi-level indexed DataFrame that has been grouped by two columns: **'Genre'** and **'Released_Year'**. The **'IMDB_Rating'** column shows the calculated mean IMDb rating for movies within each genre and released year combination, and the **'No_of_Votes'** column displays the sum of votes received by movies in each group.

For example, in the **'Action'** genre for the year **1924**, the average IMDb rating was **8.2**, and the total number of votes was **41,985**. Similarly, for the 'Action' genre in the year **1926**, the average rating was **8.1**, and the total votes were **81,156**. This pattern continues for each unique combination of genre and released year, providing a comprehensive breakdown of IMDb ratings and votes for movies within different categories and years. The hierarchical index created by grouping allows for a structured and organized presentation of this information, making it easier to analyze and interpret.

Aggregation with User-defined Functions

Aggregation with user-defined functions (UDFs) in data analysis involves applying custom-built functions to groups of data in order to derive meaningful insights. While built-in aggregation functions (for example, sum, mean) serve common needs, UDFs provide flexibility for more specific analysis requirements. This approach allows you to define your own logic for summarizing and extracting information from grouped data.

Benefits:

- **Tailored Analysis:** UDFs enable you to tailor the aggregation process to your specific analysis objectives. This flexibility is crucial for exploring unique patterns or performing specialized calculations.

- **Complex Computation:** For complex calculations that cannot be achieved with standard aggregation functions, UDFs provide the means to implement intricate logic and obtain accurate results.

- **Domain-Specific Insights:** Different domains have distinct metrics and measurements. UDFs let you create custom metrics that align with your domain's specific requirements, leading to more relevant insights.

- **Feature Engineering:** UDFs can generate new features from existing data, enhancing the dataset's richness for subsequent analysis or machine learning tasks.

- **Handling Missing Data:** UDFs can handle missing data within groups, providing more robust analysis compared to built-in functions that might ignore or incorrectly treat missing values.

- **Advanced Analysis:** UDFs are particularly useful when dealing with advanced statistical analysis, outlier detection, or data transformation that cannot be achieved with standard aggregations.

- **Reusable Logic:** Once defined, UDFs can be reused across different projects or datasets, saving time and promoting consistency in analysis methodologies.

Suppose we have a dataset containing information about movies, including their genres and ratings. We want to find the average rating of movies within each genre, but with a custom twist: we want to consider a movie as "**highly rated**" if its rating is above **8.0** and "**low rated**" otherwise. We'll define a function to perform this custom aggregation:

In the following code, we defined the **custom_aggregation** function that takes a group of movies as input and calculates the count of movies with ratings above 8.0 (highly rated) and below or equal to 8.0 (low rated) within each genre.

Then we group the data by the "**Genre**" column using the **groupby** operation and apply the **custom_aggregation** function to each genre group.

```
# Define a custom aggregation function
def custom_aggregation(group):
```

```
high_rated = sum(group['IMDB_Rating'] > 8.0)
low_rated = sum(group['IMDB_Rating'] <= 8.0)
return pd.Series({'High_Rated': high_rated, 'Low_Rated': low_rated})
```

```
# Grouping data by Genre and applying the custom aggregation function
grouped_data = df.groupby('Genre').apply(custom_aggregation)
```

```
# Display the result
print(grouped_data)
```

Output:

Genre	High_Rated	Low_Rated
Action	52	120
Adventure	23	49
Animation	25	57
Biography	27	61
Comedy	39	116
Crime	42	65
Drama	101	188
Family	0	2
Fantasy	1	1
Film-Noir	1	2
Horror	3	8
Mystery	5	7
Thriller	0	1
Western	3	1

Figure 6.16: Group by custom aggregate function

We can see the output displays table with two columns: **High_Rated** and **Low_Rated**. For each genre, the **High_Rated** column indicates the count of movies within that genre that have an IMDb rating above **8.0**, and the "**Low_Rated**" column indicates the count of movies with an IMDb rating of **8.0** or below.

For instance, in the "**Action**" genre, there are 52 highly rated movies (with ratings above **8.0**) and 120 low-rated movies (with ratings **8.0** or below). Similarly, in the "**Adventure**" genre, there are 23 highly rated movies and 49 low-rated movies. This pattern continues for all other genres, providing a breakdown of movie counts based on the custom rating classification.

The output helps us understand how many movies within each genre are considered highly rated or low rated according to the custom aggregation function. This information can be valuable for analyzing the distribution of movie ratings across different genres and identifying trends in audience preferences.

Let's explore another example that involves identifying the most prolific director in the IMDb movie dataset. In this case, we want to determine the director who has directed the highest number of movies. We'll achieve this using a custom aggregation function and **groupby** operations.

```python
# Define a custom aggregation function to find most prolific director
def most_prolific_director(group):
    director_count = group.shape[0]  # Count of movies directed by the
    director
    return pd.Series({'Total_Movies': director_count})


# Grouping data by Director and applying the UDF
grouped_by_director = df.groupby('Director')
prolific_director_stats = grouped_by_director.apply(most_prolific_director)


# Find the director with the most movies
most_prolific = prolific_director_stats['Total_Movies'].idxmax()
print(f"The most prolific director is '{most_prolific}' with {prolific_
director_stats['Total_Movies'].max()} movies.")
```

Output:

```
The most prolific director is 'Alfred Hitchcock' with 14 movies.
```

Figure 6.17: Find the prolific director using custom aggregate function

The output shows that the most prolific director in the dataset is **'Alfred Hitchcock'**, who has directed a total of 14 movies. This information is obtained by applying the custom aggregation function to the grouped data based on the director. The function calculates the count of movies directed by each director, and then we identify the director with the highest count, which in this case is Alfred Hitchcock with 14 movies.

Iterating Through Groups

Iterating through groups refers to the process of systematically traversing subsets of data that have been grouped based on specific criteria in a DataFrame. After applying a grouping operation, the data is split into smaller groups based on common values in one or more columns. Iterating through these groups allows you to perform targeted actions or computations on each group, which can provide valuable insights and facilitate customized analysis.

Example 1: Average Rating by Decade

In this example, let's calculate the average IMDb rating for movies in each decade using the IMDb dataset. We will group the data by the release year's decade and then iterate through the groups to compute the average rating for each decade.

```
# Grouping data by release decade
def group_by_decade(year):
    return f"{(int(year) // 10) * 10}s"


grouped_by_decade = df.groupby(df['Released_Year'].apply(group_by_decade))


# Calculate average rating for each decade
average_rating_by_decade = {}
for decade, group in grouped_by_decade:
    average_rating = group['IMDB_Rating'].mean()
    average_rating_by_decade[decade] = average_rating


# Print the average ratings by decade
for decade, avg_rating in average_rating_by_decade.items():
    print(f"Decade: {decade}, Average Rating: {avg_rating:.2f}")
```

Output:

```
Decade: 1920s, Average Rating: 8.13
Decade: 1930s, Average Rating: 7.97
Decade: 1940s, Average Rating: 8.03
Decade: 1950s, Average Rating: 8.06
Decade: 1960s, Average Rating: 7.97
Decade: 1970s, Average Rating: 7.97
Decade: 1980s, Average Rating: 7.95
Decade: 1990s, Average Rating: 7.96
Decade: 2000s, Average Rating: 7.90
Decade: 2010s, Average Rating: 7.92
Decade: 2020s, Average Rating: 8.13
```

Figure 6.18: Calculate average rating by decade

In the preceding example, we begin by categorizing movies into distinct groups determined by their release years, such as the **1960s** or **1970s**. The function **group_by_decade** helps with this grouping.

It then calculates the average rating for each group of movies in a particular decade. It goes through each group and figures out their average rating by adding up the ratings and dividing by the number of movies in the group. These calculated average ratings are stored in a special container called a dictionary, which acts like a mini storage unit.

After this, it iterates through the stored average ratings and shows them on the screen. It displays the average rating for movies from each decade. So, by using this code, you can learn about the trends in movie ratings over different decades without having to do all the calculations manually. It's like having a friendly helper that quickly crunches the numbers for you and tells you the results.

Let us look into another example to enhance our understanding of iterating through groups.

```
# Grouping data by movie genres
grouped_by_genre = df.groupby('Genre')


# Calculating the total number of votes for each genre
total_votes_by_genre = {}
for genre, group in grouped_by_genre:
    total_votes = group['No_of_Votes'].sum()
    total_votes_by_genre[genre] = total_votes


# Print the total votes for each genre
for genre, total_votes in total_votes_by_genre.items():
    print(f"Genre: {genre}, Total Votes: {total_votes}")
```

Output:

```
Genre: Action, Total Votes: 72282412
Genre: Adventure, Total Votes: 22306966
Genre: Animation, Total Votes: 21978630
Genre: Biography, Total Votes: 24006844
Genre: Comedy, Total Votes: 27620327
Genre: Crime, Total Votes: 33533615
Genre: Drama, Total Votes: 61367304
Genre: Family, Total Votes: 551221
Genre: Fantasy, Total Votes: 146222
Genre: Film-Noir, Total Votes: 367215
Genre: Horror, Total Votes: 3742556
Genre: Mystery, Total Votes: 4203004
Genre: Thriller, Total Votes: 27733
Genre: Western, Total Votes: 1289665
```

***Figure 6.19:** Calculate total votes by Genre*

In this example, we're taking a closer look at movie genres. We group the data by genre and then calculate the total number of votes received by movies in each genre. The for loop iterates through the grouped data, computing the total votes for each genre and storing it in the **total_votes_by_genre** dictionary. Finally, we print out the total votes for each genre to better understand the audience engagement across different movie genres.

Discretization and Binning

Discretization and binning are techniques used to group continuous data into discrete intervals or bins. This process can be helpful when dealing with numerical data that has a wide range and needs to be categorized for analysis. Discretization helps simplify data, reduce noise, and facilitate analysis by creating meaningful categories.

Syntax

```
pd.cut(data_series, bins, labels=labels, right=False)
```

- **pd.cut:** This is the function provided by the pandas library for performing binning and discretization.

- **data_series:** This is the continuous numerical data that you want to discretize. It can be a pandas Series or a NumPy array.

- **bins:** This parameter defines the bin edges or intervals. It can be specified as a list of values representing the edges of the bins. For example, [0, 25, 50, 75, 100] represents four bins with the intervals [0, 25), [25, 50), [50, 75), [75, 100).

- **labels:** This is an optional parameter that allows you to assign labels to the discrete intervals. It should have the same length as the number of bins minus one. These labels represent the categories or groups that data points will be assigned to.

- **right:** Another optional parameter that determines whether the right bin edge is open or closed. By default, it's set to True, making intervals closed on the right. Setting it to False makes intervals left-closed and right-open.

The **pd.cut()** function returns a new categorical Series containing the bin labels for each data point based on the specified bins and labels.

Remember that discretization and binning are helpful when you want to convert continuous data into categorical or ordinal data, allowing you to analyze patterns and relationships more effectively, especially when you're interested in group-wise analysis.

```
# Define bins and labels for IMDB ratings
rating_bins = [0, 6.5, 7.5, 8.5, 10]
rating_labels = ['Low', 'Average', 'Good', 'Excellent']


# Discretize IMDB ratings
```

```
df['Rating_Category'] = pd.cut(df['IMDB_Rating'], bins=rating_bins, la-
bels=rating_labels, right=False)
```

```
# Display the result
```

```
print(df[['Series_Title', 'IMDB_Rating', 'Rating_Category']])
```

Output:

```
              Series_Title  IMDB_Rating Rating_Category
0      The Shawshank Redemption          9.3       Excellent
1                 The Godfather          9.2       Excellent
2               The Dark Knight          9.0       Excellent
3          The Godfather: Part II        9.0       Excellent
4                 12 Angry Men          9.0       Excellent
..                       ...          ...             ...
995        Breakfast at Tiffany's        7.6            Good
996                       Giant          7.6            Good
997          From Here to Eternity        7.6            Good
998                    Lifeboat          7.6            Good
999                 The 39 Steps          7.6            Good

[999 rows x 3 columns]
```

Figure 6.20: *Discretization and binning*

The provided code snippet demonstrates the process of discretizing IMDb ratings into distinct rating categories using the Pandas library. First, bins and corresponding labels are defined to categorize the IMDb ratings. The **'rating_bins'** list defines the numerical ranges for each category, and the **'rating_labels'** list assigns labels to these categories.

The output showcases a portion of the IMDb movie dataset with three relevant columns: **'Series_Title'**, **'IMDB_Rating'**, and **'Rating_Category'**. Each row represents a movie and its corresponding IMDb rating category. The **'IMDB_Rating'** column displays the numerical IMDb rating of each movie, while the **'Rating_ Category'** column provides a categorical classification of the movies' ratings. This classification is determined through the process of binning, where IMDb ratings are grouped into predefined rating ranges.

For example, **'The Shawshank Redemption'** has an IMDb rating of **9.3**, which falls into the "**Excellent**" rating category. Similarly, '**The Godfather**' and '**The Dark Knight**' also have high IMDb ratings of **9.2** and **9.0**, respectively, and are categorized as "**Excellent**". On the other hand, movies like **'Breakfast at Tiffany's'** and **'Giant'** have IMDb ratings of **7.6**, placing them in the "**Good**" rating category.

This categorical representation of IMDb ratings allows for a broader understanding of the overall quality of movies based on their ratings, making it easier to compare and analyze them without focusing on precise numerical differences.

Conclusion

Aggregation serves as a powerful tool in Pandas, enabling the synthesis and analysis of data in diverse ways. By grouping data based on specified criteria and applying functions to these groups, we derive summary statistics that facilitate insightful analysis. Throughout this chapter, we've comprehensively explored aggregation techniques in Pandas. From understanding the basics of groupby and aggregation to iterating through groups, utilizing user-defined functions, and applying various aggregation methods to DataFrame columns, we've gained a deep understanding of this crucial data manipulation process.

Moving ahead, in the chapter, we will delve into reshaping and pivoting data–essential techniques in data analysis. These methods allow us to transform data into different formats that better suit our analytical needs. By the end of this chapter, you'll be equipped with the skills to effectively reshape and pivot data, enhancing your data analysis capabilities.

Exercise

- Load the Boston Housing dataset and group the data by the **'RAD'** column. Calculate the average **'TAX'** and **'NOX'** values for each group.

- Split the data into groups based on the **'CHAS'** column. Count the occurrences of houses along the Charles River (**CHAS = 1**) and those not along the river (**CHAS = 0**).

- Group the data by the **'TAX'** column. Iterate through the groups and find the tax range with the highest average **'CRIM'** (per capita crime rate by town).

- Define a custom aggregation function that calculates the range of **'RM'** (average number of rooms per dwelling) within each group. Apply this function to find the range of **'RM'** for each **'RAD'** group.

- Discretize the **'TAX'** column into bins. Count the number of occurrences in each bin and display the results.

CHAPTER 7
Reshaping and Pivoting in Pandas

Welcome to *Chapter 7, Reshaping and Pivoting in Pandas*, where we embark on an exploration of the pivotal techniques that Pandas, a cornerstone library in the Python data ecosystem, offers for reshaping and pivoting data. The ability to restructure data efficiently and meaningfully is a superpower in the world of data analysis. In this chapter, we'll delve into the intricate art of reshaping and pivoting, equipping you with the tools to wield this power effectively.

This chapter is your guide to the transformative techniques of reshaping and pivoting data using the powerful toolkit.

Structure

In this chapter, we will discuss the following topics:

- MultiIndexing
- Long and Wide Formats
- Stacking and Unstacking
- Melting Data
- Exploding Data
- Creating Pivot Tables
- Advanced Pivot Table Techniques

MultiIndexing in Series and DataFrame

MultiIndex (also known as hierarchical indexing) is a feature in pandas that allows you to have multiple levels of indexing for a Series or Dataframe. It is especially useful when dealing with data that has multiple dimensions or hierarchies. A MultiIndex structure enables you to organize and work with complex data in a more structured and efficient manner.

Advantages of Using MultiIndex:

- **Hierarchical Organization:** MultiIndex provides a natural way to organize data hierarchically. You can represent data with multiple dimensions or levels of detail, such as time series data with different granularities or data categorized into multiple dimensions like region, product, and time.

- **Efficient Slicing and Indexing:** MultiIndexing allows for easy and efficient slicing and indexing of data. You can access data at specific levels, making it simpler to extract subsets of your data that match particular criteria.

- **Clearer Code:** It makes your code more self-explanatory. You can use meaningful labels for each level of the index, which makes it easier for others (or your future self) to understand your data and code.

- **Aggregation and Grouping:** MultiIndexing pairs well with pandas' powerful grouping and aggregation functions, making it easier to perform complex data manipulations and calculations.

Creating a MultiIndex using a list of tuples:

We can create a MultiIndex using a list of tuples, where each tuple represents a unique combination of index values at each level of the hierarchy. Each level in the MultiIndex corresponds to a different dimension or category of your data.

Let's consider a scenario that represents sales of three products (**Laptops**, **Smartphones**, **Headphones**) across four different years (**2020** to **2023**). The sales numbers are recorded in four different currencies (**USD**, **EUR**, **GBP**, **JPY**).

```python
import pandas as pd


# Sample data
sales_data = [100, 90, 105, 115, 85, 88, 95, 80, 110, 120, 100, 105]


# Indices as tuples
index_tuples = [
    ('Laptops', 2020, 'USD'),
    ('Smartphones', 2020, 'EUR'),
    ('Headphones', 2020, 'GBP'),
    ('Laptops', 2021, 'USD'),
    ('Smartphones', 2021, 'EUR'),
    ('Headphones', 2021, 'GBP'),
    ('Laptops', 2022, 'USD'),
```

```
('Smartphones', 2022, 'EUR'),

('Headphones', 2022, 'JPY'),

('Laptops', 2023, 'USD'),

('Smartphones', 2023, 'JPY'),

('Headphones', 2023, 'GBP')

]
```

This list defines a set of indices, each of which is a tuple containing three pieces of information: the product type, the year, and the currency.

```
# Create a Series with a MultiIndex

series = pd.Series(sales_data, index=index_tuples)

series
```

Output:

```
(Laptops, 2020, USD)        100
(Smartphones, 2020, EUR)     90
(Headphones, 2020, GBP)     105
(Laptops, 2021, USD)        115
(Smartphones, 2021, EUR)     85
(Headphones, 2021, GBP)      88
(Laptops, 2022, USD)         95
(Smartphones, 2022, EUR)     80
(Headphones, 2022, JPY)     110
(Laptops, 2023, USD)        120
(Smartphones, 2023, JPY)    100
(Headphones, 2023, GBP)     105
dtype: int64
```

Figure 7.1: Create a series with a multiindex

The output presents a situation where the index is a combination of three separate pieces of information, fused into one: the product (Laptops, Smartphones, Headphones), the year (2020, 2021, 2022, 2023), and the currency (USD, EUR, GBP, JPY). This composite tuple structure poses challenges.

Problem:

When we have the three dimensions mashed together into a single tuple index, performing operations based on just one of those dimensions can be cumbersome. For instance, if you wish to fetch the first row, you'd need to sift through the entire tuple. This isn't just inefficient from a computational standpoint, but it also makes the code less readable and harder to maintain.

```
row_data = series[('Laptops', 2020, 'USD')]
print(row_data)
```

Output:

```
100
```

Figure 7.2: *Fetch the first row using entire tuple*

- **Tuple-Based Indexing**: The primary issue with this approach is that the entire tuple must be known and used to fetch data. If you only have partial information (e.g., you only know the fruit and year but not the currency), you'd have difficulty accessing the desired data directly.

- **Error-Prone**: As in the provided code, if you try to fetch data with a tuple that doesn't exist in the index (like (Laptops, 2020, NY)), it will result in a KeyError. This makes the process error-prone and requires additional code to handle exceptions.

- **Inefficient Filtering**: If you want to filter data based on a specific element of the tuple (e.g., all sales from 2021), you'll have to write custom filtering logic, making the process slower and less intuitive.

Solution: Hierarchical Indexing (MultiIndex):

Hierarchical indexing, also known as multi-indexing, allows for indexing on multiple levels, thereby structuring the data more effectively. Instead of having one complex index (a tuple of three values), we can have a multi-level index where each level corresponds to one of our dimensions (Product, Year, Currency).

Using hierarchical indexing, we can quickly and easily filter and access data based on any level of the index without having to wrestle with tuple parsing.

`MultiIndex.from_tuples`: This method is used to create a multi-level (hierarchical) index in pandas from a list of tuples. Each tuple typically represents one multi-index data point.

We will be using the same data as above and create a hierarchical index using the `index_tuples`

```
multiindex = pd.MultiIndex.from_tuples(index_tuples, names=['Product', 'Year', 'Currency'])
```

Here, the **names** parameter provides labels to the different levels of the hierarchy (in order). This helps in understanding and referring to the specific levels later on.

We can then apply this **multiindex** to our series:

```
series = pd.Series(sales_data, index=multiindex)
series
```

Output:

```
Product       Year  Currency
Laptops       2020  USD         100
Smartphones   2020  EUR          90
Headphones    2020  GBP         105
Laptops       2021  USD         115
Smartphones   2021  EUR          85
Headphones    2021  GBP          88
Laptops       2022  USD          95
Smartphones   2022  EUR          80
Headphones    2022  JPY         110
Laptops       2023  USD         120
Smartphones   2023  JPY         100
Headphones    2023  GBP         105
dtype: int64
```

Figure 7.3: Create series using multiindex

As we can see, the resulting **multiindex** object is a hierarchical index with three levels: Product, Year, and City. This allows for more advanced indexing and slicing operations.

For instance, if you want to get all sales data for **2020**, you can easily do that with this MultiIndex structure. This kind of granular access becomes challenging if we are using a flat index structure or if we treat each tuple as a single index.

```
# Get all sales data for the year 2020
data_2020 = series[:, 2020, :]
data_2020
```

Output:

```
Product       Currency
Laptops       USD         100
Smartphones   EUR          90
Headphones    GBP         105
dtype: int64
```

Figure 7.4: Fetch the sales data for the year 2020

Let's see another example to fetch sales data related to smartphones, regardless of the year or currency.

```
# Get sales data for Smartphones across all years and currencies
Smartphones_sales = series['Smartphones']
Smartphones_sales
```

Output:

```
Year  Currency
2020  EUR          90
2021  EUR          85
2022  EUR          80
2023  JPY         100
dtype: int64
```

Figure 7.5: Fetch the sales data for smartphones

MultiIndex from Products

When working with hierarchical indices in pandas, there is one more method to create a MultiIndex is by using the **from_product** method. This is particularly useful when you have several categories and you want to produce a MultiIndex that represents all possible combinations of these categories.

pd.MultiIndex.from_product is a class method that creates a MultiIndex from the cartesian product of multiple iterables.

Instead of manually writing out all the combinations as tuples (like in the **from_tuples** method), **from_product** automates this process by generating all possible combinations of the provided categories. It's particularly handy when you have many combinations.

Let's consider that we have three separate lists: one for products, one for years, and one for currencies. We want a MultiIndex that represents all combinations of these lists.

```python
sales_data = [100, 90, 105, 115]


# Separate lists
products = ['Smartphones', 'Laptops']
years = [2020, 2021]
currencies = ['USD', 'EUR']


# Create MultiIndex using `from_product`
index = pd.MultiIndex.from_product([products, years, currencies],
names=['Product', 'Year', 'Currency'])


# Adjust the sales_data to fit the index size
series = pd.Series(sales_data * 2, index=index)
```

In this example, the **from_product** method creates a MultiIndex from the cartesian product of the three lists: products, years, and currencies. The resulting series has an index that represents every combination of product, year, and currency.

Output:

```
Product       Year  Currency
Smartphones   2020  USD         100
                    EUR          90
              2021  USD         105
                    EUR         115
Laptops       2020  USD         100
                    EUR          90
              2021  USD         105
                    EUR         115
dtype: int64
```

Figure 7.6: MultiIndex series

Now, you can access data in the same hierarchical manner as before. For instance, if you want to get sales data for smartphones across all years and currencies:

smartPhones_sales = series['Smartphones']

smartPhones_sales

Output:

```
Year  Currency
2020  USD         100
      EUR          90
2021  USD         105
      EUR         115
dtype: int64
```

Figure 7.7: Fetch sales data for smartphones across all years and currencies

This approach using **from_product** simplifies the process of creating a MultiIndex, especially when there are numerous combinations.

Previously, we looked at how to represent hierarchical data using a MultiIndex in a series. However, real-world datasets are often multi-dimensional, making it necessary to work with DataFrames, which are two-dimensional labeled data structures in pandas.

A MultiIndex DataFrame is essentially a DataFrame with hierarchical indexing on its rows or columns or both. This hierarchical indexing allows for data organization and representation in a way where you can have multiple levels of indices, making it more versatile for certain types of data structures.

Let's use the products, years, and currencies example to create a MultiIndex DataFrame.

```
# Sample data
data = [
    [100, 101, 102, 103],
    [90, 91, 92, 93],
    [105, 106, 107, 108],
    [115, 116, 117, 118]
]


# Separate lists for indices and columns
products = ['Smartphones', 'Laptops']
years = [2020, 2021]
currencies = ['USD', 'EUR', 'GBP', 'JPY']  # Added two more currencies
to match the data columns


# Create row MultiIndex
row_index = pd.MultiIndex.from_product([products, years], names=['Prod-
uct', 'Year'])


# Create a dataframe with the row MultiIndex and currency columns
df = pd.DataFrame(data, index=row_index, columns=currencies)
```

The resultant DataFrame looks like

Output:

Product	Year	USD	EUR	GBP	JPY
Smartphones	2020	100	101	102	103
	2021	90	91	92	93
Laptops	2020	105	106	107	108
	2021	115	116	117	118

Figure 7.8: *MultiIndex DataFrame*

Unlike a Series, which has just one column of data and an index, a DataFrame allows for multiple columns of data, each potentially having its own data type. In the preceding example, we took advantage of this by adding sales figures for four different currencies (**USD**, **EUR**, **GBP**, **JPY**) as separate columns.

Accessing data in a multi-index DataFrame is slightly different from a regular DataFrame due to the hierarchical structure of the indices. Here are some methods you can use to access data in a multi-index DataFrame.

1. Using .loc[ ]:

You can use **.loc[ ]** to access rows based on the hierarchical indices.

For instance, given our **df**:

```
df.loc['Smartphones']
```

Output:

Year	USD	EUR	GBP	JPY
2020	100	101	102	103
2021	90	91	92	93

Figure 7.9: Fetch data using .loc for product smartphone

The resultant DataFrame would show the sales data for all years and currencies related to smartphones.

To access sales data for smartphones in 2020:

```
df.loc[('Smartphones', 2020)]
```

Output:

```
USD     100
EUR     101
GBP     102
JPY     103
Name: (Smartphones, 2020), dtype: int64
```

Figure 7.10: Fetch data using .loc for product smartphone and year 2020

2. Accessing specific columns:

Columns can be accessed as usual, even in a multi-index DataFrame. Let's access sales data of Smartphones in 2020 in USD:

```
df.loc[('Smartphones', 2020), 'USD']
```

Output:

```
100
```

Figure 7.11: Fetch data from a specific column

3. Slicing:

You can slice a multi-index DataFrame as well. To get data for smartphones for the years **2020** and **2021**:

```
df.loc[('Smartphones', slice(None)), :]
```

Output:

Product	Year	USD	EUR	GBP	JPY
Smartphones	2020	100	101	102	103
	2021	90	91	92	93

Figure 7.12: Slicing multiIndex DataFrame

4. Accessing columns:

You can simply call the column if you wish to access a specific currency.

```
print(df['USD'])
```

Output:

```
Product      Year
Smartphones  2020    100
             2021     90
Laptops      2020    105
             2021    115
Name: USD, dtype: int64
```

Figure 7.13: Fetch data using a specific column

Long and Wide Formats

Data comes in various shapes and sizes, and understanding the distinctions between these shapes is fundamental in data analysis. Two common formats are long and wide, each with its own merits and use cases. In this section, we'll explore the differences between these formats and when to employ them, and we'll learn how Pandas can be utilized to seamlessly transform data between these two formats.

Long Format

The long format, often referred to as the "tidy" format, is designed to facilitate analysis and manipulation. In this format, each row typically represents a unique observation, and each column represents a distinct variable or dimension. Here are some key characteristics of the long format:

- **Multiple Rows per Entity**: Long format data often has multiple rows for each entity (e.g., individual, time point, location). These rows contain observations related to the entity.

- **Variable Names in a Single Column**: Instead of having different columns for each variable, the variable names are typically stored in a single column, often referred to as the "**variable**" or "**feature**" column.

- **Values Correspond to Observations**: The actual values of the variables are stored in a separate column, often referred to as the "**value**" column.

The long format is particularly useful for:

- **Data Analysis**: It facilitates various data analysis tasks such as aggregation, filtering, and grouping.

- **Visualization**: Many data visualization tools and libraries, including Seaborn and Plotly, work seamlessly with data in this format.

- **Time Series Data**: The long format is well-suited for time series data with multiple time points for each entity.

```
# Create a sample long-format DataFrame
data = {
    'Student': ['Alice', 'Bob', 'Alice', 'Bob'],
    'Subject': ['Math', 'Math', 'Science', 'Science'],
    'Score': [90, 88, 85, 92]
}

df_long = pd.DataFrame(data)
print("Long-format DataFrame:")
df_long
```

Output:

```
Long-format DataFrame:

   Student  Subject  Score
0   Alice    Math     90
1   Bob      Math     88
2   Alice    Science  85
3   Bob      Science  92
```

Figure 7.14: *Long-format DataFrame*

Wide Format

Conversely, the wide format is characterized by having a separate column for each variable or dimension. In this format, each row typically represents a single entity or case. Key features of the wide format include:

- **Single Row per Entity:** Each entity has a single row, making it easy to compare variables across entities.

- **Columns Represent Variables:** Variables are stored as columns, and each column header indicates the variable's name or category.

- **Values Correspond to Variables:** The values in each cell correspond to the observations for a specific variable.

The wide format is well-suited for:

- **Data Visualization:** It is often more intuitive to visualize data using tools like Excel or Tableau, which expect data in this format.

- **Modeling:** Some machine learning algorithms and statistical models may require data in a wide format.

```
# Create a sample wide-format DataFrame
data_wide = {
    'Student': ['Alice', 'Bob'],
    'Math': [90, 88],
    'Science': [85, 92]
}

df_wide = pd.DataFrame(data_wide)
print("\nWide-format DataFrame:")
df_wide
```

Output:

```
Wide-format DataFrame:

    Student  Math  Science
0    Alice    90       85
1      Bob    88       92
```

Figure 7.15: Wide format DataFrame

Choosing the Right Format

The choice between long and wide formats depends on the specific goals of your analysis or project:

- Use the **long format** for most data analysis tasks, as it provides flexibility and compatibility with various analysis and visualization tools.

- Consider converting data into a **wide format** when you need it for specific modeling purposes or when creating summary tables for reporting and visualization.

Stacking and Unstacking

Reshaping data is a fundamental aspect of data manipulation, and Pandas provides powerful tools for accomplishing this, including the stack and unstack functions. These functions allow you to transform data between long and wide formats, facilitating various analytical tasks. In this section, we'll delve into stacking and unstacking, offering real-world examples, and demonstrating how to use Pandas' **stack and unstack** functions for efficient data reshaping.

Stacking

Stacking, sometimes referred to as *"vertical transformation,"* involves converting wide-format data into a long-format. It's the process of moving columns into rows, resulting in a vertically extended dataset. Stacking is useful for tasks like data aggregation and filtering.

To illustrate stacking, let's consider the following scenario.

Stacking Example: Quarterly Sales Data

Imagine having a dataset with quarterly sales data for different product categories represented in a wide format:

Quarter	Product_A	Product_B	Product_C
Q1	1000	800	1200
Q2	1100	820	1300

Table 7.1: *Quarterly sales data – wide format*

By applying stacking, we transform it into a long format like this

Quarter	Product	Sales
Q1	Product_A	1000
Q1	Product_B	800

Q1	Product_C	1200
Q2	Product_A	1100
Q2	Product_B	820
Q2	Product_C	1300

Table 7.2: *Quarterly sales data – long format*

Let's see how using the **stack** function in Python, we can convert this data into a long format:

```
# Creating the wide-format DataFrame
data_wide = {
    'Quarter': ['Q1', 'Q2'],
    'Product_A': [1000, 1100],
    'Product_B': [800, 820],
    'Product_C': [1200, 1300]
}


df_wide = pd.DataFrame(data_wide)


df_wide
```

Output:

	Quarter	Product_A	Product_B	Product_C
0	Q1	1000	800	1200
1	Q2	1100	820	1300

Figure 7.16: *Create a wide DataFrame*

The preceding code creates a wide-format DataFrame containing quarterly sales data for different products. Each product category (**Product_A**, **Product_B**, **Product_C**) has its own column, and the sales figures are separated by quarters (Q1 and Q2).

```
# Stacking (vertical transformation) the data
stacked_df = df_wide.set_index('Quarter').stack().reset_index-
(name='Sales')
print("Stacked DataFrame:")
stacked_df
```

Output:

	Quarter	level_1	Sales
0	Q1	Product_A	1000
1	Q1	Product_B	800
2	Q1	Product_C	1200
3	Q2	Product_A	1100
4	Q2	Product_B	820
5	Q2	Product_C	1300

Figure 7.17: Stacking the DataFrame

Upon applying the stack function with **set_index**, the result is a vertically transformed DataFrame, often referred to as a "**stacked**" DataFrame. In the **stacked DataFrame**:

- The **'Quarter'** column is retained as an identifier variable, and the DataFrame is indexed by **'Quarter.'**

- The **'stack'** function transforms the columns (**Product_A**, **Product_B**, **Product_C**) into rows, effectively creating a multi-level index where **'Quarter'** and **'Product'** become the levels.

- The '**reset_index**' function is used to reset the index and create a new column named 'Sales' to store the sales figures.

The result is a long-format DataFrame, which is a more suitable format for various types of analysis and visualization. It allows for easier data manipulation and provides a structured representation of sales data by product category and quarter.

Unstacking

Unstacking, known as "*horizontal transformation*," pivots long-format data into a wide format. It entails moving rows into columns, leading to a horizontally expanded dataset. Unstacking is often used for clear data visualization or to prepare data for modeling.

Unstacking Example: Monthly Temperature Data

Consider a long-format dataset containing monthly temperature data for different cities:

Month	City	Temperature
January	New York	32
January	Boston	30

February	New York	35
February	Boston	32

Table 7.3: *Monthly temperature data*

After unstacking,

Month	New York	Boston
January	32	30
February	35	32

Table 7.4: *Unstacking*

We can transform this data from a long format back into a wide format using the unstack function in Python. Let's explore how to achieve this.

```
# Creating the long-format DataFrame
data_long = {
    'Month': ['January', 'January', 'February', 'February'],
    'City': ['New York', 'Boston', 'New York', 'Boston'],
    'Temperature': [32, 30, 35, 32]
}


df_long = pd.DataFrame(data_long)
df_long
```

Output:

Figure 7.18: *Create a long-format DataFrame*

The code begins with a long-format DataFrame containing temperature data for cities in different months.

```
# Unstacking (horizontal transformation) the data
unstacked_df = df_long.set_index(['Month', 'City'])['Temperature'].un-
stack().reset_index()
```

```
print("\nUnstacked DataFrame:")
unstacked_df
```

Output:

```
Unstacked DataFrame:

City    Month   Boston  New York

    0   February    32        35

    1   January     30        32
```

Figure 7.19: Unstacking the DataFrame

After applying horizontal transformation using **set_index**, **unstack**, and **reset_index**, the result is an unstacked DataFrame where **'Month'** and **'City'** columns become regular columns, and each city (**'New York'** and **'Boston'**) has its own column displaying temperature values for each month. This format simplifies data comparison between cities and months.

With these functions, we can seamlessly transform data to suit various analytical requirements, whether it's for in-depth analysis, visualization, or modeling.

Melting Data

Melting is the process of converting wide-format data into a long format by reshaping it. It's similar to stacking, as discussed earlier, and involves transforming columns into rows, resulting in a vertically extended dataset.

The Melt Function in Pandas

In Pandas, the **melt** function is used to melt data efficiently. Let's explore the key parameters of the melt function:

- **id_vars:** This parameter specifies which columns should remain as-is (**unmelted**) and not be transformed into rows.

- **value_vars:** Here, you specify which columns should be melted into rows. If not specified, all columns not mentioned in **id_vars** are **melted**.

- **var_name:** This parameter allows you to specify the name of the column that will store the variable names after melting.

- **value_name:** You use this parameter to name the column that will store the values after melting.

To understand the significance of melting data, consider the following real-world scenarios:

Time Series Data Transformation:

Suppose you have time series data in a wide format:

Date	Temperature	Humidity
2023-01-01	32	45
2023-01-01	30	48
2023-01-03	35	42

Table 7.5: *Time series data*

```
# Creating a sample wide-format DataFrame
data_wide = {
    'Date': ['2023-01-01', '2023-01-02', '2023-01-03'],
    'Temperature': [32, 30, 35],
    'Humidity': [45, 48, 42]
}


df_wide = pd.DataFrame(data_wide)
df_wide
```

Output:

	Date	Temperature	Humidity
0	2023-01-01	32	45
1	2023-01-02	30	48
2	2023-01-03	35	42

Figure 7.20: *Create a wide-format DataFrame*

In the preceding code snippet, we constructed a DataFrame in a wide format that depicts time series data, including dates, temperature readings, and humidity levels.

```
# Melting the time series data
melted_df = df_wide.melt(id_vars=['Date'], var_name='Variable', val-
ue_name='Value')


print("Melted Time Series DataFrame:")
melted_df
```

Output:

```
Melted Time Series DataFrame:

        Date       Variable   Value

0   2023-01-01   Temperature    32

1   2023-01-02   Temperature    30

2   2023-01-03   Temperature    35

3   2023-01-01     Humidity     45

4   2023-01-02     Humidity     48

5   2023-01-03     Humidity     42
```

Figure 7.21: *Time series data using Melt*

In the preceding data transformation process shown, we employ the **melt** function to reshape our dataset. Specifically, we designate the **'Date'** column as the identifier variable (**id_vars**), which remains unaltered. We also set the '**var_name**' parameter to **'Variable'** and the '**value_name**' parameter to **'Value'** for the resulting melted DataFrame. This transformation results in '**melted_df**,' a long-format DataFrame that is more conducive for subsequent analysis and visualization tasks.

Exploding Data

In data analysis, you often encounter nested structures or lists within your data that need to be expanded for further exploration. Pandas' explode function is a valuable tool for efficiently handling such situations. In this section, we will demonstrate how to use explode to unnest data, providing examples that highlight its usefulness in scenarios involving JSON-like structures or hierarchical data.

Exploding data refers to the process of transforming nested or list-like structures within a DataFrame into separate rows. This operation expands the data, making it more accessible for analysis.

The Explode Function in Pandas

In Pandas, the explode function is used to perform this operation efficiently. The key parameter of the explode function is:

column: This parameter specifies which column contains the nested structure that you want to explode.

Let's see an example to demonstrate how to use the explode function in Pandas to expand nested or list-like data.

Suppose you have a dataset of students and the courses they are enrolled in. Each student can be enrolled in multiple courses, and this information is stored on a list. Here's a sample dataset:

Student ID	Name	Courses
1	Alice	["Math", "Science"]
2	Bob	["History", "Geography"]
3	Charlie	["English"]

Table 7.6: Time series data

In this dataset, the **'Courses'** column contains lists of courses for each student. To analyze this data more effectively, you can use the **explode** function to expand the **'Courses'** column, creating separate rows for each course for each student.

Exploded Data:

Student ID	Name	Course
1	Alice	Math
1	Alice	Science
2	Bob	History
2	Bob	Geography
3	Charlie	English

Table 7.7: Exploded data

Now, let's provide a Python example using the explode function in Pandas to achieve this:

```
# Creating a DataFrame with the original data

data = {
    'Student ID': [1, 2, 3],
    'Name': ['Alice', 'Bob', 'Charlie'],
    'Courses': [['Math', 'Science'], ['History', 'Geography'],
['English']]
}

df = pd.DataFrame(data)
df
```

Output:

	Student ID	Name	Courses
0	1	Alice	[Math, Science]
1	2	Bob	[History, Geography]
2	3	Charlie	[English]

Figure 7.22: Create a sample DataFrame

In this code snippet, we start with a DataFrame called **df**, which contains student information, including their names and courses in a nested list format.

```
# Using explode to expand the 'Courses' column
exploded_df = df.explode('Courses', ignore_index=True)


print("Exploded DataFrame:")
exploded_df
```

Output:

```
Exploded DataFrame:
```

	Student ID	Name	Courses
0	1	Alice	Math
1	1	Alice	Science
2	2	Bob	History
3	2	Bob	Geography
4	3	Charlie	English

Figure 7.23: Explode DataFrame

By using the explode function on the 'Courses' column with **ignore_index=True**, we transform this data into a new **DataFrame** called **exploded_df**. This operation expands the nested lists in **'Courses'** into separate rows, resulting in individual rows for each student-course pairing. The **'exploded_df'** DataFrame is a flattened representation of the original data, making it more suitable for analysis and reporting tasks.

Creating Pivot Tables

Pivot tables are versatile tools that allow you to reshape data, reorganize it, and generate meaningful summaries. They are particularly useful for aggregating data, providing a condensed view of large datasets by grouping and summarizing information based on specific criteria. Pivot tables are widely used in data analysis and reporting to gain insights and make data-driven decisions.

Key Concepts in Creating Pivot Tables

- **Index:** The index of a pivot table determines the rows of the table. It represents the categorical variables by which you want to group and summarize data.

- **Columns:** The columns represent the variables you want to compare or categorize the data by.

- **Values:** The values are the data you want to summarize or aggregate, typically through functions like sum, mean, count, or custom aggregation functions.

- **Aggregation Functions:** These functions define how data is summarized within the pivot table. Common aggregation functions include sum, mean, count, min, and max.

Let's explore scenarios where pivot tables are invaluable:

Sales Data Analysis:

Imagine you have a dataset of sales transactions with columns like **'Product Category,'** **'Sales Region,'** and **'Revenue.'** You can create a **pivot** table to quickly analyze total revenue by product category and sales region, providing insights into the best-performing categories and regions.

```
# Creating a sample DataFrame
data = {
    'Product Category': ['Electronics', 'Clothing', 'Electronics',
'Clothing'],
    'Sales Region': ['North', 'South', 'North', 'South'],
    'Revenue': [5000, 3000, 6000, 4000]
}


df = pd.DataFrame(data)
df
```

Output:

	Product Category	Sales Region	Revenue
0	Electronics	North	5000
1	Clothing	South	3000
2	Electronics	North	6000
3	Clothing	South	4000

Figure 7.24: Sample DataFrame

```
# Creating a pivot table to summarize revenue by category and region
pivot_table = pd.pivot_table(df, values='Revenue', index='Product
Category', columns='Sales Region',
                                    aggfunc='sum', fill_value=0)
```

```
print("Pivot Table:")
```

```
pivot_table
```

Output:

```
Pivot Table:

    Sales Region    North   South

Product Category

        Clothing        0    7000

     Electronics    11000       0
```

Figure 7.25: Create a pivot table to summarize revenue by category and region

In the preceding code, the pivot table summarizes the total revenue by **'Product Category'** and '**Sales Region**' and uses the aggregation function **'sum'** to calculate the sum of revenues. Any missing values in the pivot table are filled with **0** using the **fill_value=0** parameter. This pivot table provides a clear and concise view of revenue distribution across product categories and sales regions, making it valuable for sales data analysis and decision-making.

Advanced Pivot Table Techniques

In this section, we will explore advanced techniques for working with pivot tables in Pandas. These techniques are particularly useful for handling complex data structures and performing specialized analyses. Here are the key topics we will cover:

- **Multi-Index Pivot Tables:**

Multi-index pivot tables allow you to create pivot tables with a hierarchical row and column indices. This means you can have multiple levels of categorization, which is useful for in-depth data summarization. For example, if you're analyzing sales data, you can have multi-index rows with levels like **'Year'** and **'Quarter**,' and multi-index columns with levels like **'Product Category'** and **'Region**.' This way, you can drill down into your data with greater granularity.

```
# Creating a sample DataFrame for sales data
data = {
    'Year': [2021, 2021, 2022, 2022],
```

```
        'Quarter': ['Q1', 'Q2', 'Q1', 'Q2'],
        'Product Category': ['Electronics', 'Clothing', 'Electronics',
    'Clothing'],
        'Region': ['North', 'South', 'North', 'South'],
        'Revenue': [5000, 3000, 6000, 4000]
}
```

```
df = pd.DataFrame(data)
df
```

Output:

	Year	Quarter	Product Category	Region	Revenue
0	2021	Q1	Electronics	North	5000
1	2021	Q2	Clothing	South	3000
2	2022	Q1	Electronics	North	6000
3	2022	Q2	Clothing	South	4000

Figure 7.26: Create a DataFrame with sales data

Let's explore how to create a pivot table with hierarchical row and column indices.

```
# Creating a multi-index pivot table with hierarchical row and column
indices
pivot_table = df.pivot_table(index=['Year', 'Quarter'], columns=['Prod-
uct Category', 'Region'], values='Revenue', aggfunc='sum', fill_value=0)
```

```
print("Multi-Index Pivot Table:")
pivot_table
```

Output:

```
Multi-Index Pivot Table:
```

Product Category		Clothing	Electronics
	Region	South	North
Year	Quarter		
2021	Q1	0	5000
	Q2	3000	0
2022	Q1	0	6000
	Q2	4000	0

Figure 7.27: Pivot table with hierarchical row and column indices

The output of this code will be a multi-index pivot table. Rows are hierarchically indexed by **'Year'** and **'Quarter',** while columns have a multi-index structure with levels **'Product Category'** and **'Region'.** The values in the table represent the total revenue for each combination of **'Year'** and **'Quarter',** further categorized by **'Product Category'** and **'Region'.** This provides a detailed and structured summary of revenue data, making it easier to analyze sales performance over different time periods and across various product categories and regions.

- **Hierarchical Column Structures:**

Hierarchical column structures in pivot tables involve organizing columns in a nested or hierarchical manner. This is particularly useful when you have data with multiple levels of information that you want to present in a structured way. For instance, you might have a pivot table with **'Product Category'** as the first-level column and 'Region' as the second-level column, allowing you to view data in a more organized fashion.

```
# Creating a pivot table with hierarchical columns
pivot_table = df.pivot_table(index='Year', columns=['Product Category',
'Region'],

                          values='Revenue', aggfunc='sum', fill_val-
ue=0)


print("hierarchical columns Pivot Table:")
pivot_table
```

Output:

```
hierarchical columns Pivot Table:

Product Category  Clothing  Electronics
        Region     South       North
          Year
          2021      3000        5000
          2022      4000        6000
```

Figure 7.28: *Hierarchical columns pivot table*

The output of the preceding code is a pivot table with hierarchical column structures with **'Year'** as the index and **'Product Category'** and **'Region'** forming hierarchical columns. It presents the total revenue for each year (**'2021'** and **'2022'**) and further breaks it down by product category (**'Clothing'** and **'Electronics'**) and region (**'South'** and **'North'**). For example, in the cell where **'Year'** is **'2021',** **'Product Category'** is **'Clothing',** and **'Region'** is **'South',** the value **'3000'** represents the total revenue for that specific combination. This hierarchical structure provides a clear summary of revenue figures, making it easy to compare sales across different years, product categories, and regions.

Conclusion

In this chapter, we've delved deep into reshaping and pivoting data using Pandas, essential techniques for data analysis. We've covered MultiIndexing, transforming between Long and Wide Formats, Stacking, Unstacking, Melting Data, Exploding Data, and Creating Pivot Tables. These techniques empower data professionals to efficiently structure data for in-depth analysis. In the next chapter, we'll delve into joining and merging data, covering topics such as concatenation, Inner Joins, Outer Joins, Left Joins, joining on index, and merging on multiple columns. This chapter equips us with the skills to seamlessly integrate datasets, a critical aspect of data analysis.

Exercise Questions

- Given a long-format DataFrame with data about student test scores in different subjects and years, demonstrate how to convert it into a wide-format DataFrame for better analysis.

  ```
  data = {
  'Student': ['Alice', 'Alice', 'Bob', 'Bob', 'Charlie', 'Charlie'],
  'Year': [2021, 2022, 2021, 2022, 2021, 2022],
  'Subject': ['Math', 'Math', 'Math', 'Math', 'Math', 'Math'],
  'Score': [85, 88, 90, 92, 78, 82]
  }
  ```

- Given a dataset that records quarterly sales data for various products and regions, apply stacking and unstacking operations to better understand the quarterly performance of each product across different regions.

  ```
  data = {
      'Product': ['A', 'B', 'A', 'B'],
      'Region': ['North', 'North', 'South', 'South'],
      'Q1 Sales': [1000, 1200, 800, 950],
      'Q2 Sales': [1100, 1300, 850, 980]
  }
  ```

- Given a dataset containing sales data for different products and regions. Use the Pandas melt function to transform this data into a long format, allowing for an in-depth analysis of product performance across regions.

```
data = {
    'Product': ['A', 'B', 'C'],
    'North Sales': [1000, 1200, 800],
    'South Sales': [1100, 1300, 850]
}
```

- Use the following dataset with nested structures, representing survey responses including multiple-choice questions. Utilize the Pandas explode function to flatten the nested data, making it suitable for thorough analysis.

```
data = {
    'Respondent': [1, 2, 3],
    'Responses': [
        ['Option A', 'Option B'],
        ['Option B'],
        ['Option A', 'Option C']
    ]
}
```

- The following dataset features customer purchase information, including purchase dates, products, and prices. Construct a pivot table to summarize total spending by product category and purchase date, offering valuable insights into purchasing trends.

```
data = {
    'Purchase Date': ['2022-01-01', '2022-01-01', '2022-01-02',
'2022-01-02'],
    'Product': ['A', 'B', 'A', 'C'],
    'Price': [50, 30, 45, 25]
}
```

Joining and Merging Data in Pandas

Welcome to the eighth chapter of our data manipulation journey! In this installment, we delve into the art of combining datasets through the powerful techniques of joining and merging using Pandas. These techniques are the bridges that connect individual datasets into a unified whole, paving the way for deeper insights and comprehensive analyses.

Structure

In this chapter, we will discuss the following topics:

- Introduction to Joining and Merging
- Concatenating Data Along Rows and Columns
- Merging Dataframes
  - Inner Join
  - Outer Join
  - Left Join
  - Right Join
- Joining Dataframes on Their Index
- Merging on Multiple Columns

Introduction to Joining and Merging

In data analysis, datasets are rarely isolated entities. Often, valuable insights lie in the connections between different datasets. Joining and merging are data manipulation techniques that allow us to bring together these datasets, creating a more comprehensive and enriched source of information. In this section, we'll explore the foundational concepts of joining and merging data using Pandas.

Understanding the Basics: Joining vs. Merging

Before getting into the technical aspects, let's clarify the distinction between joining and merging:

- **Joining:** Joining refers to the process of combining datasets based on a shared column, known as a *"key."* This key serves as a common identifier that links corresponding rows across datasets. Joining is similar to combining information from different spreadsheets using a common field.

- **Merging:** Merging is a broader term that encompasses joining. It involves combining datasets based on one or more keys, and the keys can be located in columns other than the index. Merging can involve more complex operations, such as combining datasets on multiple columns or indices.

Why Join and Merge?

The motivation behind joining and merging is clear: to uncover insights that wouldn't be apparent when analyzing datasets in isolation. Consider a scenario where you have one dataset containing customer information and another dataset containing purchase history. By joining or merging these datasets, you can analyze which customers made which purchases, revealing patterns and correlations that contribute to a deeper understanding of customer behavior.

Key Aspects of Joining and Merging

Several key aspects are crucial to understand before diving into joining and merging:

- **Key Columns:** In both joining and merging, the key column(s) are the basis for combining datasets. These columns should contain common values that link corresponding rows across datasets.

- **Types of Joins:** There are several types of joins: inner join, outer join, left join, and right join. Each type specifies which rows to retain from the datasets being merged based on the key columns.

- **Duplicate Values:** It's important to handle duplicate values in the key columns, as these can impact the results of the merge. Pandas provides methods to handle duplicates, such as aggregating them or selecting a specific one.

Concatenating Data Along Rows and Columns

Concatenating data involves combining multiple datasets together to create a larger dataset. This operation is akin to stacking or extending datasets, and it can be performed either along rows (vertically) or columns (horizontally). Concatenation is particularly useful when you have datasets with the same structure but different instances or time periods.

Syntax:

Pandas provides the **pd.concat()** function for concatenating dataframes. The basic syntax is as follows:

```
result = pd.concat([dataframe1, dataframe2, ...], axis=0)
```

- **dataframe1, dataframe2, ...:** A list of dataframes you want to concatenate.
- **axis**: Specifies the axis along which the concatenation will occur. Use **axis=0** to concatenate along rows (vertical concatenation) and **axis=1** to concatenate along columns (horizontal concatenation).

Concatenate Data Along Rows

Concatenating data along rows, also known as vertical concatenation or stacking, involves combining multiple datasets by appending their rows one after another. This is useful when you have datasets with the same columns and want to extend the number of rows in your resulting dataset.

Syntax:

To concatenate along rows, set the axis parameter to **0**. The syntax is as follows:

```
result = pd.concat([dataframe1, dataframe2, ...], axis=0)
```

Let's consider an example where we have two datasets, **dataframe1** and **dataframe2**, both containing information about employees.

```
import pandas as pd


# Create two dataframes
dataframe1 = pd.DataFrame({
    'Employee_ID': [101, 102],
    'Name': ['Alice', 'Bob'],
    'Department': ['HR', 'Finance']
})


dataframe2 = pd.DataFrame({
    'Employee_ID': [103, 104],
    'Name': ['Charlie', 'David'],
    'Department': ['Marketing', 'IT']
})
```

In this example, the **pd.concat()** function combines the two dataframes, **dataframe1** and **dataframe2**, along rows. The resulting **concatenated_rows** dataframe contains all the rows from both **dataframe1** and **dataframe2**. The columns remain the same, and the index values are retained from the original dataframes.

```
# Concatenate along rows
concatenated_rows = pd.concat([dataframe1, dataframe2], axis=0)
concatenated_rows
```

Output:

	Employee_ID	Name	Department
0	101	Alice	HR
1	102	Bob	Finance
0	103	Charlie	Marketing
1	104	David	IT

Figure 8.1: *Concatenate along rows*

Concatenating data along rows is a straightforward way to extend the dataset with additional observations while maintaining the column structure. This technique is particularly useful when we have datasets with the same column names and want to stack their rows together.

Concatenate Data Along Columns

Concatenating data along columns involves combining multiple datasets by adding their columns side by side. This operation is useful when you have datasets with different instances or observations, and you want to expand the information by appending new attributes.

Syntax:

To concatenate dataframes along columns, set the axis parameter to **1** in the **pd.concat()** function. The syntax is as follows:

```
result = pd.concat([dataframe1, dataframe2, ...], axis=1)
```

Let's consider a scenario where you have two datasets, **dataframe1** and **dataframe2**, both containing information about employees. These datasets have the same index (representing employees), but they contain different attributes.

```
# Create two dataframes
dataframe1 = pd.DataFrame({
    'Employee_ID': [101, 102],
    'Name': ['Alice', 'Bob']
})
```

```
dataframe2 = pd.DataFrame({
    'Salary': [50000, 60000],
    'Department': ['HR', 'Finance']
})
```

In this example, **dataframe1** contains employee IDs and names, while **dataframe2** includes department names and corresponding salaries. The **pd.concat()** function aligns the columns from both **dataframes** side by side, creating the **concatenated_columns** that don't have corresponding data in both **dataframes**.

```
# Concatenate along columns
concatenated_columns = pd.concat([dataframe1, dataframe2], axis=1)
concatenated_columns
```

Output:

	Employee_ID	Name	Salary	Department
0	101	Alice	50000	HR
1	102	Bob	60000	Finance

Figure 8.2: Concatenate along columns

Concatenating data along columns enriches your dataset with additional attributes while maintaining the same number of rows. This technique is ideal for combining datasets that share a common index and adding more information to your existing observations.

Concatenating Dataframes with Missing Values

Concatenating dataframes with missing values involves combining multiple datasets where not all columns have corresponding data in every dataframe. This operation is commonly used to merge datasets with differing attributes, resulting in aligned rows but potential gaps in columns.

Let's explore concatenation with missing values through an example. Consider two datasets, **dataframe1** and **dataframe2**, representing employee information.

In this example, **dataframe1** contains employee IDs and names, while dataframe2 includes names and corresponding salaries. The **pd.concat()** function aligns the columns based on their names. As a result, the **Salary** column from **dataframe2** does not have corresponding data in dataframe1, leading to missing values in the **Employee_ID** and Salary columns in the concatenated dataframe.

```
# Create two dataframes
dataframe1 = pd.DataFrame({
    'Employee_ID': [101, 102],
    'Name': ['Alice', 'Bob']
})


dataframe2 = pd.DataFrame({
    'Name': ['Charlie', 'David'],
    'Salary': [60000, 75000]
})


# Concatenate dataframes with missing values
concatenated_with_missing = pd.concat([dataframe1, dataframe2])


print(concatenated_with_missing)
```

Output:

```
   Employee_ID    Name    Salary
0        101.0    Alice      NaN
1        102.0      Bob      NaN
0          NaN  Charlie  60000.0
1          NaN    David  75000.0
```

Figure 8.3: Concatenate dataframes with missing values

When concatenating dataframes, the columns are aligned based on their names. If a column exists in one dataframe but not in another, Pandas inserts **NaN** (Not a Number) values in the corresponding cells to indicate missing data.

We can observe from the output, the **Employee_ID** column is present in the first dataframe but not in the second, leading to NaN values in the **Employee_ID** column for the rows from the second dataframe. Conversely, the **Salary** column is present in the second dataframe but not in the first, resulting in **NaN** values in the Salary column for the rows from the first.

Merging Dataframes

Merging dataframes involves combining datasets based on shared columns, also known as keys. This operation is akin to a database join, where you align rows from different dataframes based on common values in specified columns. Merging allows you to consolidate data from multiple sources into a single dataframe.

Syntax:

Pandas provides the **pd.merge()** function for merging dataframes. The basic syntax is as follows:

```
result = pd.merge(left_dataframe, right_dataframe, on='key_column')
```

- **left_dataframe:** The dataframe you want to merge from the left side.
- **right_dataframe:** The dataframe you want to merge from the right side.
- **on:** The column(s) used as the key for the merge.

Inner Joins

Inner joins are a type of merging operation that combines dataframes based on a common key, retaining only the rows where the key values exist in both dataframes. In other words, an inner join focuses on the intersection of the key values between the dataframes, discarding non-matching rows.

Syntax:

Pandas provides the **pd.merge()** function for performing inner joins. The basic syntax is as follows:

```
result = pd.merge(left_dataframe, right_dataframe, on='key_column',
how='inner')
```

- **left_dataframe:** The dataframe to merge from the left side.
- **right_dataframe:** The dataframe to merge from the right side.
- **on:** The column(s) used as the key for the merge.
- **how:** Specifies the type of join; use **'inner'** for inner joins.

Suppose we have two datasets, **orders_data** and **customers_data**, containing information about orders and customer details.

```
# Create orders_data dataframe
orders_data = pd.DataFrame({
    'Order_ID': [101, 102, 103],
    'Customer_ID': [201, 202, 203],
    'Product': ['A', 'B', 'C']
})


# Create customers_data dataframe
customers_data = pd.DataFrame({
    'Customer_ID': [201, 202, 204],
```

```
    'Name': ['Alice', 'Bob', 'Charlie'],
    'Location': ['New York', 'San Francisco', 'Los Angeles']
})
```

Output:

Figure 8.4: *Create order and customer dataframes*

In this example, we're performing an inner join on the **'Customer_ID'** column between **orders_data** and **customers_data** dataframes. The resulting **inner_join_result** dataframe retains only the rows where the **'Customer_ID'** values exist in both dataframes. Non-matching rows are omitted from the output.

```
# Perform inner join based on 'Customer_ID'
inner_join_result = pd.merge(orders_data, customers_data, on='Customer-ID', how='inner')
print(inner_join_result)
```

Output:

```
   Order_ID  Customer_ID Product   Name      Location
0      101          201       A  Alice      New York
1      102          202       B    Bob  San Francisco
```

Figure 8.5: *Inner joins*

Inner join emphasizes shared information and provides a consolidated view of data intersections. Inner joins are particularly useful for extracting insights about elements common to multiple datasets, allowing for more focused analysis and understanding of relationships.

Outer Joins

An outer join is a merging operation that combines two dataframes based on a specified key column, retaining all rows from both dataframes while filling in missing values with **NaN** (Not a Number) where necessary. Outer joins emphasize the union of data, allowing you to capture information from both datasets, even when key values don't match perfectly.

Syntax:

To perform an outer join in Pandas, you use the **pd.merge()** function with the how parameter set to **'outer'**. The syntax is as follows:

```
result = pd.merge(left_dataframe, right_dataframe, on='key_column',
how='outer')
```

- **left_dataframe:** The dataframe you want to merge from the left side.
- **right_dataframe:** The dataframe you want to merge from the right side.
- **on:** The column(s) used as the key for the merge.
- **how:** Specifies the type of join. Use **'outer'** for an outer join.

```
# Create employees dataframe
employees = pd.DataFrame({
    'Employee_ID': [101, 102, 103, 104],
    'Name': ['Alice', 'Bob', 'Charlie', 'David'],
    'Department_ID': [1, 2, 1, 3]
})


# Create departments dataframe
departments = pd.DataFrame({
    'Department_ID': [1, 2, 4],
    'Department_Name': ['HR', 'Finance', 'Marketing']
})
```

Output:

	Employee_ID	Name	Department_ID
0	101	Alice	1
1	102	Bob	2
2	103	Charlie	1
3	104	David	3

departments

	Department_ID	Department_Name
0	1	HR
1	2	Finance
2	4	Marketing

Figure 8.6: *Create employees and departments dataframes*

In this example, an outer join is executed between the **employees** and **departments** dataframes using the shared **'Department_ID'** column. The **pd.merge()** function combines all rows from both dataframes, filling in missing values with **NaN** where appropriate. The resulting **outer_joined** dataframe captures all employees and departments, even when **department IDs** do not match perfectly.

```
# Perform an outer join based on 'Department_ID'
```

```
outer_joined = pd.merge(employees, departments, on='Department_ID', how='outer')
```

```
print(outer_joined)
```

Output:

```
   Employee_ID     Name  Department_ID Department_Name
0        101.0    Alice              1              HR
1        103.0  Charlie              1              HR
2        102.0      Bob              2         Finance
3        104.0    David              3             NaN
4          NaN      NaN              4       Marketing
```

Figure 8.7: Outer joins

Outer joins offer a comprehensive way to unite data from different datasets, accommodating discrepancies in key values. The resulting dataframe contains all rows from both dataframes, with **NaN** values in columns where data is missing. Outer joins are valuable for capturing a broad view of relationships between elements, even when complete matches are not present in the data.

Left Outer Join

A left outer join is a merging operation that combines two dataframes based on a specified key column, retaining all rows from the left dataframe. When key values match, data from the right dataframe is included; otherwise, missing values are filled with **NaN**. Left outer joins emphasize preserving data from the left dataframe while adding relevant information from the right dataframe.

Syntax:result = pd.merge(left_dataframe, right_dataframe, on='key_column', how='left')

Let's illustrate a left outer join using the same dataframes, **employees** and **departments**, based on the common column **'Department_ID'**.

```
# Perform an outer join based on 'Department_ID'
```

```
left_joined = pd.merge(employees, departments, on='Department_ID', how='left')
```

```
print(left_joined)
```

Output:

```
    Employee_ID      Name  Department_ID Department_Name
0           101     Alice              1              HR
1           102       Bob              2         Finance
2           103   Charlie              1              HR
3           104     David              3             NaN
```

Figure 8.8: Left join

In this example, a left join is performed using the **pd.merge()** function with the how parameter set to **'left'**. As a result, all rows from the **employees** dataframe are retained in the merged output. When the **'Department_ID'** values match between the **employees** and **departments** dataframes (such as for employees **Alice, Bob,** and **Charlie),** their corresponding 'Department_Name' values are included in the merged result. For the employee with 'Department_ID' 3 (**David**), which has no corresponding entry in the **departments** dataframe, the 'Department_Name' is filled with **NaN**.

Right Join

A right join is a merging operation that combines two dataframes based on a specified key column, retaining all rows from the right dataframe. When key values match, data from the left dataframe is included; otherwise, missing values are filled with **NaN**. Right joins emphasize preserving data from the right dataframe while integrating relevant information from the left dataframe.

Now, let's perform a right join based on the common column 'Department_ID'.

```
right_joined = pd.merge(employees, departments, on='Department_ID',
how='right')

right_joined
```

Output:

	Employee_ID	Name	Department_ID	Department_Name
0	101.0	Alice	1	HR
1	103.0	Charlie	1	HR
2	102.0	Bob	2	Finance
3	NaN	NaN	4	Marketing

Figure 8.9: Right join

In this example, a right join is performed and all rows from the **departments** dataframe are retained in the merged output. When the **'Department_ID'** values match between the **employees** and **departments** dataframes **(for HR** and **Finance),** their corresponding **employee** information is included in the merged result. For the department with

'**Department_ID**' **4**, which has no corresponding entry in the **employees** dataframe, the '**Employee_ID**' and '**Name**' columns are filled with **NaN**.

Right joins are valuable for preserving data from the right dataframe while incorporating relevant information from the left dataframe. This ensures that no information from the right dataframe is lost during the merging process, providing a balanced view of the relationship between the datasets.

Joining Dataframes on Their Index

When merging dataframes, you can also use their indices as the basis for the merge operation. This allows you to align data based on the index values of the dataframes instead of using a specific column for merging. Here's how you can achieve this using Pandas.

Syntax:

```
result = pd.merge(left_dataframe, right_dataframe, left_index=True,
right_index=True, how='...')
```

- **left_dataframe:** The dataframe you want to merge from the left side.
- **right_dataframe:** The dataframe you want to merge from the right side.
- **left_index:** Set to True to indicate that you want to use the left dataframes index for merging.
- **right_index:** Set to True to indicate that you want to use the right dataframes index for merging.
- **how:** Specifies the type of join (for example, '**inner**', '**outer**', '**left**', '**right**').

Now let us Consider two dataframes, students and scores, where the indices represent student IDs, and you want to merge them based on their indices.

```
# Create students dataframe
students = pd.DataFrame({
    'Name': ['Alice', 'Bob', 'Charlie'],
    'Age': [21, 22, 20]
}, index=[101, 102, 103])


# Create scores dataframe
scores = pd.DataFrame({
    'Math': [95, 85, 78],
    'Science': [89, 92, 81]
}, index=[101, 102, 104])  # Note the missing index 103
```

Output:

```
students

        Name  Age

101    Alice   21

102      Bob   22

103  Charlie   20


scores

       Math  Science

101      95       89

102      85       92

104      78       81
```

Figure 8.10: Create students and scores dataframes

Let's use **pd.merge()** function with **left_index=True** and **right_index=True** to merge the two dataframes based on their indices.

By specifying **how='inner'**, we are indicating that we want an **inner join**.

```
# Perform an inner join based on indices
inner_joined = pd.merge(students, scores, left_index=True, right_index=True, how='inner')


print("Inner Joined:")
print(inner_joined)
```

Output:

```
Inner Joined:
        Name  Age  Math  Science
101    Alice   21    95       89
102      Bob   22    85       92
```

Figure 8.11: Inner join based on Indices

The resulting **inner_joined** dataframe will only contain rows with indices that are common to both students and scores, which are **101** and **102** in this case.

The rows corresponding to indices **103** (present only in students) and **104** (present only in scores) are excluded because they do not have a counterpart in the other dataframe.

Merging on Multiple Columns

Merging on multiple columns involves combining two dataframes based on more than one column. By specifying multiple key columns, you ensure a more precise alignment of rows, which can be useful in scenarios where a single column is not sufficient to determine a unique match.

Syntax:

Pandas' **pd.merge()** function is employed for this purpose. The syntax for merging based on multiple columns is:

```
result = pd.merge(left_dataframe, right_dataframe, on=['key_column1',
'key_column2', ...], how='...')
```

- **left_dataframe**: The dataframe you want to merge from the left side.
- **right_dataframe**: The dataframe you want to merge from the right side.
- **on:** A list of column names used as keys for the merge.
- **how:** Specifies the type of join (for example, **'inner'**, **'outer'**, **'left'**, **'right'**).

Let's use a practical example for better understanding. Assume you have two dataframes - one with student details and another with their scores. Both **dataframes** have **'StudentID'** and **'Subject'** as columns, and you want to merge them based on both these columns.

```
# Sample dataframes
students = pd.DataFrame({
    'StudentID': [1, 1, 2, 2],
    'Subject': ['Math', 'History', 'Math', 'History'],
    'Name': ['Alice', 'Alice', 'Bob', 'Bob']
})


scores = pd.DataFrame({
    'StudentID': [1, 1, 2, 2],
    'Subject': ['Math', 'History', 'Math', 'History'],
    'Score': [90, 85, 78, 88]
})
```

Let's merge the **students** and **scores** dataframes using an inner join. This merge operation will focus on aligning the records based on common values in both the **StudentID** and Subject columns.

```
# Merging on multiple columns

merged_df = pd.merge(students, scores, on=['StudentID', 'Subject'],
how='inner')

print(merged_df)
```

Output:

```
    StudentID  Subject   Name  Score
0           1     Math  Alice     90
1           1  History  Alice     85
2           2     Math    Bob     78
3           2  History    Bob     88
```

Figure 8.12: *Merging on multiple columns*

In the preceding code, the dataframes **students** and **scores** are being merged based on both **'StudentID'** and **'Subject'**. This means a row in students with, say, **StudentID=1** and **Subject='Math'** will be combined with a row in scores with the same **StudentID** and Subject values. The resultant dataframe will have rows with **'StudentID'**, **'Subject'**, **'Name'**, and **'Score'** columns.

This way, by merging on multiple columns, you can obtain a comprehensive dataframe with information aligned based on two (or more) criteria. It's a powerful tool, especially when working with complex datasets where a single column doesn't offer a unique identifier for rows.

Conclusion

This chapter provided a deep dive into the process of joining and merging datasets using Pandas. The ability to combine datasets is crucial in data analysis as it allows for more comprehensive insights and integrated data exploration. Through a series of hands-on examples and explanations, we've unraveled the differences between joins and merges and explored various join types, including inner, outer, left, and right joins. We also delved into more advanced topics, such as merging on multiple columns and using indices as the basis for merging.

The upcoming chapter, *Chapter 9*, is set to introduce us to Time Series Analysis in Pandas. Time series data, with its unique temporal nature, offers a wealth of insights. In this chapter, we'll explore Pandas' tools tailored for this data type. We'll learn about Python and Pandas' datetime capabilities, handle time-indexed data, and delve into techniques like resampling. By the end, you'll be well-versed in managing and analyzing time series data in Pandas.

Exercise Questions

1. Given two **dataframes**, **df1**, and **df2**, with identical columns, concatenate them vertically (that is, by rows).

2. Given two dataframes, employees with columns 'Employee_ID', 'Name', and 'Department_ID', and departments with columns 'Department_ID' and 'Department_Name', demonstrate the results of (a) Inner Join, (b) Left Join, (c) Right Join, and (d) Outer Join.

3. Given two dataframes, employees with columns 'Employee_ID', 'Name', and 'Department_ID', and departments with columns 'Department_ID' and 'Department_Name', demonstrate the results of (a) Inner Join, (b) Left Join, (c) Right Join, and (d) Outer Join.

4. You have a dataframe **student_scores** that has 'Student_ID', 'Subject', and 'Score', and another dataframe **student_teachers** that has 'Student_ID', 'Subject', and 'Teacher'. Merge them based on both 'Student_ID' and 'Subject'. What can you deduce about the resulting dataframe?

Introduction to Time Series Analysis in Pandas

Introduction

Welcome to the ninth chapter of our data manipulation journey! In this chapter, we will explore how to efficiently handle time series data using the Pandas library in Python. Time series analysis is a crucial aspect of data analysis, especially when dealing with data that is indexed by time. Time series data consists of observations or measurements recorded at regular intervals over a specific period.

Structure

In this chapter, we will discuss the following topics:

- Introducing the Timestamp Object
- Timestamp Attributes and Properties
- How Python Works with Datetimes
- Handling Time Series Data in Pandas
- Common Operations
  - Indexing and Slicing
  - Resampling
  - Shifting and Lagging
  - Rolling Windows
- Assembling Datetime from Multiple DataFrame Columns

Introducing the Timestamp Object

In data analysis and time series modeling, timestamps play a critical role in representing moments in time. A timestamp is a specific point in time, typically recorded with date and time information. For example, 2023-10-19 14:30:00 is a timestamp representing October 19, 2023, at 2:30 PM.

In Python, the datetime module provides various tools for working with timestamps. The Pandas library extends these capabilities further by introducing the Timestamp object. This object is part of the Pandas datetime module and serves as a versatile and efficient way to handle timestamps within data structures like DataFrames and Series.

Creating Timestamps in Pandas

You can create Timestamp objects in Pandas in several ways as follows:

From a String

Creating Timestamps in Pandas from a string is a common and convenient way to represent timestamps in your data. Pandas is flexible in recognizing various timestamp formats, making it user-friendly for parsing dates and times from string representations. Let's dive into the details of creating Timestamp objects from a string:

```
import pandas as pd


# Creating a Timestamp from a string
timestamp_str = "2023-10-19 14:30:00"
timestamp = pd.Timestamp(timestamp_str)
print(timestamp)
```

Output:

```
2023-10-19 14:30:00
```

Figure 9.1: Create TimeStamp from a string

In the provided code snippet, we utilize the Pandas library to create a Timestamp object from a string representation of a timestamp, which is 2023-10-19 14:30:00. This string follows the common format of YYYY-MM-DD HH:MM:SS. With Pandas, we achieve this conversion effortlessly. We define the timestamp string in the variable **timestamp_str** and then employ the **pd.Timestamp()** constructor to create a Pandas Timestamp object named timestamp. The Timestamp object encapsulates the parsed timestamp information

Timestamp Recognition

Pandas is quite flexible when it comes to recognizing various timestamp formats. It can handle different formats, including:

`YYYY-MM-DD HH:MM:SS`

`YYYY/MM/DD HH:MM:SS`

`YYYY.MM.DD HH:MM:SS`

`YYYY-MM-DD`

`YYYY/MM/DD`

`YYYY.MM.DD`

Pandas will automatically parse these string representations and create the corresponding Timestamp object. For example, the following code would produce the same result as above:

```
timestamp_str = "2023/10/19 14:30:00"
timestamp = pd.Timestamp(timestamp_str)
print(timestamp)
```

Output:

```
2023-10-19 14:30:00
```

Figure 9.2: TimeStamp recognition

Pandas also recognizes variations in the order of date components, including whether the date starts with the year, month, or day.

```
timestamp_str = "10-19-2023 14:30:00"
timestamp = pd.Timestamp(timestamp_str)
print(timestamp)
```

Output:

```
2023-10-19 14:30:00
```

Figure 9.3: TimeStamp variations

In this example, the order of the date components is month-day-year, but Pandas still correctly interprets it as October 19, 2023.

Pandas can also handle timestamps with fractional seconds, time zones, and other variations in timestamp representation.

Using Parameters

Creating a Timestamp object using parameters in Pandas allows you to specify the individual components of a timestamp, such as year, month, day, hour, minute, and second. This method provides precise control over the creation of timestamps and is particularly useful when you have separate variables representing date and time components. Let's define this method and explain it with examples:

Creating a Timestamp Using Parameters

To create a Timestamp object using parameters, you can use the **pd.Timestamp()** constructor and provide values for each of the following components:

year: The year component of the timestamp.

month: The month component (1-12) of the timestamp.

day: The day component (1-31) of the timestamp.

hour: The hour component (0-23) of the timestamp.

minute: The minute component (0-59) of the timestamp.

second: The second component (0-59) of the timestamp.

```
# Creating a Timestamp using parameters
timestamp = pd.Timestamp(year=2023, month=10, day=19, hour=14, minute=30, second=0)
print(timestamp)
```

Output:

```
2023-10-19 14:30:00
```

Figure 9.4: Create Timestamp using parameters

In the provided code snippet, **pd.Timestamp()** constructor is employed, and parameters are passed to define the **year (2023), month (10 for October), day (19), hour (14), minute (30),** and **second (0)** components of the timestamp. The resulting timestamp object represents October 19, 2023, at 2:30 PM. This approach provides precise control over timestamp creation, making it particularly useful when you need to specify exact datetime values for various data analysis and time-related tasks.

Timestamp Attributes and Properties

The Timestamp object provides various attributes and properties to access different components of the timestamp, such as year, month, day, hour, minute, second, and more. Here are some common attributes and properties:

Year, Month, Day, Hour, Minute, Second: You can access each of these individual components of a timestamp using attributes such as `.year`, `.month`, `.day`, `.hour`, `.minute`, and `.second`. For example, `timestamp.year` returns the year component of the timestamp.

- **Microsecond**: The `.microsecond` attribute provides the microsecond component of the timestamp, allowing you to work with high-precision timestamps.

- **Day of the Week**: The `.dayofweek` attribute returns the day of the week as an integer, where Monday is `0` and Sunday is `6`. This is useful for tasks involving day-specific analysis or filtering.

- **Day of the Year**: The `.dayofyear` attribute provides the day of the year, which can be valuable when analyzing data over an annual cycle.

- **Is Leap Year**: The `.is_leap_year` property returns a boolean value indicating whether the year of the timestamp is a leap year or not.

Here's a brief code example demonstrating the use of these attributes and properties:

```
# Creating a Timestamp
timestamp = pd.Timestamp("2023-10-19 14:30:00")


# Accessing timestamp attributes and properties
print("Year:", timestamp.year)
print("Month:", timestamp.month)
print("Day:", timestamp.day)
print("Hour:", timestamp.hour)
print("Minute:", timestamp.minute)
print("Second:", timestamp.second)
print("Microsecond:", timestamp.microsecond)
print("Day of the week (0=Monday, 6=Sunday):", timestamp.dayofweek)
print("Day of the year:", timestamp.dayofyear)
print("Is it a leap year?", timestamp.is_leap_year)
```

Output:

```
Year: 2023
Month: 10
Day: 19
Hour: 14
Minute: 30
Second: 0
Microsecond: 0
Day of the week (0=Monday, 6=Sunday): 3
Day of the year: 292
Is it a leap year? False
```

Figure 9.5: *Accessing Timestamp attributes and properties*

In this code, we create a Timestamp object representing October 19, 2023, at 2:30 PM. We then access and print various attributes and properties to extract specific components and characteristics of the timestamp. These attributes and properties are essential for performing detailed analysis and manipulation of time-related data in Pandas.

Working with Datetimes in Python

In Python, the datetime module provides a comprehensive set of tools for working with dates and times. The module allows you to create, manipulate, and format datetime objects, making it a powerful tool for various applications, including data analysis, time series modeling, and more.

Creating Datetimes

You can create datetime objects in Python using the datetime class constructor. A datetime object represents a specific point in time, including both date and time components.

```
from datetime import datetime


# Creating a datetime object for a specific date and time
dt = datetime(2023, 10, 19, 14, 30, 0)
print(dt)
```

Output:

```
2023-10-19 14:30:00
```

Figure 9.6: *Create datetime object*

In the provided Python code snippet, a datetime object is created using the datetime module. The datetime constructor is used to specify a specific date and time. In this case, the datetime object dt is set to represent the date and time of October 19, 2023, at 2:30 PM (14:30:00 in 24-hour format).

Extracting Components

In Python's datetime module, you can extract various components of a datetime object by accessing its attributes. Here's a breakdown of how to extract different components:

- **year**: This attribute retrieves the year component of the datetime object.
- **month**: It retrieves the month component, ranging from 1 (January) to 12 (December).
- **day**: This attribute gets the day component of the datetime.
- **hour**: It extracts the hour component from 0 to 23.
- **minute**: Retrieves the minute component, ranging from 0 to 59.
- **second**: It gets the second component, ranging from 0 to 59.
- **microsecond**: Extracts the microsecond component, representing fractions of a second.

```python
# Creating a datetime object for a specific date and time
dt = datetime(2023, 10, 19, 14, 30, 0)


# Extracting components
year = dt.year
month = dt.month
day = dt.day
hour = dt.hour
minute = dt.minute
second = dt.second
microsecond = dt.microsecond


# Printing the extracted components
print(f"Year: {year}")
print(f"Month: {month}")
print(f"Day: {day}")
print(f"Hour: {hour}")
print(f"Minute: {minute}")
print(f"Second: {second}")
```

Output:

```
Year: 2023
Month: 10
Day: 19
Hour: 14
Minute: 30
Second: 0
```

Figure 9.7: Extract Datetime components

In this code, we first create a datetime object dt representing October 19, 2023, at 2:30 PM. Then, we use the attributes such as **.year**, **.month**, **.day**, **.hour**, **.minute**, **.second**, and **.microsecond** to extract and print each component's value. This allows you to work with specific date and time information in your Python programs.

Formatting Datetimes

Formatting datetime objects as strings using the **.strftime()** method in Python is a powerful way to display dates and times in a custom format. The **.strftime()** method stands for "**string format time**" and allows you to specify a format string that defines how you want the datetime to be represented.

Here's a brief explanation of how it works:

- You call the **strftime()** method on a datetime object.
- You pass a format string as an argument to **strftime()**.
- The format string contains placeholders for various datetime components, such as **%Y** for year, **%m** for month, **%d** for day, **%H** for hour, **%M** for minute, **%S** for second, and many more. These placeholders are replaced with the corresponding values from the datetime object.
- You can include other characters in the format string, such as slashes, colons, spaces, or any text you want to appear in the formatted output.

Let's see an example how to format a datetime object using **strftime()**:

```
# Creating a datetime object for a specific date and time
dt = datetime(2023, 10, 19, 14, 30, 0)


# Formatting the datetime as a string
formatted_datetime = dt.strftime("%Y-%m-%d %H:%M:%S")


# Printing the formatted datetime
print(formatted_datetime)
```

Output:

```
2023-10-19 14:30:00
```

Figure 9.8: *Format Datetime*

In this example, we first create a datetime object representing October 19, 2023, at 2:30 PM. Then, we use **strftime()** with the format string **"%Y-%m-%d %H:%M:%S"** to format it as "2023-10-19 14:30:00". You can customize the format string according to your preferences to display the datetime in the desired format. The **%Y, %m, %d, %H, %M,** and **%S** placeholders correspond to the year, month, day, hour, minute, and second components, respectively.

Handling Time Series Data in Pandas

Time series data refers to a sequence of observations recorded at specific time intervals or timestamps. Examples of time series data include stock prices, weather measurements, sensor readings, and economic indicators, among others. Managing and analyzing time series data is a crucial task in data science. Pandas, a powerful data manipulation library in Python, provides extensive tools and techniques to handle such data efficiently. In this discussion, we will explore how to handle time series data in Pandas, covering key concepts, data structures, and common operations.

Key Concepts

Before delving into Pandas-specific functionality, let's briefly review some fundamental concepts related to time series data:

- **Timestamp**: A timestamp represents a specific point in time, typically with date and time information. It's the fundamental unit in time series data.

- **Frequency**: Frequency refers to the time interval between consecutive data points in a time series. Common frequencies include daily, hourly, and monthly.

- **DateTime Index**: In Pandas, a datetime index is a specialized index that allows for efficient time-based indexing and slicing of time series data. It consists of Timestamp objects.

Data Structures in Pandas for Time Series

Pandas provides two primary data structures for handling time series data:

Series with Datetime Index

A Series with a datetime index is a data structure in pandas that associates a time-based index with a sequence of data values. This is particularly useful for time series data, where observations are indexed by timestamps. The datetime index allows for easy time-based slicing, filtering, and aggregation of data.

Suppose you have a dataset containing daily temperature records for a month. You can create a Series with a datetime index to represent this data. Here's a step-by-step breakdown:

```
import random

# Generate a datetime index for a month, starting from October 1, 2023
start_date = datetime(2023, 10, 1)
end_date = datetime(2023, 10, 15)
date_index = pd.date_range(start=start_date, end=end_date, freq='D')

# Generate random temperature data for each day
temperature_data = [random.uniform(60, 80) for _ in date_index]

# Create a Series with a datetime index
temperature_series = pd.Series(temperature_data, index=date_index)
temperature_series
```

Output:

```
2023-10-01    75.550854
2023-10-02    70.950306
2023-10-03    75.152774
2023-10-04    66.079876
2023-10-05    78.399431
2023-10-06    73.326583
2023-10-07    77.636648
2023-10-08    73.080332
2023-10-09    75.388359
2023-10-10    76.166928
2023-10-11    69.887674
2023-10-12    71.412684
2023-10-13    60.059215
2023-10-14    76.170724
2023-10-15    62.794483
Freq: D, dtype: float64
```

Figure 9.9: *Format Datetime*

Now, we have a Series that represents daily temperature records for 15 days of October 2023.

With a Series that has a datetime index, you can perform various time-based operations and analyses, such as:

- **Time Series Plotting:** Visualize the temperature data over time to identify trends, seasonal patterns, or anomalies.

- **Data Aggregation:** Calculate statistics like daily averages, maximum and minimum temperatures, or weekly summaries.

- **Time-based Slicing:** Select specific time intervals or date ranges from the series, making it easy to focus on specific periods of interest.

- **Resampling:** Change the frequency of the data (for example, convert daily data to monthly data) using methods such as `.resample()`.

- **Calculations Across Time:** Compute differences between consecutive timestamps, calculate rolling averages, or determine the rate of change over time.

- **Date Filtering:** Filter data based on conditions related to timestamps (for example, selecting all days with temperatures above a certain threshold).

DataFrame with Datetime Index

A DataFrame with a datetime index is a pandas data structure that combines tabular data with a datetime-based index. This structure is particularly useful for managing and analyzing time series data, where observations are indexed by timestamps. Here's how to create and work with a DataFrame with a datetime index:

We can create a DataFrame with a datetime index in several ways, including reading data from external sources such as CSV files, but here's a basic example of how to create one manually:

```
# Create a datetime index
date_index = pd.date_range(start='2023-01-01', end='2023-01-05', fre-
q='D')


# Create a DataFrame with a datetime index and sample data
data = {
    'Temperature (°C)': [20.1, 21.3, 19.8, 22.5, 20.9],
    'Humidity (%)': [50, 48, 52, 47, 49]
}


df = pd.DataFrame(data, index=date_index)
```

```
# Print the DataFrame
df
```

Output:

	Temperature (°C)	Humidity (%)
2023-01-01	20.1	50
2023-01-02	21.3	48
2023-01-03	19.8	52
2023-01-04	22.5	47
2023-01-05	20.9	49

Figure 9.10: DataFrame with datetime index

In the preceding code, a pandas DataFrame with a datetime index is created. The datetime index is generated using **pd.date_range()**, spanning from January 1, 2023, to January 5, 2023, with a daily frequency. This index is then associated with two columns of sample data: '**Temperature (°C)**' and '**Humidity (%)**'. The resulting DataFrame, **df**, effectively organizes and associates time-stamped data, making it easier to work with and analyze time series data.

This is useful because it allows us to maintain the temporal context of your data, making it easier to perform time-based operations and analyses. With this DataFrame, you can easily perform tasks, such as plotting temperature and humidity trends over time, calculating daily averages, filtering data for specific date ranges, and conducting various time series analyses. It provides a structured way to manage and explore time-stamped data, which is essential in fields such as meteorology, finance, IoT, and many others where time series data is common.

Common Operations

Now, let's explore some common operations and techniques for working with time series data in Pandas.

Indexing and Slicing

Pandas provides various ways to index and slice time series data based on datetime indexes, including:

Single Timestamp Selection: We can use a single datetime value to select data for a specific timestamp:

```
# Select data for a specific date
specific_date_data = df.loc['2023-01-02']
specific_date_data
```

Output:

```
Temperature (°C)    21.3
Humidity (%)        48.0
Name: 2023-01-02 00:00:00, dtype: float64
```

Figure 9.11: *Single timestamp selection*

We use **.loc[]** to select data from the DataFrame df for a specific date, '**2023-01-02**'.

Here, you see the temperature and humidity values for January 2, 2023. The index is the timestamp, and the values are associated with that specific point in time.

This operation is useful for retrieving data for a particular timestamp in a time series dataset, allowing you to analyze and extract information for specific moments in time.

Date Range Selection: We can select data for a specific date range using slicing:

```
# Select data for a range of dates
date_range_data = df['2023-01-02':'2023-01-04']
date_range_data
```

Output:

	Temperature (°C)	Humidity (%)
2023-01-02	21.3	48
2023-01-03	19.8	52
2023-01-04	22.5	47

Figure 9.12: *Date range selection*

In the preceding code snippet, we use slicing on the DataFrame **df** to select data for a specific date range, which is from '**2023-01-02**' to '**2023-01-04**'.

The output will be a DataFrame and we can see the temperature and humidity data for the dates ranging from January 2, 2023, to January 4, 2023. The index consists of timestamps, and the values correspond to the data within the specified date range.

Selecting by Year, Month, or Day:

You can use **.loc[]** with partial datetime indexing to select data for specific years, months, or days:

Let's create a DataFrame with different months and years to demonstrate how to select data by year, month, or day. In this example, we'll create a DataFrame with temperature and humidity data for various dates spanning different months and years. Afterward, we'll illustrate how to select data for specific periods using the techniques discussed earlier:

```
# Create a datetime index with various dates
date_index = pd.to_datetime(['2022-12-15', '2023-01-02', '2023-02-10',
'2023-03-25', '2024-01-05'])


# Create a DataFrame with temperature and humidity data
data = {
    'Temperature (°C)': [18.5, 20.1, 19.8, 21.5, 22.0],
    'Humidity (%)': [55, 50, 48, 53, 49]
}


df = pd.DataFrame(data, index=date_index)


# Print the DataFrame
print(df)
```

Output:

```
            Temperature (°C)  Humidity (%)
2022-12-15              18.5            55
2023-01-02              20.1            50
2023-02-10              19.8            48
2023-03-25              21.5            53
2024-01-05              22.0            49
```

Figure 9.13: Selecting by year, month or day

Let's explore the "**Selecting by Year, Month, or Day**" operation for time series data.

To select data for January 2023, you can use **.loc[]** with a partial datetime index:

```
# Select data for January 2023
january_data = df.loc['2023-01']
print(january_data)
```

Output:

```
            Temperature (°C)  Humidity (%)
2023-01-02              20.1            50
```

Figure 9.14: Select data for January 2023

To select data for all January 2nd dates across years, you can use a boolean condition with **.index.day**:

```
january_2nd_data = df[df.index.day == 2]

print(january_2nd_data)
```

Output:

	Temperature (°C)	Humidity (%)
2023-01-02	20.1	50

Figure 9.15: Select data for January 2nd

To select data for the year 2023, you can use `.loc[]` with a partial datetime index for the entire year:

```
year_2023_data = df.loc['2023']
print(year_2023_data)
```

Output:

	Temperature (°C)	Humidity (%)
2023-01-02	20.1	50
2023-02-10	19.8	48
2023-03-25	21.5	53

Figure 9.16: Select data for year 2023

These operations will allow you to extract and analyze data for specific years, months, or days within your time series dataset, making it easier to perform targeted analysis and gain insights from your temporal data.

Resampling

Resampling is the process of changing the frequency of time series data. You can resample data to a lower frequency (downsampling) or a higher frequency (upsampling) based on your analysis needs. The **resample()** method in pandas is a powerful tool for performing resampling operations.

Downsampling: Reducing Frequency

Downsampling involves reducing the frequency of your time series data by aggregating or summarizing values over longer time periods. This can be useful for simplifying your data, **reducing noise, and gaining a broader overview of trends and patterns over larger time intervals**.

Let's see this with an example, suppose you have daily temperature data, and you want to reduce it to weekly averages for a smoother overview of temperature trends.

We will create a datetime index representing 15 days of January 2023 using **pd.date_range()**.

```
# Create a datetime index for daily data
date_index = pd.date_range(start='2023-01-01', end='2023-01-15',
freq='D')
```

```
# Generate random daily temperature data
temperature_data = [20.1 + i * 0.2 for i in range(len(date_index))]
```

```
# Create a DataFrame with daily data
df = pd.DataFrame({'Temperature (°C)': temperature_data}, index=date_index)
```

```
df
```

Output:

	Temperature (°C)
2023-01-01	20.1
2023-01-02	20.3
2023-01-03	20.5
2023-01-04	20.7
2023-01-05	20.9
2023-01-06	21.1
2023-01-07	21.3
2023-01-08	21.5
2023-01-09	21.7
2023-01-10	21.9
2023-01-11	22.1
2023-01-12	22.3
2023-01-13	22.5
2023-01-14	22.7
2023-01-15	22.9

Figure 9.17: Create Dataframe for 15 days of January

To downsample this daily data to weekly averages, we use the **.resample('W')** method. 'W' represents the weekly frequency, and we apply the **.mean()** method to calculate the average temperature for each week.

```
# Downsample to weekly data with mean aggregation
weekly_mean = df['Temperature (°C)'].resample('W').mean()
weekly_mean
```

Output:

```
2023-01-01    20.1
2023-01-08    20.9
2023-01-15    22.3
Freq: W-SUN, Name: Temperature (°C), dtype: float64
```

Figure 9.18: Downsample data to weekly

In this output, you see the weekly average temperatures for each week in January 2023. Downsampling to weekly data provides a clearer view of the temperature trends over the month compared to the daily fluctuations.

Downsampling is valuable when you want to reduce noise in your data, highlight longer-term patterns, or prepare your time series data for higher-level analysis while retaining the important trends and patterns.

Upsampling: Increasing Frequency

Upsampling is a data transformation technique used in time series analysis, signal processing, and data manipulation to increase the frequency of data points in a time series or signal. It involves converting data from a lower frequency to a higher frequency, typically by interpolating or generating new data points between existing data points.

The primary goal of upsampling is to provide a more detailed or fine-grained view of the data at a higher time resolution

Let's create a DataFrame **df** with monthly temperature data for January, February, and March 2023 and convert the '**Date**' column to a datetime data type and set it as the index of the DataFrame.

```
# Create a DataFrame with monthly temperature data
data = {
    'Date': ['2023-01-01', '2023-02-01', '2023-03-01'],
    'Temperature (°C)': [20.1, 21.5, 22.0]
}

df = pd.DataFrame(data)
df['Date'] = pd.to_datetime(df['Date'])

# Set the 'Date' column as the index
df.set_index('Date', inplace=True)
df
```

Output:

Date	Temperature (°C)
2023-01-01	20.1
2023-02-01	21.5
2023-03-01	22.0

Figure 9.19: *Create Dataframe with monthly temperature data*

To upsample this monthly data to daily data, we use the **resample**('D') method to resample it to daily frequency and **asfreq()** to ensure that the index includes all daily dates and then use **interpolate(method='linear')** to perform linear interpolation between the available monthly values to fill in the missing daily temperature values.

```
# Upsample to daily data with linear interpolation

df_upsampled = df.resample('D').asfreq().interpolate(method='linear')


# Print the upsampled DataFrame

print(df_upsampled)
```

Output:

```
                Temperature (°C)
Date
2023-01-01       20.100000
2023-01-02       20.145161
2023-01-03       20.190323
2023-01-04       20.235484
2023-01-05       20.280645
2023-01-06       20.325806
2023-01-07       20.370968
2023-01-08       20.416129
2023-01-09       20.461290
2023-01-10       20.506452
2023-01-11       20.551613
2023-01-12       20.596774
2023-01-13       20.641935
2023-01-14       20.687097
2023-01-15       20.732258
2023-01-16       20.777419
2023-01-17       20.822581
2023-01-18       20.867742
2023-01-19       20.912903
2023-01-20       20.958065
2023-01-21       21.003226
2023-01-22       21.048387
2023-01-23       21.093548
2023-01-24       21.138710
2023-01-25       21.183871
2023-01-26       21.229032
2023-01-27       21.274194
2023-01-28       21.319355
2023-01-29       21.364516
2023-01-30       21.409677
2023-01-31       21.454839
2023-02-01       21.500000
2023-02-02       21.517857
2023-02-03       21.535714
2023-02-04       21.553571
2023-02-05       21.571429
2023-02-06       21.589286
2023-02-07       21.607143
```

Figure 9.20: *Upsample to daily data with linear interpolation*

In this output, we see daily temperature values interpolated from the available monthly values. This upsampling process allows you to work with higher-frequency data for more detailed analysis and visualization while filling in missing values using interpolation methods.

Upsampling is valuable when you need to increase the granularity of your time series data or align it with data of a higher frequency for further analysis or modeling.

Shifting and Lagging

In time series analysis, "`shifting`" or "`lagging`" refers to the operation of moving data points forward or backward in time within a time series. It is a common technique used to create new time series datasets or to perform time-based comparisons. Two key terms related to shifting and lagging are:

Lag: A lag refers to the number of time periods by which data is shifted backward in time. A positive lag value means shifting data to the past, while a negative lag value means shifting data into the future.

Lead: A lead is essentially a negative lag, meaning data is shifted forward in time.

Creating Lagged Features

Lagged features are features that capture the values of a variable at earlier time points, which can be useful for predictive modeling and time series analysis. In this example, we'll create a lagged feature for temperature data.

Suppose you have a time series DataFrame with temperature data:

```
# Create a DataFrame with temperature data
data = {
    'Date': ['2023-01-01', '2023-01-02', '2023-01-03', '2023-01-04',
'2023-01-05'],
    'Temperature (°C)': [20.1, 21.5, 22.0, 23.2, 22.8]
}

df = pd.DataFrame(data)
df['Date'] = pd.to_datetime(df['Date'])
df.set_index('Date', inplace=True)
df
```

Output:

Date	Temperature (°C)
2023-01-01	20.1
2023-01-02	21.5
2023-01-03	22.0
2023-01-04	23.2
2023-01-05	22.8

Figure 9.21: Create Dataframe with temperature and date columns

Now, let's create a lagged feature for the temperature with a lag of 1 time period:

```
# Creating a lagged feature for temperature with a lag of 1 time period
df['Temperature (°C)_lag1'] = df['Temperature (°C)'].shift(1)
```

We use the `.shift(1)` method to shift the **'Temperature (°C)'** column by 1 time period (in this case, one day). This creates a new column, **'Temperature (°C)_lag1'**, which contains the temperature values from the previous day.

The resulting DataFrame, **df**, will now have an additional column representing the lagged feature:

Date	Temperature (°C)	Temperature (°C)_lag1
2023-01-01	20.1	NaN
2023-01-02	21.5	20.1
2023-01-03	22.0	21.5
2023-01-04	23.2	22.0
2023-01-05	22.8	23.2

Figure 9.22: Dataframe with lagged output

In the resulting DataFrame, you can see that the **'Temperature (°C)_lag1'** column contains the temperature values from the previous day, effectively creating a lagged feature. This can be valuable for time series forecasting or analysis because it allows you to incorporate historical values as input features for predictive models.

Creating lagged features is a fundamental technique in time series analysis and can help capture temporal dependencies and patterns in your data, which can improve the accuracy of predictive models.

Creating Lead Features

To create lead features, you shift the values of a variable forward in time by a specified number of time periods (leads). These lead features can be valuable for predicting future values of the variable.

Suppose you have a time series DataFrame with **temperature** data:

We will be using the same dataframe we created for Lag. Now, let's create a lead feature for the temperature with a lead of 1 time period (one day ahead):

```
# Creating a lead feature for temperature with a lead of 1 time period
df['Temperature (°C)_lead1'] = df['Temperature (°C)'].shift(-1)
```

In the preceding code, we use the **.shift(-1)** method to shift the **Temperature (°C)** column forward by 1 time period (in this case, one day). This creates a new column, **Temperature (°C)_lead1**, which contains the temperature values from the following day.

The resulting DataFrame, df, will now have an additional column representing the leaded feature:

Date	Temperature (°C)	Temperature (°C)_lag1	Temperature (°C)_lead1
2023-01-01	20.1	NaN	21.5
2023-01-02	21.5	20.1	22.0
2023-01-03	22.0	21.5	23.2
2023-01-04	23.2	22.0	22.8
2023-01-05	22.8	23.2	NaN

***Figure 9.23:** Dataframe with lead output*

In the resulting DataFrame, you can see that the **'Temperature (°C)_lead1'** column contains the temperature values from the following day, effectively creating a leaded feature. This can be valuable for time series forecasting tasks where you want to predict future values based on historical data.

Creating lead features allows you to incorporate future values of a variable as input features for predictive models or to analyze how changes in the variable relate to future outcomes.

Rolling Windows

Rolling windows, also known as moving windows or rolling averages, are a powerful technique in time series analysis. They involve creating subsets of data by "**rolling**" a fixed-size window or time frame across a time series. Within each window, various calculations or operations can be applied, such as calculating moving averages, standard deviations, or other statistical metrics.

Rolling windows are valuable for:

- **Smoothing Data:** Rolling windows can help smooth out noisy or volatile time series data by calculating moving averages or other aggregates within the window.

- **Identifying Trends and Patterns:** They are used to identify trends, patterns, or anomalies in time series data by analyzing statistics calculated within the rolling window.

- **Feature Engineering:** Rolling windows can be used to create lagged features or other time-dependent features for predictive modeling.

Here are a few common operations and examples related to rolling windows:

Rolling Mean (Moving Average)

The rolling mean, also referred to as a moving average, calculates the average value of a time series within a rolling or moving window of a specified size. This rolling window moves along the time series, and at each time point, it calculates the mean of the data points within that window.

We will be using the same dataframe we created earlier.

To calculate a rolling mean, we use the `.rolling(window=3)` method, which creates a rolling window of size three days. This means that for each day, the rolling window includes the current day and the two previous days.

We then apply the `.mean()` method to calculate the mean temperature within the rolling window.

```
# Calculate a 3-day rolling mean of daily temperature data
rolling_mean_3d = df['Temperature (°C)'].rolling(window=3).mean()
```

The resulting **rolling_mean_3d Series** will contain the 3-day rolling mean of the daily temperature data:

```
Date
2023-01-01          NaN
2023-01-02          NaN
2023-01-03    21.200000
2023-01-04    22.233333
2023-01-05    22.666667
Name: Temperature (°C), dtype: float64
```

Figure 9.24: Rolling mean output

In this output, you can see that the rolling mean starts as **NaN** for the first two days because there aren't enough data points to calculate the mean. From the third day onward, it provides a smoothed representation of the temperature data, highlighting trends and patterns while reducing the impact of daily fluctuations.

Rolling Standard Deviation

The rolling standard deviation calculates the standard deviation of a time series within a rolling or moving window of a specified size. This rolling window moves along the time series, and at each time point, it calculates the standard deviation of the data points within that window.

Here's how you can calculate a rolling standard deviation using pandas:

```
# Calculate a 3-day rolling standard deviation of daily temperature data
rolling_std_3d = df['Temperature (°C)'].rolling(window=3).std()
```

In the preceding code, we calculate a 3-day rolling standard deviation of the **'Temperature (°C)'** column using the **.rolling(window=3).std()** method.

The resulting **rolling_std_3d Series** will contain the 3-day rolling standard deviation of the daily temperature data:

```
Date
2023-01-01          NaN
2023-01-02          NaN
2023-01-03     0.984886
2023-01-04     0.873689
2023-01-05     0.611010
Name: Temperature (°C), dtype: float64
```

Figure 9.25: Rolling standard deviation output

In this output, you can see that the rolling standard deviation starts as **NaN** for the first two days because there aren't enough data points to calculate it. From the third day onward, it provides a measure of the variability or dispersion of the temperature data within the 3-day rolling window.

Rolling Sum

The rolling sum calculates the cumulative sum of a time series within a rolling window. It's useful for understanding the total or accumulated values over a specific period.

Here's how you can calculate a rolling sum using pandas:

```python
# Create a DataFrame with monthly sales data
data = {
    'Date': ['2023-01-01', '2023-02-01', '2023-03-01', '2023-04-01',
'2023-05-01'],
    'Monthly Sales': [1000, 1200, 900, 1100, 950]
}

df = pd.DataFrame(data)
df['Date'] = pd.to_datetime(df['Date'])
df.set_index('Date', inplace=True)

# Calculate a 3-month rolling sum of monthly sales data
rolling_sum_3m = df['Monthly Sales'].rolling(window=3).sum()
```

In the preceding code, we created a DataFrame **df** with monthly sales data and set the '**Date**' column as the index.

To calculate a rolling sum, we use the **.rolling(window=3)** method, which creates a rolling window of size 3 months. This means that for each month, the rolling window includes the current month and the two previous months.

We then apply the **.sum()** method to calculate the sum of the monthly sales within the rolling window.

Output:

```
Date
2023-01-01        NaN
2023-02-01        NaN
2023-03-01     3100.0
2023-04-01     3200.0
2023-05-01     2950.0
Name: Monthly Sales, dtype: float64
```

Figure 9.26: *Rolling sum output*

In this output, you can see that the rolling sum starts as **NaN** for the first two months because there aren't enough data points to calculate it. From the third month onward, it provides the cumulative sum of the monthly sales within the 3-month rolling window.

The rolling sum is useful for tracking the accumulation of values over time, such as total sales, inventory levels, or other cumulative metrics. It can help in identifying trends or patterns related to cumulative data in time series analysis.

Exponential Moving Average (EMA)

The Exponential Moving Average (EMA) is a type of moving average that assigns exponentially decreasing weights to the values in the time series. It is particularly useful for capturing recent trends and is more responsive to recent data compared to a simple moving average.

```
# Create a DataFrame with daily closing price data
data = {
    'Date': ['2023-01-01', '2023-01-02', '2023-01-03', '2023-01-04',
'2023-01-05'],
    'Closing Price': [100.2, 101.0, 101.5, 100.8, 101.2]
}


df = pd.DataFrame(data)
df['Date'] = pd.to_datetime(df['Date'])
df.set_index('Date', inplace=True)


df
```

Output:

Date	Closing Price
2023-01-01	100.2
2023-01-02	101.0
2023-01-03	101.5
2023-01-04	100.8
2023-01-05	101.2

Figure 9.27: Exponential moving average

In the preceding code. we create a DataFrame **df** with daily closing price data and set the **'Date'** column as the index. To calculate an EMA, we use the **.ewm(span=3)** method, which creates an Exponential Moving Window with a span of three days. The span represents the smoothing factor or the number of time periods over which the EMA is calculated.

We then apply the **.mean()** method to calculate the Exponential Moving Average of the daily closing prices within the specified window.

```
# Calculate a 3-day Exponential Moving Average (EMA) of daily closing prices
ema_3d = df['Closing Price'].ewm(span=3).mean()
# Print the result
ema_3d
```

Output:

```
Date
2023-01-01    100.200000
2023-01-02    100.733333
2023-01-03    101.171429
2023-01-04    100.973333
2023-01-05    101.090323
Name: Closing Price, dtype: float64
```

Figure 9.28: *Exponential moving average output*

In this output, you can see that the EMA is calculated for each day, with greater weight given to recent closing prices. The EMA responds more quickly to price changes compared to a simple moving average.

Assembling Datetime from Multiple DataFrame Columns

Assembling datetime from multiple DataFrame columns involves combining separate date and time components into a single datetime object within a pandas DataFrame. This is a common data manipulation task when dealing with time-related data distributed across different columns, such as year, month, day, hour, minute, and second.

First, we start with a DataFrame that has date and time information distributed across separate columns. For this example, we'll create a DataFrame with columns **'Year'**, **'Month'**, **'Day'**, **'Hour'**, **'Minute'**, and **'Second'** to represent date and time components.

```
# Create a DataFrame with date and time information in separate columns
data = {
    'Year': [2023, 2023, 2023],
    'Month': [1, 2, 3],
    'Day': [15, 20, 25],
```

```
    'Hour': [10, 15, 18],

    'Minute': [30, 45, 0],

    'Second': [0, 0, 0]

}


df = pd.DataFrame(data)

df
```

Output:

	Year	Month	Day	Hour	Minute	Second
0	2023	1	15	10	30	0
1	2023	2	20	15	45	0
2	2023	3	25	18	0	0

Figure 9.29: Dataframe with date and time information

To assemble a datetime column from these separate columns, you use the **pd.to_datetime()** function. This function takes the date and time components and combines them into a single datetime column.

```
# Assemble a datetime column from multiple columns
```

df['Datetime'] = pd.to_datetime(df[['Year', 'Month', 'Day', 'Hour', 'Minute', 'Second']], format='%Y-%m-%d %H:%M:%S')

We selected the relevant columns (**'Year'**, **'Month'**, **'Day'**, **'Hour'**, **'Minute'**, **'Second'**) by passing them as a DataFrame slice (**df[['Year'**, **'Month'**, **'Day'**, **'Hour'**, **'Minute'**, **'Second']]**) to the **pd.to_datetime()** function.

Next, we specify the format parameter as **'%Y-%m-%d %H:%M:%S'** to match the order of the columns and their format. The format string indicates the order of year, month, day, hour, minute, and second components.

Output:

	Year	Month	Day	Hour	Minute	Second	Datetime
0	2023	1	15	10	30	0	2023-01-15 10:30:00
1	2023	2	20	15	45	0	2023-02-20 15:45:00
2	2023	3	25	18	0	0	2023-03-25 18:00:00

Figure 9.30: DateTime column from multiple columns

DataFrame df will have a new **'Datetime'** column that combines the date and time information into a single datetime object.

This assembled datetime column makes it easier to work with datetime objects for various time-based analyses and is a fundamental step in preparing time series data for analysis.

Conclusion

This chapter was a deep dive into the essentials of handling time series data using Pandas. We began by introducing the Timestamp object, gaining a solid grasp of datetime manipulation. Throughout the chapter, we explored a wide range of crucial operations, from indexing to resampling and rolling windows, empowering us to analyze time-based data effectively. Additionally, we learned to assemble datetime objects from separate DataFrame columns, streamlining data preparation. This chapter equipped us with a comprehensive toolbox for mastering time series analysis in Pandas, setting the stage for insightful insights and visualizations.

In *Chapter 10, Visualization using Matplotlib*, we will explore the world of data visualization in Pandas. This chapter will equip you with the skills to create a wide range of plots, from basic line plots to advanced visualizations with datetime objects. You will learn how to customize plot aesthetics, create subplots, and save your plots for sharing insights effectively. By the end of the chapter, you will be well-versed in Pandas' plotting capabilities, enabling you to visually convey data patterns and findings with confidence.

Exercise Questions

1. List and briefly describe at least three attributes or properties of a Timestamp object that you can use to extract information such as year, month, and day.

2. Suppose you have hourly temperature data for a month. Explain how you can use Pandas' resampling techniques to convert this data into daily temperature averages.

3. You have a DataFrame `temperature_data` containing daily temperature measurements for a month, with a `'Date'` index. Your goal is to upsample this data to an hourly frequency, filling in the gaps with the previous day's temperature value.

4. Differentiate between downsampling and upsampling, and provide examples of when each might be used.

5. Given a DataFrame with separate columns for `year`, `month`, `day`, `hour`, `minute`, and `second`, outline the steps to assemble a datetime column using Pandas. Provide sample code.

CHAPTER 10
Visualization Using Matplotlib

Introduction

Welcome to *Chapter 10* of our journey through data analysis and Python programming. In this chapter, we will immerse ourselves in the captivating realm of data visualization using Matplotlib.

Data visualization is the art and science of transforming raw data into insightful, meaningful, and aesthetically pleasing visuals. It's a skill that every data enthusiast and analyst should master because, as the saying goes, "A *picture is worth a thousand words*". Effective data visualization can make complex data accessible, reveal hidden patterns, and aid in decision-making.

Our tool of choice for this exciting journey is Matplotlib, a versatile and powerful library in the Python ecosystem. Matplotlib empowers you to create an array of visualizations, from simple line charts to intricate 3D plots, all with fine-grained control over every aspect of your visual masterpiece.

In this chapter, we will take you from the very basics of Matplotlib to advanced techniques, guiding you through the art of crafting stunning and insightful visualizations. By the end of this chapter, you will be equipped with the skills to tell compelling data-driven stories using Matplotlib.

So, let's embark on this visual journey, where we will unlock the full potential of Matplotlib, one plot at a time.

Structure

In this chapter, we will discuss the following topics:

- Importance of Data Visualization in Data Analysis
- Matplotlib - Key Tool for Data Visualization in Python
- Basic Structure of a Matplotlib Plot

- Customizing Plot Visuals
- Exploring Various Plot Types
  - ○ Line Plots
  - ○ Bar Plots
  - ○ Scatter Plots
  - ○ Histograms
  - ○ Density Plot
  - ○ Box Plots
  - ○ Violin Plots
  - ○ Area Plots
- Subplots Using Matplotlib
- Effective Visualization of Time Series Data
- Exporting and Saving Plots: Saving Plots as Image Files and Interactive HTML Files

Importance of Data Visualization in Data Analysis

In the realm of data analysis, the significance of data visualization cannot be overstated. Data is often complex, multidimensional, and filled with information that might be challenging to decipher when presented in its raw form. This is where data visualization comes to the rescue. It serves as a bridge between the data and human understanding, enabling us to extract insights and identify patterns with ease.

Data visualization brings several key advantages, including:

- **Simplification of Complexity:** Visualizations simplify complex datasets, making them more accessible and digestible for analysts and stakeholders. Complex relationships and trends become evident through well-crafted visuals.

- **Effective Communication:** Visual representations of data are universally understood and transcend language barriers. They facilitate effective communication and insights to both technical and non-technical audiences, aiding in informed decision-making.

- **Exploratory Data Analysis:** Data visualization is an essential component of exploratory data analysis (EDA). It allows data scientists to interact with data visually, quickly spotting outliers, anomalies, and trends, which guide further investigation.

- **Pattern Recognition:** Visualizations can reveal hidden patterns, correlations, and anomalies that might remain concealed in numerical tables. This aids in hypothesis generation and testing.

Benefits of Visualizing Data for Understanding and Communication

Data visualization offers a plethora of benefits, enhancing our ability to comprehend and communicate data effectively, such as:

- **Clarity:** Visuals provide a clear representation of data, making it easier to grasp complex information at a glance.

- **Comparison:** Visualizations facilitate the comparison of data points, allowing us to identify trends and differences effortlessly.

- **Storytelling:** Visualizations are powerful storytelling tools. They enable us to convey a narrative, guiding the audience through the data and highlighting key points.

- **Engagement:** Visuals capture attention and engage the viewer, making data more memorable and impactful.

- **Decision-Making:** Well-constructed visualizations aid in informed decision-making by presenting data in a format that is intuitive and persuasive.

Matplotlib - Key Tool for Data Visualization in Python

Matplotlib, a Python library, plays a pivotal role in the world of data visualization. It offers a rich set of tools for creating a wide variety of static, animated, and interactive plots and charts. Matplotlib's flexibility and customization options make it a favorite among data scientists and analysts.

In this section, we will explore Matplotlib's capabilities and dive into the art of crafting meaningful and visually appealing data visualizations. We'll start by understanding its installation and basic usage.

Getting Started with Matplotlib

To kickstart our exploration of data visualization with Matplotlib, we will first install and import the essential libraries. While Matplotlib takes center stage for plotting, we'll also be making use of two indispensable libraries: Pandas and NumPy.

Installation of Matplotlib

To install Matplotlib, you can use Python's package manager, **pip**. Open your command prompt or terminal and run the following command:

```
pip install matplotlib
```

This command will download and install the latest version of Matplotlib.

Importing Matplotlib

Once you have Matplotlib installed, you can import it into your Python script or Jupyter Notebook using the following line of code:

```
import matplotlib.pyplot as plt
```

The **plt** alias is commonly used for Matplotlib, making it easier to reference Matplotlib functions and objects in your code.

Once Matplotlib is installed, you can import it, along with other crucial libraries, into your Python script or Jupyter Notebook. Here's how you can import Matplotlib, NumPy, and Pandas:

```
import matplotlib.pyplot as plt
import numpy as np
import pandas as pd
```

Using %matplotlib inline (or %matplotlib notebook)

For those working in a Jupyter Notebook environment, we recommend using the **%matplotlib** inline magic command at the beginning of your notebook. This command ensures that Matplotlib plots are displayed directly within the notebook, making your data visualization workflow seamless and interactive.

Include the following line in a cell at the beginning of your notebook:

```
%matplotlib inline
```

Basic Structure of a Matplotlib Plot

Now that we have introduced the figure and axes, let's delve into the fundamental structure of a Matplotlib plot. Every Matplotlib plot, regardless of its complexity, shares the following core components:

- **Data:** At the heart of every plot are the data points you intend to visualize. These data points can come in various forms, such as lists, arrays, or data loaded from external sources. The type of data you have will influence the choice of plot and the way you customize it.

- **Plot Type:** Next, you choose the type of plot that best represents your data and your visualization goals. Matplotlib offers an array of plot types, including line plots, bar plots, scatter plots, histograms, and more. The choice of plot type should align with the nature of your data and the message you want to convey.

- **Customizations:** Matplotlib provides extensive customization options, allowing you to tailor your plot to your specific needs. You can modify various aspects of the plot, such as colors, markers, line styles, labels, titles, axis properties, and more. This level of customization empowers you to create visually appealing and informative visualizations.

- **Display or Saving:** After crafting your plot, you have the option to either display it on the screen for immediate analysis or save it to a file for later use or sharing. The `plt.show()` function is used to display the plot, while functions such as `plt.savefig()` enable you to save it in various formats (for example, PNG and PDF).

Understanding this fundamental structure enables you to create a wide range of visualizations in Matplotlib. It is the foundation upon which you will build as you explore different plot types and customization options in the pages that follow.

Customizing Plot Visuals

Customizing plot visuals refers to the process of modifying various aspects of a data visualization to make it visually appealing, informative, and tailored to your specific needs. This customization can include adjusting colors, fonts, labels, markers, axes, and other elements of the plot to improve its clarity and effectiveness in conveying information. By customizing plot visuals, you can create more engaging and informative data visualizations.

The Figure

At the top level of this structure, we have the figure. Think of it as the blank canvas upon which your data visualizations will come to life. The figure serves as the overarching container, encompassing the entire area where your plots and subplots will be rendered.

When you create a figure, you establish the foundation for your visualization. You can think of it as if you're defining the size and shape of the canvas where your artwork; in this case, your data will be displayed.

The Axes

Within each figure, we have one or more axes. An "**axis**" (plural: "**axes**") is not the familiar x-or y-axis you may associate with a plot. Instead, in the context of Matplotlib, an "**axis**" represents an individual plot or subplot within the figure. Axes provide a space where you can visualize your data, set up coordinate systems, and apply various customizations.

To create a single set of axes within a figure, you can use the **plt.subplots()** function as follows:

```
import matplotlib.pyplot as plt
```

```
# Create a figure with a single set of axes
fig, ax = plt.subplots()
```

If you need multiple subplots within a single figure, you can specify the number of rows and columns, creating a grid of axes:

```
# Create a 2x2 grid of subplots within a single figure
fig, axs = plt.subplots(2, 2)
```

Each **ax** in **axs** represents an individual set of axes within the figure. These axes provide the canvas on which you'll craft your data visualizations, allowing you to organize and customize your plots effectively.

Understanding the relationship between the figure and axes is crucial as it forms the backbone of creating various types of plots using Matplotlib.

Labels and Titles

Now that we've explored the Matplotlib figure and axes, let's shift our focus to two crucial components that enhance the interpretability and clarity of your plots: labels and titles.

Labels

X-axis Label: The x-axis label, also known as the x-label, describes the data dimension represented along the horizontal axis. It clarifies what the values on the x-axis represent, providing essential context for viewers. Adding an x-axis label is critical for ensuring that viewers correctly interpret the variable or category displayed. For example, if you're plotting time series data, an appropriate x-axis label might be Time.

```
ax.set_xlabel('Time')
```

Y-axis Label: The y-axis label, or y-label, serves a similar purpose but for the vertical axis. It describes the data dimension represented along the y-axis and provides information about the unit of measurement. For instance, if you're plotting temperature data in degrees Celsius, an appropriate y-axis label would be "**Temperature (°C)**."

```
ax.set_ylabel('Temperature (°C)')
```

Customizing Labels: Labels can be further customized by specifying attributes such as font size, font family, color, and rotation. Customizations enhance the aesthetics and readability of your plot. For instance, you can adjust the font size to make labels more prominent:

```
ax.set_xlabel('Time', fontsize=12)
```

Title

A title serves as the narrative or context for your entire plot. It is a concise, informative text element placed above the plot to convey the purpose or subject of the visualization. A well-crafted title provides clarity and guidance to viewers, enabling them to understand the plot's content and message.

Adding a title to your Matplotlib plot is accomplished using the **ax.set_title()** method:

```
ax.set_title('Temperature Trends Over Time')
```

Customizing Titles

Titles can be customized to match your preferred style and enhance their visual impact. You can modify attributes such as font size, font family, font weight, color, and alignment. Customized titles contribute to the overall professionalism and visual appeal of your visualizations.

```
ax.set_title('Temperature Trends Over Time', fontsize=16, font-
weight='bold', color='blue', loc='center')
```

In this example, we've increased the font size, made the title bold, changed its color to blue, and aligned it to the center of the plot.

Labels and titles are essential for providing context, clarity, and professionalism to your Matplotlib plots. They guide viewers in interpreting the data correctly and communicate the plot's purpose effectively.

Ticks and Gridlines

In this section, we will explore additional ways to enhance the appearance and readability of your Matplotlib plots by customizing ticks and gridlines.

Ticks

X-axis Ticks: Ticks are the marks and labels along the x-axis that indicate specific data points or intervals. Customizing x-axis ticks allows you to control their appearance and positioning. You can set custom tick positions and labels using the **ax.set_xticks()** and **ax.set_xticklabels()** methods, respectively:

```
ax.set_xticks([0, 1, 2, 3, 4])
ax.set_xticklabels(['Jan', 'Feb', 'Mar', 'Apr', 'May'])
```

Y-axis Ticks: Similarly, you can customize y-axis ticks by specifying custom tick positions and labels using **ax.set_yticks()** and **ax.set_yticklabels()**:

```
ax.set_yticks([0, 10, 20, 30, 40])
ax.set_yticklabels(['0%', '10%', '20%', '30%', '40%'])
```

Tick Parameters: You can adjust various tick parameters, including tick length, tick label rotation, tick label font size, and tick label alignment, to tailor the appearance of ticks to your preferences:

```
ax.tick_params(axis='x', length=5, labelrotation=45, labelsize=10)
```

Gridlines

Gridlines are horizontal and vertical lines that span the plot, aiding in data interpretation and alignment. You can customize gridlines to improve the overall appearance and guide viewers' eyes across the plot.

Adding Gridlines: You can add gridlines to your plot using the **ax.grid()** method. By default, both major and minor gridlines are shown. You can customize which gridlines are displayed and their appearance using parameters such as which, axis, and linestyle:

```
ax.grid(True, which='major', axis='both', linestyle='--')
```

Customizing Grid Parameters: Further customization of gridlines includes modifying their color, thickness, and transparency. These customizations contribute to the aesthetics of your plot:

```
ax.grid(True, which='major', axis='both', linestyle='--', color='gray',
linewidth=0.5, alpha=0.7)
```

Customizing ticks and gridlines enhances the readability and aesthetics of your Matplotlib plots. These elements help viewers navigate the plot, understand data points, and maintain clarity, ultimately improving the overall quality of your visualizations.

Adding Legends and Annotations

In this section, we will explore two additional elements that can elevate your Matplotlib plots: legends and annotations. These elements provide valuable information and context to your visualizations.

Legends

Creating a Legend: Legends are crucial when your plot displays multiple datasets or elements, as they clarify which data corresponds to each line or marker. To create a legend, you should assign labels to each plotted element using the label parameter and then invoke `ax.legend()`:

```
ax.plot(x1, y1, label='Dataset A')
```

```
ax.plot(x2, y2, label='Dataset B')
```

```
ax.legend()
```

Legend Placement: By default, Matplotlib places legends in the "**best**" location to avoid overlapping with data. However, you can specify the legend's location using the loc parameter with values such as '**upper right**', '**lower left**', or '**center**':

```
ax.legend(loc='upper right')
```

Customizing Legend Appearance: You can customize the legend's appearance by adjusting properties such as font size, font family, background color, border, and more:

```
ax.legend(fontsize=12, frameon=True, framealpha=0.8)
```

Annotations

Annotations are text or markers added to specific data points or regions of the plot to provide additional information or highlight key features.

Text Annotations: You can add text annotations using the `ax.text()` function. Specify the coordinates where the text should be placed and the text content:

```
ax.text(2, 15, 'Peak Value', fontsize=12, color='red', ha='center',
va='center')
```

Arrow Annotations: Arrow annotations can be used to draw attention to specific data points. You can create arrow annotations with `ax.annotate()`. Define the text, arrow's starting point, arrow's end point, and customize its appearance:

```
ax.annotate('Important Event', xy=(3, 25), xytext=(2, 35), fontsize=12,
            arrowprops=dict(arrowstyle='->', color='blue'))
```

Legends and annotations are valuable tools for adding context and insights to your Matplotlib plots. They help viewers identify and understand the data, making your visualizations more informative and compelling.

Displaying Your Plots

In this final section, we'll cover the practical aspects displaying your Matplotlib plots, ensuring that your visualizations reach your audience effectively.

After crafting your plot, you can use the **plt.show()** function to display it on your screen:

```
plt.show()
```

This command renders the plot in a graphical window, allowing you to interact with it, zoom in, and explore the details. It's especially useful during the plotting process to visualize your work in progress.

Incorporating Everything in an Example

Let's consolidate all the concepts discussed in this section into a comprehensive example. In this example, we'll create a line plot to visualize the monthly temperature trends, add labels, a title, customize ticks and gridlines, include a legend, and annotate key events:

```
import matplotlib.pyplot as plt
import numpy as np


# Sample data
months = np.arange(1, 13)
temperatures = np.random.randint(0, 30, 12)
```

Figure and Axes

We begin by creating a figure and a single set of axes using **plt.subplots()**. The figure serves as our canvas, while the axes define the plotting area.

```
# Create a figure and a single set of axes
fig, ax = plt.subplots()
```

Customizing the Plot

We proceed to plot our temperature data as a line plot with customizations. We specify markers, line styles, and colors to make our plot visually appealing. The label parameter is used to identify the dataset.

```
# Plot temperature data as a line plot with customization
ax.plot(months, temperatures, marker='o', linestyle='-', color='b', la-
bel='Monthly Temperature')
```

Labels and Title

We add labels to the x-axis and y-axis, describing the data dimensions. Additionally, we set a descriptive title for our plot to provide context and understanding.

```
# Add labels and a title
ax.set_xlabel('Month')
ax.set_ylabel('Temperature (°C)')
ax.set_title('Monthly Temperature Trends')
```

Customizing Ticks

We customize the x-axis ticks by specifying their positions and labels. This helps in displaying month abbreviations instead of numerical values.

```
# Customize x-axis ticks
ax.set_xticks(np.arange(1, 13))
```

```
ax.set_xticklabels(['Jan', 'Feb', 'Mar', 'Apr', 'May', 'Jun', 'Jul',
'Aug', 'Sep', 'Oct', 'Nov', 'Dec'])
```

Similarly, we customize the y-axis ticks to display specific intervals.

```
# Customize y-axis ticks
ax.set_yticks(np.arange(0, 30, 5))
```

Gridlines

Gridlines are added to both major and minor axes, enhancing the readability and alignment of our plot.

```
# Add gridlines
ax.grid(True, which='major', axis='both', linestyle='--', color='gray',
linewidth=0.5, alpha=0.7)
```

Legend

Although we have only one dataset in this example, we include a legend to demonstrate its usage. Legends are vital when multiple datasets are displayed on the same plot.

```
# Add a legend
ax.legend()
```

Annotations

We add a text annotation to highlight a specific data point. Annotations are valuable for drawing attention to key information.

```
# Text annotation
ax.annotate('Record High', xy=(7, 28), xytext=(7, 26), fontsize=10,
            arrowprops=dict(arrowstyle='->', color='red'))
```

Displaying the Plot

Finally, we use **plt.show()** to display the plot on the screen, making it accessible for visualization and analysis.

```
# Display the plot
plt.show()
```

Output:

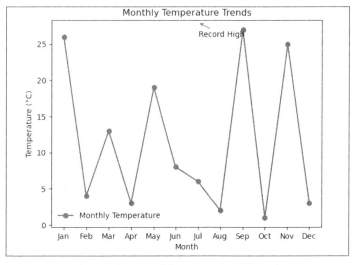

***Figure* 10.1:** *Monthly temperature trends*

Exploring Various Plot Types

In this section, we will explore a variety of plot types, each tailored for visualizing and conveying different aspects of data. By examining these plot types, we aim to understand their characteristics, and how they can effectively represent data patterns, relationships, and insights. Whether it's tracking trends over time, comparing categories, or exploring data distributions, each plot type offers unique capabilities to help data analysts make informed decisions and draw meaningful conclusions.

Line Plots

Line plots, also known as line charts or line graphs, are a type of data visualization used to display data points as a series of data markers connected by straight lines. They are particularly useful for visualizing trends, changes over time, and continuous data.

Components of a Line Plot

- **Data points:** Each data point represents an observation or measurement at a specific point in time or along a continuous scale.

- **Axes:** Line plots have two axes, the x-axis (horizontal) and the y-axis (vertical). The x-axis represents the independent variable (for example, time), while the y-axis represents the dependent variable (for example, values or measurements).

- **Connecting lines:** The lines that connect data points help visualize trends and changes in the data over the specified scale.

- **Labels:** Labels for the x-axis and y-axis describe what the axes represent. Clear labeling is essential for understanding the context of the data.

- **Legends:** Legends are used to identify different data series when multiple lines are plotted on the same graph.

Interpreting Line Plots

- **Trend Identification:** Line plots are excellent for identifying trends in data. Rising or falling lines indicate upward or downward trends, while flat lines suggest stability.

- **Data Patterns**: Line plots can reveal patterns, cycles, or fluctuations in data over time or along a continuous scale.

- **Outlier Detection**: Outliers, data points that deviate significantly from the overall pattern, can be spotted in line plots.

Let's create a simple line plot in Python with random data:

```python
# Sample data: Year and annual average temperatures in Celsius

years = np.arange(2010, 2022)

temperatures = [14.2, 14.5, 14.8, 15.2, 15.7, 16.3, 16.8, 17.2, 17.6,
17.9, 18.2, 18.5]


# Create a line plot

plt.figure(figsize=(8, 5))  # Set the figure size

plt.plot(years, temperatures, marker='o', linestyle='-', color='b',
label='Annual Average Temperature')


# Add labels and a title

plt.xlabel('Year')

plt.ylabel('Temperature (°C)')
```

```
plt.title('Annual Average Temperature Changes (2010-2021)')

# Add gridlines for clarity
plt.grid(True, linestyle='--', alpha=0.7)

# Add a legend
plt.legend()

# Display the plot
plt.tight_layout()
plt.show()
```

Output:

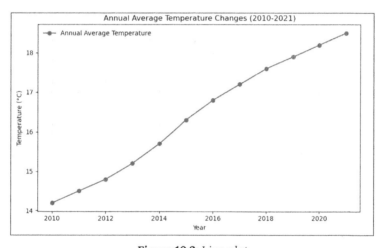

Figure 10.2: *Line plot*

Bar Plots

Bar plots are an essential tool for visualizing categorical data, making them suitable for comparing different categories. In this section, we will explore how to create bar plots using Matplotlib, covering both vertical and horizontal bar plots. Additionally, we'll delve into customization options to make your bar plots more informative and visually appealing.

Components of a Bar Plot

- **Bars:** The bars are the central visual elements of a bar plot. Each bar represents a specific category or group, and the length or height of the bar corresponds to a numerical value or count associated with that category.

- **Category Axis (x-axis or y-axis):** The category axis, also known as the x-axis (for vertical bar plots) or y-axis (for horizontal bar plots), represents the categories or groups being compared. Each category is displayed along this axis, providing context for the data.

- **Value Axis (y-axis or x-axis):** The value axis, also known as the y-axis (for vertical bar plots) or x-axis (for horizontal bar plots), represents the numerical values or counts associated with each category. It provides a scale for interpreting the heights or lengths of the bars.

- **Bar Width:** The width of the bars determines how much space each bar occupies along the category axis. Customizing the bar width can affect the visual appearance and readability of the plot.

Interpretation of Bar Plots

- **Comparison:** Bar plots are used to compare data values across different categories or groups. They make it easy to identify which categories have higher or lower values.

- **Distribution:** The distribution of values within each category can be observed. Bar plots help visualize the spread or concentration of data within each group.

- **Ranking:** Categories can be ranked based on their associated values. This ranking can highlight the most significant or least significant categories.

- **Patterns:** Patterns, such as trends, variations, and anomalies, can be identified. Bar plots are useful for spotting irregularities or specific patterns in the data.

- **Group Comparison:** When multiple datasets or groups are displayed on the same plot, bar plots facilitate comparing the performance or characteristics of these groups.

In this example, we'll create a vertical bar plot to visualize the sales data of different product categories.

```
# Sample data
categories = ['Category A', 'Category B', 'Category C', 'Category D']
sales = [4500, 6200, 3000, 7500]


# Create a vertical bar plot
plt.bar(categories, sales, color='skyblue')


# Add labels and a title
plt.xlabel('Product Categories')
plt.ylabel('Sales (in USD)')
```

```
plt.title('Sales by Product Category')


# Show the plot
plt.show()
```

Output:

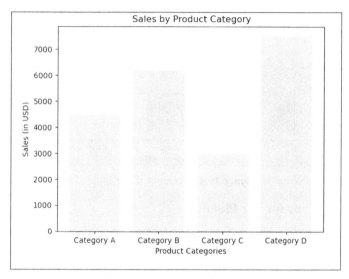

Figure 10.3: *Vertical bar plot*

Horizontal Bar Plots

Let's create a horizontal bar plot to visualize the same sales data.

```
# Create a horizontal bar plot
plt.barh(categories, sales, color='lightcoral')


# Add labels and a title
plt.xlabel('Sales (in USD)')
plt.ylabel('Product Categories')
plt.title('Sales by Product Category (Horizontal Bar Plot)')


# Show the plot
plt.show()
```

Output:

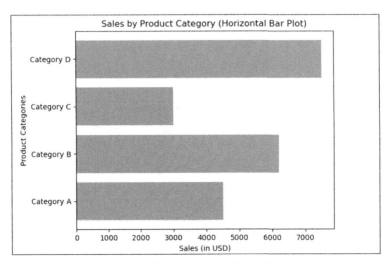

Figure 10.4: Horizontal bar plot

Customization Options for Bar Plots:

Bar plots offer a canvas for creative customization, allowing you to transform ordinary data representation into visually compelling insights. In the following example, we will explore how to harness the power of customization with techniques such as color selection, bar width adjustments, and the inclusion of error bars. These enhancements not only make your bar plots more visually appealing but also provide valuable context for better data interpretation:

```
import matplotlib.pyplot as plt


# Sample data
categories = ['Category A', 'Category B', 'Category C', 'Category D']
sales = [4500, 6200, 3000, 7500]


# Create a figure with a specific size (e.g., 8 inches wide and 6 inches
tall)
plt.figure(figsize=(10, 8))


# Create a vertical bar plot with customizations
plt.bar(categories, sales, color=['skyblue', 'lightcoral', 'lightgreen',
'lightsalmon'], edgecolor='black', linewidth=2, alpha=0.7)
```

```
# Customize the x-axis tick labels
plt.xticks(rotation=45, fontsize=12, fontweight='bold', color='gray')


# Customize the y-axis tick labels
plt.yticks(fontsize=12, fontweight='bold', color='gray')


# Add data labels above each bar
for i, v in enumerate(sales):
    plt.text(i, v + 100, str(v), ha='center', va='bottom', fontsize=10,
fontweight='bold')


# Add a legend
plt.legend(['Sales'], loc='upper left', fontsize=12)


# Add a grid for reference
plt.grid(axis='y', linestyle='--', alpha=0.5)


# Add labels and a title with custom font and size
plt.xlabel('Product Categories', fontsize=14, fontweight='bold',
color='black')
plt.ylabel('Sales (in USD)', fontsize=14, fontweight='bold',
color='black')
plt.title('Monthly Sales by Product Category', fontsize=16,
fontweight='bold', color='black')


# Show the customized plot
plt.show()
```

Output:

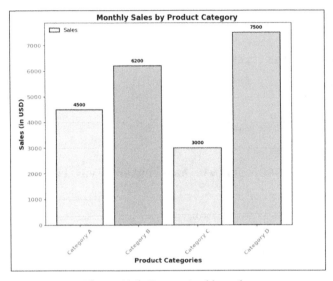

Figure 10.5: *Customized bar plot*

Scatter Plots

A scatter plot is a fundamental visualization technique used to explore relationships between two numerical variables. It displays data points as individual markers on a two-dimensional plane, with one variable plotted on the x-axis and the other on the y-axis. Scatter plots are particularly useful for identifying patterns, correlations, and potential outliers in your data.

Components of a Scatter Plot

- **X-axis and Y-axis:** These axes represent the two variables that the data is being compared on.

- **Data Points:** Each dot or mark represents an individual record from the dataset, plotted according to its x-value (horizontal axis) and y-value (vertical axis).

- **Axis Labels:** Descriptive labels for the x-axis and y-axis, typically including units of measurement.

- **Scale:** The range of values on the axes, which can be linear or logarithmic, depending on the nature and scale of the data.

- **Trend Line (Optional):** Sometimes, a line of best fit (regression line) is added to a scatter plot to indicate the trend in the data.

Interpretation of Scatter Plot

- **Correlation:** Scatter plots can suggest various kinds of correlation between variables with a certain confidence interval. Correlation may be positive (as one variable increases, so does the other), negative (as one variable increases, the other decreases), or null (no correlation).

- **Outliers:** Points that lie far from the main group of data can indicate outliers in the data.
- **Clusters and Gaps:** The arrangement of points can indicate clustering and gaps, which can suggest subgroups or patterns within the data.

```
# Generate some data
np.random.seed(5)
x = np.random.rand(50) * 100  # Random data for x-axis
y = x * 0.5 + np.random.normal(size=x.size) * 10  # Positive correlation
with some noise


# Create scatter plot
plt.figure(figsize=(10, 6))
plt.scatter(x, y, c='blue', marker='o', alpha=0.7)  # Scatter plot


# Add a trend line
m, b = np.polyfit(x, y, 1)  # Fit line
plt.plot(x, m*x + b, color='red')  # Add line to plot


# Label the axes
plt.xlabel('Variable X')
plt.ylabel('Variable Y')


# Add a title
plt.title('Scatter Plot with Trend Line')


# Show the plot
plt.show()
```

Output:

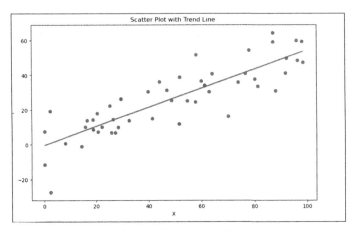

Figure 10.6: *Scatter plot*

Histograms

Histograms are essential tools for visualizing the distribution of numerical data. They help you understand the frequency or probability of data points falling into specific intervals or bins. Histograms are particularly useful when you want to explore the central tendency, variability, and shape of a dataset.

Components of a Histogram

- **X-Axis (Bins):** This axis represents the intervals that the data is divided into. The range of data is segmented into "**bins**" or "**buckets**," which cover equal ranges of values. The choice of bin size and range can drastically affect the histogram's appearance and its interpretive value.

- **Y-Axis (Frequency):** This axis shows the number of data points within each bin. The "**height**" of a bar corresponds to the frequency or count of data points it represents.

- **Bars:** Each bar in a histogram represents the tabulated frequency or occurrence of data points for each bin, with the height reflecting the frequency.

Interpretation of Histogram

- **Distribution Shape:** The shape of the histogram can provide a lot of information regarding the statistical distribution of the data. It can be symmetrical, skewed to the left or right, unimodal, bimodal, and more.

- **Central Tendency:** It describes where most of the data lies and the peak of the histogram can give an indication of the mean or median of the data.

- **Spread:** The range of the bins that the histogram covers indicates the variability or spread of the data.

- **Outliers and Gaps:** Sparse bars or a pattern of long-tailed distribution in one of the tails of the histogram can suggest outliers or gaps in data.

- **Comparison:** When multiple histograms are plotted over each other or side by side, you can compare different datasets or distribution properties such as central tendency, spread, and shape.

```python
# Generate random data with a normal distribution
data = np.random.randn(1000)


# Set up the figure and axis
fig, ax = plt.subplots(figsize=(10, 6))


# Calculate the optimal number of bins based on the Freedman-
Diaconis rule
q25, q75 = np.percentile(data, [25, 75])
bin_width = 2 * (q75 - q25) * len(data) ** (-1/3)
bins = int((data.max() - data.min()) / bin_width)


# Create the histogram with optimal bins and a nice color
n, bins, patches = ax.hist(data, bins=bins, color='skyblue',
edgecolor='black', alpha=0.7)


# Add a grid for easier reading of the histogram
ax.grid(True, which='both', linestyle='--', linewidth=0.5)


# Add titles and labels
ax.set_title('Histogram Example', fontsize=15)
ax.set_xlabel('Value', fontsize=12)
ax.set_ylabel('Frequency', fontsize=12)


# Tweak spacing to prevent clipping of ylabel
fig.tight_layout()


# Show plot
plt.show()
```

Output:

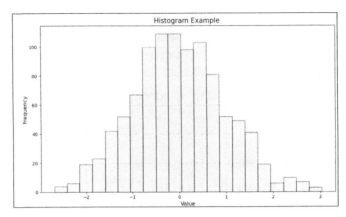

Figure 10.7: Histogram

Choosing the Right Bin Width

There's no one-size-fits-all rule for choosing bin width, but there are some commonly used rules of thumb, including:

- **Square-root rule:** Use the square root of the number of data points as the number of bins.

- **Sturges' formula:** A binning rule that suggests using a bin count of **log2(n)+1**, where **n** is the number of data points.

- **Freedman-Diaconis rule:** Chooses the bin size based on the Interquartile Range (IQR) and the number of data points, to minimize the difference between the bin and the actual data distribution.

Density Plot

A density plot, also known as a kernel density estimate (KDE) plot, visualizes the distribution of data over a continuous interval or time period. This plot is a smoothed version of a histogram, but instead of showing individual data points or bin counts, it represents data using a continuous probability density curve. Here are the key details of density plots:

Kernel Density Estimation (KDE)

At the heart of the density plot is the KDE, which smooths the data points in a way similar to how a histogram does, but without the hard binning. The KDE algorithm works by placing a kernel (a smooth, bell-shaped curve) on each data point, and then summing the kernels to create the overall density plot. The height of the curve at any point gives you an estimate of the probability density function of the variable at that point.

Interpretation of Density Plot

- **Probability Density:** The y-axis in a density plot shows the probability density, not the actual count as in histograms. The higher the curve at a point, the higher the density of data points at that value.

- **Data Distribution:** Just like histograms, density plots show the shape of the data distribution. Skewness, modality (unimodal, bimodal, multimodal), and outliers can often be identified.

- **Comparison:** Density plots can be useful for comparing the distribution of several different datasets, as they can overlap without being obscured by each other, unlike histograms.

```python
from scipy.stats import gaussian_kde


# Generate some normally distributed data for the demonstration.
data = np.random.normal(loc=0, scale=1, size=1000)


# Create a Gaussian Kernel Density Estimate (KDE)
# 'scott' factor is a rule-of-thumb for bandwidth selection, can
also use 'silverman' or a scalar
kde = gaussian_kde(data, bw_method='scott')
# Generate a range of values spanning the extent of the data for
evaluation
x_eval = np.linspace(data.min() - 3, data.max() + 3, 1000)


# Evaluate the KDE on this range to get the density estimates
density = kde(x_eval)


# Set up the plot
fig, ax = plt.subplots(figsize=(10, 6))


# Plot the density
ax.plot(x_eval, density, label='KDE', color='blue')


# Fill under the curve for better visual appeal
ax.fill_between(x_eval, density, alpha=0.5, color='blue')
```

```
# Enhance the plot with a grid, labels, and a title
ax.grid(True, linestyle='--', alpha=0.6)
ax.set_title('Density Plot of Normally Distributed Data', fon-
tsize=15)
ax.set_xlabel('Data Values', fontsize=12)
ax.set_ylabel('Density', fontsize=12)

# Optionally add the histogram for reference (commented out)
#ax.hist(data, bins=30, density=True, alpha=0.3, color='grey',
edgecolor='black', label='Histogram')

# Show legend
ax.legend()

# Tweak the layout to make room for the axis labels
plt.tight_layout()

# Display the plot
plt.show()
```

Output:

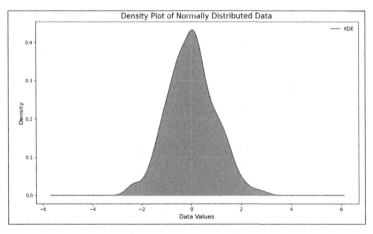

Figure 10.8: *Density plot*

Box Plots

A box plot, also known as a box-and-whisker plot, displays the distribution of data based on a five-number summary: minimum, first quartile (Q1), median, third quartile (Q3), and maximum. It can also indicate outliers.

Components of a Box Plot

- **Box:** The central rectangular box represents the interquartile range (IQR), which encompasses the middle 50% of the data. The bottom edge of the box marks the first quartile (Q1), and the top edge marks the third quartile (Q3). The length of the box represents the spread of this central portion of the data.

- **Whiskers:** The whiskers extend outward from the box to indicate the range of the data. There are two whiskers, namely:

  o **Lower Whisker:** It extends from the bottom of the box to the minimum value within a certain range (typically 1.5 times the IQR below Q1). Any data points below this range are considered outliers and are plotted individually as points.

  o **Upper Whisker:** It extends from the top of the box to the maximum value within a certain range (typically 1.5 times the IQR above Q3). Any data points above this range are also considered outliers.

- **Median Line:** Inside the box, a vertical line represents the median (or second quartile), which is the middle value when the data is sorted. It divides the data into two halves, with 50% of the data falling below and 50% above this line.

- **Outliers:** Data points that fall outside the range covered by the whiskers are considered outliers. Outliers are plotted individually as distinct points and can provide insights into potential data anomalies or extreme values.

Interpretation of Box Plot

- **Central Tendency:** The position of the median line inside the box indicates the central tendency of the data. If the median is closer to the bottom of the box, the data may be negatively skewed; if it's closer to the top, the data may be positively skewed. If the median is in the center of the box, the data may be roughly symmetrical.

- **Spread and Variability:** The length of the box and the width of the whiskers provide information about the spread or variability of the data. A wider box and longer whiskers indicate greater variability, while a narrower box and shorter whiskers suggest lower variability.

- **Potential Outliers:** The presence of individual points beyond the whiskers indicates potential outliers in the data. These values are often of interest because they may represent unusual observations or data errors.

- **Skewness:** The box plot can provide visual clues about the skewness of the data distribution. If one whisker is notably longer than the other, it suggests that the data is skewed in that direction. For example, if the upper whisker is much longer than the lower whisker, the data may be right-skewed.

```
# Set seed for reproducibility
np.random.seed(42)


# Generate random data with a few added outliers
normal_data = np.random.normal(loc=0, scale=1, size=100)
outliers = np.array([3, -3, 3.2])   # Manual outliers
data = np.concatenate((normal_data, outliers))   # Combine the
data


# Create the box plot
plt.figure(figsize=(8, 6))   # Set figure size
bp = plt.boxplot(data, vert=True, patch_artist=True,
showfliers=True)   # Box plot with patch_artist


# Customize the box properties
for box in bp['boxes']:
    # Change box color
    box.set(color='blue', linewidth=2)
    box.set(facecolor='lightgrey')


# Customize the whiskers
for whisker in bp['whiskers']:
    whisker.set(color='green', linewidth=2)


# Customize the caps
for cap in bp['caps']:
    cap.set(color='red', linewidth=2)


# Customize the median line
for median in bp['medians']:
    median.set(color='red', linewidth=2)
```

```
# Customize the fliers (outliers)
for flier in bp['fliers']:
    flier.set(marker='o', color='black', alpha=0.5)


# Add titles and labels
plt.title('Box Plot with Outliers and Annotations')
plt.ylabel('Value')


# Annotating different parts of the box plot
plt.text(x=1.15, y=data.min(), s='Min', verticalalignment=
'center', fontsize=12, color='blue')

plt.text(x=1.15, y=np.percentile(data, 25), s='Q1',
verticalalignment='center', fontsize=12, color='blue')

plt.text(x=1.15, y=np.median(data), s='Median',
verticalalignment='center', fontsize=12, color='red')

plt.text(x=1.15, y=np.percentile(data, 75), s='Q3',
verticalalignment='center', fontsize=12, color='blue')

plt.text(x=1.15, y=data.max(), s='Max', verticalalignment=
'center', fontsize=12, color='blue')

# Assuming that we define outliers using the 1.5*IQR rule, let's
annotate them.

for outlier in outliers:
    plt.text(x=1.2, y=outlier, s=f'Outlier: {outlier}',
verticalalignment='center', fontsize=9, color='black')


# Display grid
plt.grid(True, which='major', linestyle='--', linewidth=0.5,
alpha=0.7)


# Show the plot
plt.show()
```

Output:

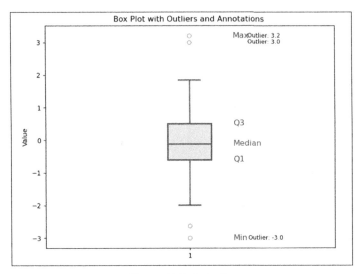

Figure 10.9: Box plot

Violin Plots

Violin plots are a method of plotting numeric data and can be understood as a combination of a box plot and a kernel density plot. They provide a visual summary of the data in the same way that box plots do, but they also include a rotated kernel density plot on each side, which gives a better sense of the distribution shape. This can be particularly useful when you have multiple groups to compare.

Components of a Violin Plot

- **Center Bar:** This shows the interquartile range, similar to the box in a box plot.
- **White Dot:** This typically represents the median of the data.
- **Thick Bar:** This represents the interquartile range, where 50% of the data points lie.
- **Thin Line:** These are similar to the "whiskers" in a box plot and represent the range of the data (excluding outliers).
- **Violin Shape:** The width of the "violin" at different values indicates the density of the data at that value. A wider section means more data points fall at that level.

Interpretation

- **Width:** The wider sections of the violin plot represent higher probability of observations at that level, with the width being proportional to the number of observations.

- **Skewness and Distribution**: The shape of the violin can show the distribution of the data (for example, skewed left/right, bimodal peaks, and more).

- **Comparisons**: Violin plots are especially useful for comparing the distribution of data across several levels or groups.

```python
# Generating some data
np.random.seed(10)
data1 = np.random.normal(100, 10, 200)
data2 = np.random.normal(90, 20, 200)
data3 = np.random.normal(80, 30, 200)
data_to_plot = [data1, data2, data3]


# Create a figure instance
fig = plt.figure(figsize=(8, 6))


# Create an axes instance and a violin plot
ax = fig.add_axes([0,0,1,1])
vp = ax.violinplot(data_to_plot)


# Customizing the violin plot
for pc in vp['bodies']:
    pc.set_facecolor('blue')
    pc.set_edgecolor('black')
    pc.set_alpha(0.75)


# Adding the median marker to the violin plot
for i in range(len(data_to_plot)):
    plt.scatter([i+1], [np.median(data_to_plot[i])], color=
'yellow')


# Customizing the box for the interquartile range
ax.boxplot(data_to_plot, notch=True, widths=0.1, patch_
artist=True,
            boxprops=dict(facecolor='red', color='black'),
            medianprops=dict(color='green'), showfliers=False)
```

```
# Labels and titles
plt.title('Violin plot')
plt.xticks([1, 2, 3], ['Group1', 'Group2', 'Group3'])
plt.ylabel('Value')

# Show the plot
plt.show()
```

Output:

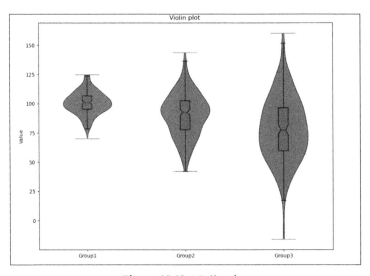

Figure 10.10: *Violin plot*

Area Plots

An area plot is a type of data visualization that displays data points as colored areas between a line (or lines) and the horizontal axis. The area between the line(s) and the axis is filled with color, making it visually easy to see the contribution of different categories or components to the whole.

Components of an Area Plot

- **X- and Y-Axes**: The x-axis typically represents time or categories, while the y-axis represents the values or proportions of the data. The filled area between the line(s) and the x-axis indicates the magnitude of each category or component.

- **Filling the Area**: The primary feature of an area plot is the filled area between the line(s) and the x-axis. This area is often shaded with colors to differentiate between different categories or components.

- **Multiple Stacked Areas**: In stacked area plots, multiple categories or components are stacked on top of each other to visualize their cumulative effect. This helps in understanding how each category contributes to the total.

Interpretation:

- **Magnitude and Proportions**: The filled areas in an area plot represent the magnitude of data values or proportions relative to the whole. Wider filled areas indicate higher values or proportions within a category, with the width being proportional to the magnitude of the data.

- **Patterns and Trends**: The direction in which the filled areas move and the presence of peaks or troughs can reveal patterns and trends within the data. Rising areas may indicate growth, while declining areas suggest a decrease.

- **Comparative Analysis**: Area plots are particularly valuable for comparing the distribution of data across different categories or components. By observing the filled areas for each category, you can assess their contributions to the overall picture.

- **Distribution Shape**: Similar to violin plots, area plots can also convey information about data distribution. The shape of the filled areas may indicate whether the data distribution is skewed left, skewed right, bimodal, or exhibits other characteristics.

```
# Simulated population data

decades = np.arange(1970, 2021, 10)

region1_population = np.array([100, 120, 130, 140, 160, 180])
# Adjusted for six decades

region2_population = np.array([80, 85, 90, 95, 100, 110])
# Adjusted for six decades

region3_population = np.array([50, 60, 75, 90, 110, 130])
# Adjusted for six decades


# Create an area plot

plt.figure(figsize=(10, 6))


# Plot the filled areas for each region

plt.fill_between(decades, region1_population, label='Region 1',
alpha=0.7)

plt.fill_between(decades, region2_population, label='Region 2',
alpha=0.7)
```

```
plt.fill_between(decades, region3_population, label='Region 3',
alpha=0.7)


# Customize the plot
plt.title('Population Distribution Over Decades')
plt.xlabel('Decades')
plt.ylabel('Population')
plt.legend(loc='upper left')


# Show the area plot
plt.grid(True)
plt.show()
```

Output:

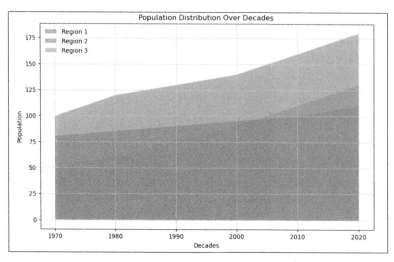

Figure 10.11: Area plot

Subplots Using Matplotlib

In Matplotlib, subplots are used to arrange multiple plots within a single figure. Each subplot is placed in a grid layout, and you have full control over the size, position, and spacing of these subplots.

What are Subplots?

Subplots are a way to create multiple smaller plots or charts within a single larger figure. Each subplot represents a distinct visual representation of data. Subplots allow you to present related information side by side, facilitating comparison and analysis.

Why Use Subplots?

- **Comparison:** Subplots are ideal for comparing different datasets or aspects of data. For example, you can visualize multiple variables or time series on separate subplots for easy comparison.

- **Clarity:** Subplots help maintain clarity in complex visualizations. Rather than creating multiple separate figures, you can consolidate information into a single figure.

- **Storytelling:** Subplots enable you to tell a more comprehensive data-driven story by presenting various facets of your data in a coherent manner.

Using plt.subplots

The **plt.subplots** function in Matplotlib is a utility wrapper that helps in creating a figure and a grid of subplots with a single call. It's very useful when you want to present multiple plots in a structured layout within the same figure. Let's break down how this function is used and how you can customize the resulting figure and array of axes.

Creating a Figure and Subplot

```
fig, ax = plt.subplots()
```

Creating Multiple Subplots

When you call **plt.subplots()**, you specify two main arguments: **nrows** and **ncols**. These arguments define the number of rows and columns of the **subplot** grid. The function returns a Figure object and an array (or a single instance) of Axes objects.

```
fig, axs = plt.subplots(nrows=2, ncols=2)
```

nrows and **ncols** specify the number of rows and columns of subplots you want to create.

axs is now an array of Axes objects, each of which can be used to plot different data.

Dividing the Figure into Subplots

The resulting **fig** object represents the entire figure, and the axes object is a 2D array of axes objects representing individual subplots. You can access and manipulate each subplot using indexing, as shown here.

Accessing Individual Subplots

You can access individual subplots similar to elements in a numpy array:

```
axs[0, 0].plot(x, y)  # Top left subplot
axs[1, 1].plot(x, y)  # Bottom right subplot
```

Sharing Axes

If you want subplots to share the same x-axis or y-axis, you can set **sharex** or **sharey** to True:

```
fig, axs = plt.subplots(2, 2, sharex='col', sharey='row')
```

This makes it easier to compare the subplots against each other since the axis scales will be identical.

Plotting in Subplots

Just like with a single plot, you can use methods like **.plot()**, **.scatter()**, **.bar()**, and so on to plot data in each Axes object:

```
axs[0, 0].plot(data_x, data_y)
```

Customizing Subplots

You can customize the spacing between subplots using **plt.subplots_adjust**, or by calling **fig.tight_layout()**, which automatically adjusts the spacing to prevent overlapping content:

```
plt.subplots_adjust(left=None, bottom=None, right=None, top=None,
wspace=None, hspace=None)
fig.tight_layout()
```

Titles, Labels, and Legends

You can also add titles, labels, and legends to each subplot:

```
axs[0, 0].set_title('Main Title')
axs[0, 0].set_xlabel('X Label')
axs[0, 0].set_ylabel('Y Label')
axs[0, 0].legend(['Dataset 1'])
```

Here's a simple complete example that creates a 2×2 grid of subplots, each with a different plot type:

```
# Create a 2x2 grid of subplots
fig, axs = plt.subplots(2, 2)


# Top-left subplot
axs[0, 0].plot([1, 2, 3], [3, 2, 1])
axs[0, 0].set_title('Line Plot')


# Top-right subplot
```

```
axs[0, 1].scatter([1, 2, 3], [3, 2, 1])
axs[0, 1].set_title('Scatter Plot')

# Bottom-left subplot
axs[1, 0].bar([1, 2, 3], [3, 2, 1])
axs[1, 0].set_title('Bar Plot')

# Bottom-right subplot
axs[1, 1].hist([1, 2, 2, 3, 3, 3, 4, 4, 4, 4])
axs[1, 1].set_title('Histogram')

# Adjust the spacing between subplots
plt.tight_layout()

# Show the plots
plt.show()
```

Output:

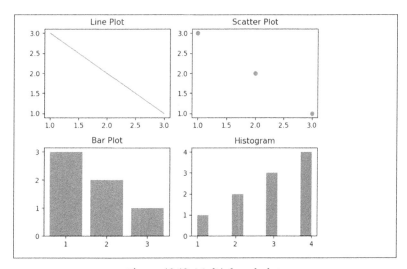

Figure 10.12: Multiple subplots

Effective Visualization of Time Series Data

Time series data represents observations collected over a sequence of equally spaced time intervals. Effective visualization of time series data is crucial for understanding trends, patterns, and anomalies. Matplotlib offers versatile tools for creating informative time series visualizations.

A **line plot** is one of the most fundamental and commonly used techniques for visualizing time series data. It is a graphical representation that displays data points as connected line segments. Line plots are particularly useful for understanding the trend and seasonality of data over time. Let's explore the details of line plots for time series data.

Key Characteristics of Line Plots

- **Time on the x-axis:** In time series data, the x-axis typically represents time or a sequence of equally spaced time intervals. Each data point corresponds to a specific time point or period.

- **Data values on the y-axis:** The y-axis represents the values or measurements associated with the data points. It could be anything from stock prices and temperature readings to sales figures and stock market indices.

- **Connected data points:** Line plots connect data points using lines, allowing you to visualize how the values change over time. This connectivity helps identify trends and patterns.

```python
# Sample time series data (Monthly average temperature)

date_rng = pd.date_range(start='2023-01-01', end='2023-12-31',
freq='M')

monthly_temperature = [25.3, 26.5, 28.7, 32.1, 35.2, 37.8, 39.5,
38.6, 36.2, 32.7, 29.1, 26.4]


# Create a Pandas DataFrame

temperature_df = pd.DataFrame({'Date': date_rng, 'Temperature
(°C)': monthly_temperature})


# Create a line plot for time series data

plt.figure(figsize=(12, 6))

plt.plot(temperature_df['Date'], temperature_df['Temperature
(°C)'], marker='o', linestyle='-', color='b', label='Monthly Avg.
Temp.')

plt.xlabel('Date')

plt.ylabel('Temperature (°C)')

plt.title('Monthly Average Temperature Over a Year')

plt.legend()

plt.grid(True)
```

```
# Customize x-axis date formatting for better readability
plt.gca().xaxis.set_major_formatter(plt.matplotlib.dates.DateFor-
matter('%b %Y'))


# Display the plot
plt.tight_layout()
plt.show()
```

Output:

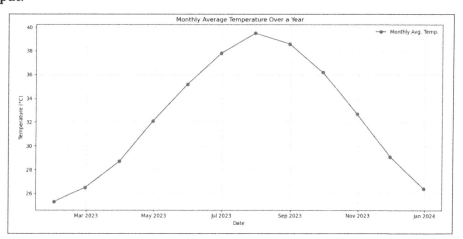

Figure 10.13: *Line plots for time series*

Bar Plots for Time Series

Bar plots are a useful visualization technique for representing time series data, especially when dealing with categorical or discrete time intervals, such as months, years, or specific events. In this explanation, we will explore how to create bar plots for time series data in detail.

Key Characteristics of Bar Plots for Time Series

- **Categorical Data on the x-axis:** In bar plots, the x-axis typically represents categorical or discrete time intervals or events. Each category or event corresponds to a bar.

- **Data Values on the y-axis:** The y-axis represents the numerical values associated with each category or event. These values can be counts, measurements, or any other relevant data.

- **Vertical or Horizontal Bars:** Bar plots can be either vertical (default) or horizontal, depending on the orientation you choose.

```
# Sample time series data (Monthly sales)
date_rng = pd.date_range(start='2023-01-01', end='2023-12-31',
freq='M')
monthly_sales = [25000, 28000, 29000, 32000, 35000, 38000, 41000,
42000, 39000, 36000, 33000, 28000]


# Create a Pandas DataFrame
sales_df = pd.DataFrame({'Month': date_rng.strftime('%b %Y'),
'Sales (USD)': monthly_sales})


# Create a vertical bar plot for time series data
plt.figure(figsize=(12, 6))
plt.bar(sales_df['Month'], sales_df['Sales (USD)'], color=
'skyblue')
plt.xlabel('Month')
plt.ylabel('Sales (USD)')
plt.title('Monthly Sales Over a Year')
plt.xticks(rotation=45)  # Rotate x-axis labels for better
readability
plt.grid(True)


# Display the plot
plt.tight_layout()
plt.show()
```

Output:

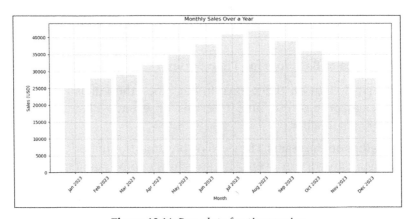

Figure 10.14: *Bar plots for time series*

Area Plot for Time Series

An **area plot**, also known as a stacked area plot or area chart, is a data visualization technique used to represent time series data or data with sequential values over time. It is similar to a line plot, but it displays the area between the line and the x-axis, filled with color or patterns. Area plots are useful for visualizing cumulative data, showing how different categories or components contribute to the whole over time.

Key Characteristics of Area Plots

- **Cumulative Representation:** An area plot represents cumulative data, where each data point's value is added to the previous data point's value. This cumulative nature makes it easy to see the total contribution of each category or component.

- **Stacked Components:** In a stacked area plot, multiple components or categories are stacked on top of each other, and the cumulative total of all categories is displayed. This helps in understanding how each category contributes to the overall trend.

- **Time on the x-axis:** Typically, area plots are used for time series data, where the x-axis represents time or sequential values. Each point on the x-axis corresponds to a specific time point or interval.

```
# Sample time series data (Cumulative monthly sales for three
product categories)

date_rng = pd.date_range(start='2023-01-01', end='2023-12-31',
freq='M')

category_a = [25000, 28000, 30000, 32000, 35000, 38000, 41000,
42000, 44000, 46000, 48000, 50000]

category_b = [15000, 16000, 17000, 18000, 19000, 20000, 21000,
22000, 23000, 24000, 25000, 26000]

category_c = [10000, 12000, 14000, 16000, 18000, 20000, 22000,
24000, 26000, 28000, 30000, 32000]


# Create a Pandas DataFrame

sales_df = pd.DataFrame({'Month': date_rng.strftime('%b %Y'),
'Category A': category_a, 'Category B': category_b, 'Category C':
category_c})


# Create a stacked area plot for time series data

plt.figure(figsize=(12, 6))

plt.stackplot(sales_df['Month'], sales_df['Category A'], sales_
```

```
df['Category B'], sales_df['Category C'], labels=['Category A',
'Category B', 'Category C'], alpha=0.7)

plt.xlabel('Month')

plt.ylabel('Cumulative Sales (USD)')

plt.title('Cumulative Monthly Sales Over a Year')

plt.legend()

plt.grid(True)


# Display the plot

plt.tight_layout()

plt.show()
```

Output:

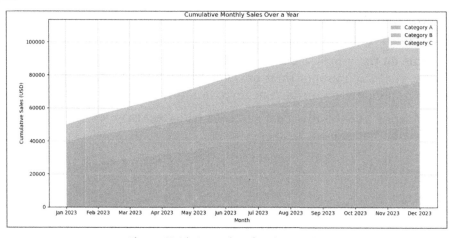

Figure 10.15: *Area plots for time series*

Exporting and Saving Plots: Saving Plots as Image Files and Interactive HTML Files

Exporting and saving plots in Matplotlib allows you to preserve your visualizations for future reference or use in reports and presentations. You can save Matplotlib plots as image files (for example, PNG, JPEG) or as interactive HTML files using the **savefig** function and other customization options. Here's a detailed explanation of how to export and save plots in Matplotlib:

Saving Plots as Image Files

1. **Choose a File Format:** Matplotlib supports various image file formats, such as PNG, JPEG, PDF, SVG, and more. Decide on the format that best suits your needs. For example, to save a plot as a PNG file, use the **.png** file extension.

2. **Use savefig:** The **savefig** function is used to save a Matplotlib figure to a file. You can call it with the desired file name and format as arguments. Here's the basic syntax:

```
plt.savefig('output.png', format='png')
```

Replace **'output.png'** with your preferred file name and format.

3. **Additional Options:** savefig provides several optional parameters for customization, such as specifying the DPI (dots per inch) for image resolution, setting the image quality (for JPEG), adjusting the bounding box, and more. For example:

```
plt.savefig('output.png', format='png', dpi=300, bbox_inches='tight')
```

- **dpi:** Sets the resolution (dots per inch) of the saved image.
- **bbox_inches:** Controls the bounding box used to save the plot. **'tight'** ensures that the entire plot is saved without cropping.

Let's see an example how to save the file as **png**:

```
# Sample data
x = np.linspace(0, 2 * np.pi, 100)
y = np.sin(x)


# Create a plot
plt.figure(figsize=(8, 4))
plt.plot(x, y, label='Sine Wave')
plt.title('Sine Wave Plot')
plt.xlabel('X-axis')
plt.ylabel('Y-axis')
plt.grid(True)
plt.legend()


# Save the plot as a PNG image
plt.savefig('sine_wave_plot.png', format='png', dpi=300)
```

Output:

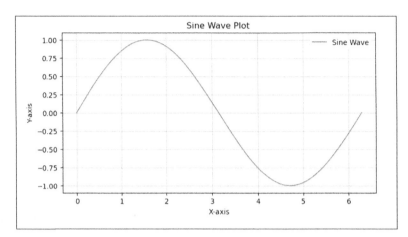

Figure 10.16: *Save fig as PNG*

After running this code, you will find a PNG image named **sine_wave_plot.png** in your current working directory. You can change the format, DPI, and file name according to your preferences.

Saving Plots as Interactive HTML Files

Saving Matplotlib plots as interactive HTML files can be achieved by converting your Matplotlib figures to Plotly figures and then saving them in an interactive format.

If you haven't already, install the **Plotly** library and run the following command:

```
pip install plotly
```

Create a Matplotlib Plot:

```
import plotly.graph_objects as go


# Sample data
x = np.linspace(0, 2 * np.pi, 100)
y = np.sin(x)


# Create a Matplotlib plot
plt.figure(figsize=(8, 4))
plt.plot(x, y, label='Sine Wave')
plt.title('Sine Wave Plot')
plt.xlabel('X-axis')
plt.ylabel('Y-axis')
```

```
plt.grid(True)
```

```
plt.legend()
```

Convert to Plotly Figure:

```
# Convert Matplotlib plot to Plotly figure
```

```
fig = go.Figure()
```

```
fig.add_trace(go.Scatter(x=x, y=y, mode='lines', name='Sine Wave'))
```

Save as Interactive HTML:

```
# Save the interactive plot as an HTML file
```

```
fig.write_html('interactive_plot.html')
```

Display the Interactive Plot:

If you want to display the interactive plot in your Jupyter Notebook or IPython environment, you can use the following code:

```
fig.show()
```

Output:

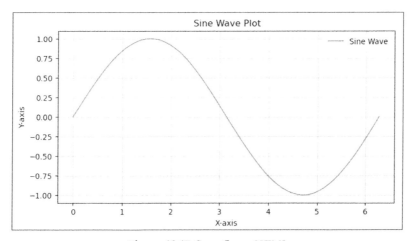

Figure 10.17: *Save fig as HTML*

Now, after running this code, you will have an interactive HTML plot named **interactive_plot.html** saved in your current working directory. You can open this file in a web browser to interact with the plot, zoom in, pan, and explore the data points.

Conclusion

In this chapter, we explored the pivotal role of data visualization in data analysis, with Matplotlib as our trusted tool. We dissected Matplotlib's structure, learned how to customize plots, and discovered various plot types, from line plots for trends to box plots for summary statistics. We even delved into the art of organizing subplots. As we conclude this chapter, we are well-prepared for *Chapter 11, Analyzing Bank Customer Churn Using Pandas*, where we'll apply out knowledge to real-world datasets, turning theory into practical insights. Stay tuned for the hands-on journey ahead.

Exercise Questions

Sample Dataset: Monthly Sales Data

```python
import pandas as pd

import numpy as np

import random


# Create a DataFrame for monthly sales data
months = pd.date_range(start="2021-01-01", end="2021-12-01", freq='MS')
sales = [random.randint(5000, 10000) for _ in range(12)]


sales_df = pd.DataFrame({'Month': months, 'Sales': sales})


# Display the dataset
print(sales_df)
```

1. Given the dataset of monthly sales figures for a retail store in 2021, create a line plot using Matplotlib. Customize the plot to include a red line, circular markers, and a title that reads "**Monthly Sales Trends (2021)**".

2. Using the provided dataset of monthly sales figures, create a horizontal bar plot using Matplotlib to visualize the sales for each month in 2021. Add appropriate labels to the axes and bars.

3. Utilizing the dataset of monthly sales figures and the corresponding months, create a scatter plot to investigate the relationship between months and sales. Analyze the scatter plot to identify any patterns or trends.

4. You have collected temperature data for three cities (**City A**, **City B**, and **City C**) over the past year. Create a subplot with three line plots (one for each city) to visualize temperature trends over time. Customize the plots with different colors, markers, and legends for each city.

CHAPTER 11

Analyzing Bank Customer Churn Using Pandas

In the preceding chapters of this book, we've journeyed through the diverse functionalities of Pandas, learning how to perform a multitude of tasks with this powerful library. Our journey has been a blend of learning through synthetic examples designed to highlight specific features of Pandas, interspersed with forays into more practical, real-world data scenarios.

This chapter will not dwell deeply into the theoretical nuances of financial concepts. Rather, our objective is to showcase how Pandas can be utilized to extract meaningful insights from time-series financial data, particularly in understanding and analyzing customer churn in the banking sector. This real-world dataset, sourced from real banking records, presents a unique opportunity to apply the concepts and techniques of Pandas in a context that is both challenging and highly pertinent to current financial analytics trends.

Structure

In this chapter, we will discuss the following topics:

- Setting Up Your Environment
- Data Used for Analysis: Bank Customer Churn
- Data Loading and Preprocessing
- Exploratory Data Analysis (EDA)
    - Descriptive Statistics Analysis
    - Churn Analysis
    - Customer Segmentation

Setting Up Your Environment

As you embark on this chapter focused on real-time data analysis using the Bank Customer Churn dataset, it's essential to have your environment ready. Since we have already covered the process of installing necessary Python packages, such as Pandas, NumPy, and Matplotlib in previous chapters, you should have these tools available in your setup. However, it's always a good practice to ensure your environment is up-to-date and prepared for the tasks ahead.

Confirming Package Installation

1. Check Installed Packages:

    •   Open your Python environment or Jupyter Notebook.

    •   Verify the installation and versions of the required packages by executing

    ```
    pip list
    ```

This command lists all installed Python packages in your environment, allowing you to confirm that Pandas, NumPy, and Matplotlib are installed.

2. Updating Packages (if necessary):

    •   If you find that any of these packages are not installed or need an update, use **pip** to install or update them. For instance:

    ```
    pip install pandas –upgrade
    pip install numpy --upgrade
    pip install matplotlib –upgrade
    ```

Setting Up a Jupyter Notebook

1. Launch Jupyter Notebook:

    •   If you prefer an interactive analysis environment, launch Jupyter Notebook (assuming it's already installed) using:

    ```
    jupyter notebook
    ```

This command will open Jupyter in your default web browser, providing a user-friendly interface for coding.

2. Create a New Notebook for the Project:

    •   In Jupyter, create a new notebook specifically for this analysis to keep your work organized.

    •   Click the **New** button in the top-right corner and select "**Python 3**" to start a new notebook.

Data Used for Analysis: Bank Customer Churn

In the analysis of bank customer churn, we utilize a specialized dataset specifically designed to understand and predict customer attrition in banking. This section outlines the key characteristics and components of the dataset, providing insight into its role in our analysis.

You can access the dataset from Kaggle: https://www.kaggle.com/code/kmalit/bank-customer-churn-prediction

Dataset Overview

Name: Bank Customer Churn Dataset

Content: The dataset comprises detailed records of bank customers, focusing on various attributes that might influence their decision to leave (or churn) the bank.

Composition of the Dataset

1. **Customer Demographics:**

    *   Age: The age of the customers.

    *   Gender: Male or Female, offering insights into gender-based trends in banking behavior.

    *   Geography: Customer's location, which could influence their banking needs and preferences.

2. **Banking Relationship:**

    *   Tenure: Duration of the customer's relationship with the bank, an essential factor in loyalty and churn.

    *   Balance: The amount of money held in the customer's bank accounts.

    *   Products Number: The number of banking products used by the customer, such as savings accounts, credit cards, or loans.

3. **Financial Behavior:**

    *   Credit Score: Provides insight into the customer's financial reliability.

    *   Estimated Salary: The customer's salary, which can impact their banking needs and potential for investments.

4. **Customer Status:**

   • IsActiveMember: Indicates whether the customer is actively using the bank's services.

   • Exited: The primary response variable, indicating whether the customer has churned or not.

Data Loading and Preprocessing

The first and crucial step in any data analysis project is to load and preprocess the data. This section will guide you through the process of loading the Bank Customer Churn dataset into a Pandas DataFrame, followed by essential preprocessing steps. These steps are critical for ensuring the quality and reliability of the data before proceeding to the analysis phase.

I. **Loading the Dataset**

    Import Libraries: Start by importing the following libraries:

    ```
    import pandas as pd

    import seaborn as sns

    import matplotlib.pyplot as plt
    ```

II. **Reading the Data:** Load the dataset into a Pandas DataFrame. Assuming the file name is **Churn_Modelling.csv**, the code is:

    ```
    churn_data = pd.read_csv('Churn_Modelling.csv')
    ```

    This command reads the CSV file and converts it into a Pandas DataFrame named **churn_data**.

III. **Initial Inspection:** After loading the dataset, it's a good practice to inspect the first few rows to understand its structure and contents.

    ```
    churn_data.head()
    ```

Output:

	RowNum	CustId	Surname	CreditScore	Geo	Gender	Age	Tenure	Balance	NumOfProducts	HasCrCard	IsActive	EstimatedSal	Exited
0	1	15634602	Hargrave	619	France	Female	42.0	2.0	0.00	1	1	1	101348.88	1
1	2	15647311	Hill	608	Spain	Female	41.0	1.0	83807.86	1	0	1	112542.58	0
2	3	15619304	Onio	502	France	Female	42.0	8.0	159660.80	3	1	0	113931.57	1
3	4	15701354	Boni	699	France	Female	39.0	1.0	0.00	2	0	0	93826.63	0
4	5	15737888	Mitchell	850	Spain	Female	43.0	2.0	125510.82	1	1	1	79084.10	0

Figure 11.1: Understanding churn data structure and contents

IV. **Finding and Filling Missing Values:** The first step in handling missing data is to identify which columns contain missing values and the extent of these missing entries. This is done using the **isnull()** and **sum()** methods in Pandas.

```
missing_values = churn_data.isnull().sum()
```

Output:

```
RowNum              0
CustId              0
Surname             0
CreditScore         0
Geo                 0
Gender              0
Age                 3
Tenure              2
Balance             0
NumOfProducts       0
HasCrCard           0
IsActive            0
EstimatedSal        0
Exited              0
dtype: int64
```

Figure 11.2: *Finding missing values*

We observed that Age and Tenure had missing values in the dataset.

- **Age** had 3 missing values (0.03% of the dataset).
- **Tenure** had 2 missing values (0.02% of the dataset).

Filling Missing Values: Once the columns with missing values are identified, the next step is to fill these gaps with appropriate values. The choice of value depends on the nature of the data and the specific column.

(a) **Choosing the Filling Strategy:**

- For numerical data, common strategies include filling with the mean, median, or a specific constant.
- The median is often preferred in cases where the data distribution is skewed or contains outliers, as it is more robust to such anomalies than the mean.

(b) **Implementation for Age and Tenure Columns:**

- In our dataset, the **Age** and **Tenure** columns have missing values.
- Given the small percentage of missing values and potential variability in these columns, we will use the median to fill these gaps.

(c) **Filling the Missing Values:**

- To fill the missing values in the **Age** column:

```
churn_data['Age'].fillna(churn_data['Age'].median(), inplace=True)
```

- Similarly, for the **Tenure** column:

```
churn_data['Tenure'].fillna(churn_data['Tenure'].median(),
inplace=True)
```

- The **fillna()** function in Pandas is used to fill missing values, and **inplace=True** ensures that the changes are made directly in the DataFrame.

(d) **Verification:** After filling the missing values, it's important to verify that the operation was successful. This can be done by rechecking for missing values:

```
churn_data.isnull().sum()
```

Output:

```
RowNum           0
CustId           0
Surname          0
CreditScore      0
Geo              0
Gender           0
Age              0
Tenure           0
Balance          0
NumOfProducts    0
HasCrCard        0
IsActive         0
EstimatedSal     0
Exited           0
dtype: int64
```

Figure 11.3: Rechecking missing values

(V) **Handling Duplicate Values:** After addressing missing values, the next critical step in data preprocessing is handling duplicate entries. Duplicate data can lead to skewed results and inaccurate analyses. Here is how you can handle duplicate values in your dataset:

Identify Duplicate Rows: Use the **duplicated()** method in Pandas to check for duplicates. This function returns a Boolean series, with True indicating a duplicate of a previous row.

```
duplicate_rows = churn_data.duplicated()
```

Counting Duplicate Rows: To understand the extent of duplication, count the number of duplicate rows.

```
number_of_duplicates = duplicate_rows.sum()
```

In our dataset, this step revealed that there are 0 duplicate rows.

a. **Analyzing Duplicate Rows:** If duplicates are found, it's crucial to analyze them before removal. Sometimes, duplicates may represent valid repeated entries.

b. **Removing Duplicate Rows:** Although our dataset does not have duplicate entries, if any were found, they could be removed using the **drop_duplicates()** method:

```
churn_data.drop_duplicates(inplace=True)
```

This method ensures that only unique rows are retained, enhancing the dataset's quality.

Dropping Columns: This step simplifies the dataset, making it more manageable and focused for analysis or modeling.

a. **Identify Irrelevant Columns**: Review each column in the dataset to determine its relevance to your analysis or modeling goals. The criteria for irrelevance can include:

- Redundancy: Columns that duplicate information present in other columns.

- Lack of Variability: Columns with little to no variation in their values.

- Non-Utility: Columns that do not contribute to the analysis or predictive modeling objectives.

b. **Dropping Columns in our Dataset:**

- In the context of the Churn Modelling dataset, certain columns might be considered for removal. Examples include:

  o **RowNum**: Likely just an index column.

  o **CustId**: Customer IDs, which may not be necessary for analysis focused on customer behavior patterns.

  o **Surname**: Customer surnames, which generally don't contribute to churn analysis.

- The decision to drop these columns should be aligned with the specific goals of your analysis.

c. **Implementing Column Removal**:

- To remove these columns, use the **drop()** method in Pandas:

```
churn_data.drop(['RowNum', 'CustId', 'Surname'], axis=1,
inplace=True)
```

Here, **axis=1** specifies that columns are being dropped, and **inplace=True** ensures that the operation modifies the DataFrame directly.

d. **Verification**: After dropping the columns, it's important to verify the structure of the DataFrame to ensure the changes are as expected.

```
churn_data.head()
```

Output:

	CreditScore	Geo	Gender	Age	Tenure	Balance	NumOfProducts	HasCrCard	IsActive	EstimatedSal	Exited
0	619	France	Female	42.0	2.0	0.00	1	1	1	101348.88	1
1	608	Spain	Female	41.0	1.0	83807.86	1	0	1	112542.58	0
2	502	France	Female	42.0	8.0	159660.80	3	1	0	113931.57	1
3	699	France	Female	39.0	1.0	0.00	2	0	0	93826.63	0
4	850	Spain	Female	43.0	2.0	125510.82	1	1	1	79084.10	0

Figure 11.4: Verify the structure of DataFrame after dropping columns

VI. **Renaming Columns:** In this section, we will see how to rename columns in the dataset to enhance clarity and facilitate ease of analysis. Properly named columns improve readability and understanding, which is crucial for effective data analysis and modeling.

Implementing the Renaming:

• Use the **rename()** function in Pandas to rename the columns.

• The process involves creating a dictionary mapping current column names to their new names and applying this mapping to the dataset.

Example of Renaming:

• **Geo** to **Geography:** To provide more clarity on the data this column represents.

• **HasCrCard** to **HasCreditCard:** To make the column's purpose more understandable.

• **IsActive** to **IsActiveMember:** To indicate the status of membership.

• **EstimatedSal** to **EstimatedSalary:** For a clearer representation of the data.

```
renamed_columns = {
'Geo': 'Geography',
'HasCrCard': 'HasCreditCard',
'IsActive': 'IsActiveMember',
'EstimatedSal': 'EstimatedSalary'
}


churn_data.rename(columns=renamed_columns, inplace=True)
```

Output:

	CreditScore	Geography	Gender	Age	Tenure	Balance	NumOfProducts	HasCreditCard	IsActiveMember	EstimatedSalary	Exited
0	619	France	Female	42.0	2.0	0.00	1	1	1	101348.88	1
1	608	Spain	Female	41.0	1.0	83807.86	1	0	1	112542.58	0
2	502	France	Female	42.0	8.0	159660.80	3	1	0	113931.57	1
3	699	France	Female	39.0	1.0	0.00	2	0	0	93826.63	0
4	850	Spain	Female	43.0	2.0	125510.82	1	1	1	79084.10	0

Figure 11.5: Renaming columns

Exploratory Data Analysis (EDA)

To explore and analyze the customer churn dataset to uncover patterns, detect anomalies, understand relationships among different features, and derive insights that could be vital for predictive modeling and business decisions.

Descriptive Statistics Analysis

Descriptive Statistics Analysis is a crucial aspect of data exploration that involves summarizing and understanding the main characteristics of a dataset. It focuses on calculating measures of central tendency, such as mean, median, and mode, to identify typical or average values within the data. Additionally, it includes measures of spread or variability, including range, variance, and standard deviation, which provide insights into how data points are distributed around central values. In Python, particularly with Pandas DataFrames, the **.describe()** method is a powerful tool for generating these statistics. It yields key metrics such as count, mean, standard deviation, minimum, maximum, and quartiles (**25%**, **50%**, **75%**) for each numerical column, offering a comprehensive overview of the dataset's numerical features. This method streamlines the process of obtaining a preliminary understanding of the data, setting the stage for more in-depth analysis.

```
churn_data.describe()
```

	CreditScore	Age	Tenure	Balance	NumOfProducts	HasCreditCard	IsActiveMember	EstimatedSalary	Exited
count	10002.000000	9999.000000	10000.000000	10002.000000	10002.000000	10002.000000	10002.000000	10002.000000	10002.000000
mean	650.554989	38.922792	5.012800	76483.606846	1.530194	0.705559	0.514997	100083.669289	0.203659
std	96.661490	10.487146	2.892174	62398.160146	0.581639	0.455814	0.499800	57508.085436	0.402739
min	350.000000	18.000000	0.000000	0.000000	1.000000	0.000000	0.000000	11.580000	0.000000
25%	584.000000	32.000000	3.000000	0.000000	1.000000	0.000000	0.000000	50983.750000	0.000000
50%	652.000000	37.000000	5.000000	97198.540000	1.000000	1.000000	1.000000	100185.240000	0.000000
75%	718.000000	44.000000	7.000000	127647.840000	2.000000	1.000000	1.000000	149383.652500	0.000000
max	850.000000	92.000000	10.000000	250898.090000	4.000000	1.000000	1.000000	199992.480000	1.000000

Figure 11.6: Descriptive statistics

Descriptive Statistics Summary

- **CreditScore:** Ranges from 350 to 850 with an average of around 650.55.
- **Age:** The average age is approximately 38.92 years, with a range from 18 to 92 years.
- **Tenure:** Tenure ranges from 0 to 10 years with an average of 5.01 years.
- **Balance:** Varies widely from 0 to 250,898.09, with an average balance of around 76,483.61.
- **NumOfProducts:** Customers use between 1 to 4 products, with an average of 1.53 products.
- **HasCreditCard:** About 70.56% of customers have a credit card.
- **IsActiveMember:** Approximately 51.50% of customers are active.
- **EstimatedSalary:** Ranges widely, with an average salary of around 100,083.67.
- **Exited (Churn Rate):** About 20.37% of customers have churned.

Univariate Analysis

Univariate analysis is a type of analysis conducted on a single variable (or attribute) at a time. It's the simplest form of data analysis where the data being analyzed consists of only one variable. This kind of analysis helps in understanding the pattern of a specific variable and can reveal insights such as range, central tendency (mean, median, mode), dispersion (variance, standard deviation), and distribution shape (normal, skewed, bimodal, and so on).

Let's analyze the numerical data:

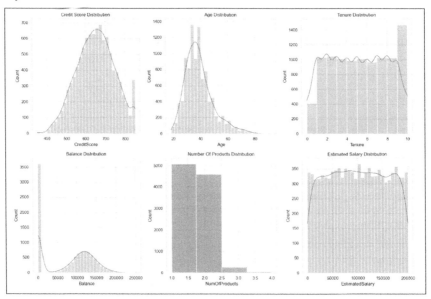

Figure 11.7: *Univariate analysis on numerical columns*

```
# Setting up the visualisation settings
sns.set(style="whitegrid")


# Creating subplots for each distribution
fig, axes = plt.subplots(nrows=2, ncols=3, figsize=(15, 10))


# Credit Score Distribution
sns.histplot(churn_data['CreditScore'], bins=30, ax=axes[0, 0],
kde=True)
axes[0, 0].set_title('Credit Score Distribution')


# Age Distribution
sns.histplot(churn_data['Age'], bins=30, ax=axes[0, 1], kde=True)
axes[0, 1].set_title('Age Distribution')


# Tenure Distribution
sns.histplot(churn_data['Tenure'], bins=10, ax=axes[0, 2], kde=True)
axes[0, 2].set_title('Tenure Distribution')


# Balance Distribution
sns.histplot(churn_data['Balance'], bins=30, ax=axes[1, 0], kde=True)
axes[1, 0].set_title('Balance Distribution')


# Number Of Products Distribution
sns.histplot(churn_data['NumOfProducts'], bins=4, ax=axes[1, 1])
axes[1, 1].set_title('Number Of Products Distribution')


# Estimated Salary Distribution
sns.histplot(churn_data['EstimatedSalary'], bins=30, ax=axes[1, 2],
kde=True)
axes[1, 2].set_title('Estimated Salary Distribution')


plt.tight_layout()
plt.show()
```

Credit Score Distribution:

- Observation: The distribution appears somewhat normal but with a slight skew to the left. Most customers have credit scores in the mid-range.

- Implication: A majority of customers seem to have an average to good credit score, which is typically desirable for a bank.

Age Distribution:

- Observation: This distribution is skewed to the right, indicating a larger proportion of younger customers, with a peak in the late 30s.

- Implication: The bank's customer base tends to be younger, which might influence the types of products and services offered.

Tenure Distribution:

- Observation: The tenure appears to be fairly evenly distributed across different lengths.

- Implication: Customers are spread across various stages of their relationship with the bank, from new to long-standing clients.

Balance Distribution:

- Observation: A large number of customers have low or zero balances, with another peak around the mid-range values.

- Implication: The bank has a significant number of customers who maintain a low balance, which might indicate a segment of customers using the bank for basic services or as a secondary banking option.

Number of Products Distribution:

- Observation: Most customers use 1 or 2 products from the bank.

- Implication: There is potential for cross-selling additional products to customers, particularly those currently using only one product.

Estimated Salary Distribution:

- Observation: The salary distribution is quite uniform across the range, without any significant peaks or troughs.

- Implication: The customer base is diverse in terms of income levels, which suggests the bank serves a wide spectrum of the market.

Output:

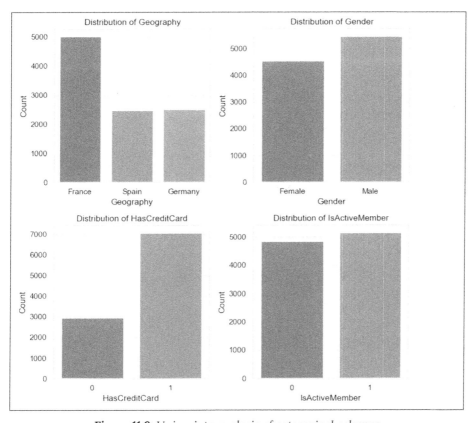

Figure 11.8: *Univariate analysis of categorical columns*

The univariate analysis of the categorical variables in the dataset provides insights into the distribution of these variables:

- **Geography**: The distribution shows the count of customers from different countries. It appears that the majority of the customers are from one specific country, likely France, based on the dataset's structure.

- **Gender**: The gender distribution shows a relatively close count between male and female customers, with a slight dominance of one gender.

- **HasCreditCard**: A significant majority of customers have a credit card. This indicates that credit card ownership is common among the bank's customers.

- **IsActiveMember**: The distribution is almost evenly split between active and inactive members, indicating a balanced mix in the customer base in terms of activity status.

Churn Analysis

Churn Analysis is the process of examining and understanding the reasons and patterns behind customers discontinuing their relationship with a business or service. In other words, it's the study of why customers `churn` or leave. This analysis is crucial for businesses to identify at-risk customers and develop strategies to improve customer retention.

Let's start with the distribution of categorical variables and their relationship with churn. We will visualize some of these variables to better understand their distribution and relationship with customer churn (Exited).

Python code:

```python
# Setting up the plot style
plt.style.use('seaborn-darkgrid')


# Plotting the distribution of categorical variables and their
relationship with churn
fig, axes = plt.subplots(3, 2, figsize=(12, 8))


# Geography
sns.countplot(ax=axes[0, 0], x='Geography', data=churn_data)
axes[0, 0].set_title('Distribution of Geography')


sns.countplot(ax=axes[0, 1], x='Geography', hue='Exited', data=churn_
data)
axes[0, 1].set_title('Churn by Geography')


# Gender
sns.countplot(ax=axes[1, 0], x='Gender', data=churn_data)
axes[1, 0].set_title('Distribution of Gender')


sns.countplot(ax=axes[1, 1], x='Gender', hue='Exited', data=churn_data)
axes[1, 1].set_title('Churn by Gender')


# IsActiveMember
sns.countplot(ax=axes[2, 0], x='IsActiveMember', data=churn_data)
axes[2, 0].set_title('Distribution of Active Membership')


sns.countplot(ax=axes[2, 1], x='IsActiveMember', hue='Exited',
```

```
data=churn_data)
axes[2, 1].set_title('Churn by Active Membership')


plt.tight_layout()
plt.show()
```

Output:

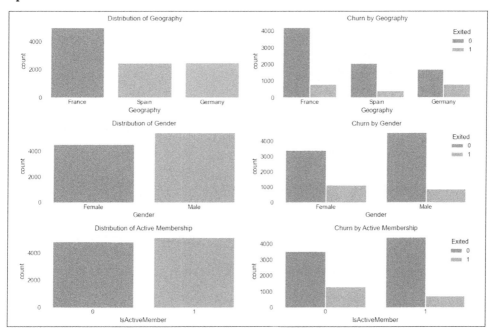

Figure 11.9: *Distribution of categorical variables and relationship with customer churn*

The visualizations provide insights into the distribution of categorical variables and their relationship with customer churn:

Geography:

- The majority of the customers are from France, followed by Spain and Germany.
- When examining churn, it appears that the proportion of churned customers is higher in France followed by Spain and Germany

Gender:

- There are more male customers than female customers in the dataset.
- The churn rate seems higher among female customers compared to male customers.

IsActiveMember:

- The number of active and inactive members is almost balanced.
- Inactive members have a noticeably higher churn rate compared to active members.

These insights suggest that geography, gender, and whether a customer is an active member play a significant role in customer churn.

Next, let's examine the distributions of numerical variables and their relationship with churn. We'll use histograms for the distributions and box plots to understand how these numerical variables relate to churn. This will help us see if there are any distinct patterns or outliers in the data.

Python code:

```python
# Visualizing the distributions of numerical variables and their
relationship with churn


# Selecting numerical columns for analysis
numerical_columns = ['CreditScore', 'Age', 'Tenure', 'Balance',
'NumOfProducts', 'EstimatedSalary']


fig, axes = plt.subplots(len(numerical_columns), 2, figsize=(15, 20))


for i, col in enumerate(numerical_columns):
    # Histogram for distribution
    sns.histplot(churn_data[col], kde=True, ax=axes[i][0])
    axes[i][0].set_title(f'Distribution of {col}')


    # Boxplot to see relationship with churn
    sns.boxplot(x='Exited', y=col, data=churn_data, ax=axes[i][1])
    axes[i][1].set_title(f'{col} vs Churn')


plt.tight_layout()
plt.show()
```

Output:

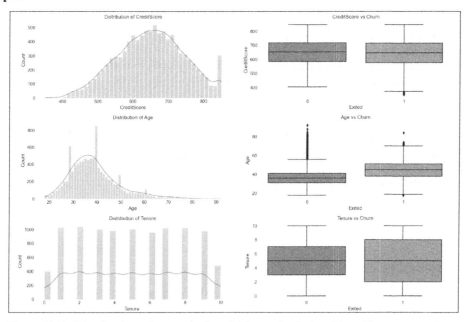

Figure 11.10: *Distribution of numerical variables and relationship with customer churn*

Continuing our exploration by focusing on the visualization of numerical variables and examining how they relate to customer churn.

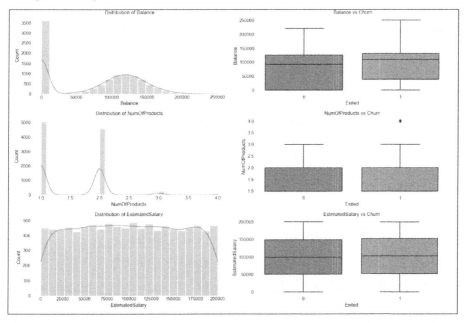

Figure 11.11: *Distribution of numerical variables and relationship with customer churn*

Credit Score:

- Mean: Churned (645.35), Not Churned (651.89)
- Median: Churned (646.00), Not Churned (653.00)

There is no significant difference in the credit scores of customers who churned and those who did not, suggesting that credit score may not be a strong predictor of churn.

Age:

- Mean: Churned (44.84), Not Churned (37.41)
- Median: Churned (45.00), Not Churned (36.00)

There's a noticeable difference in the age distribution between churned and retained customers. Churned customers tend to be older, indicating that age is a significant factor in churn.

Tenure:

- Mean: Churned (4.93), Not Churned (5.03)
- Median: Both Churned and Not Churned (5.00)

Similar tenure distributions for churned and retained customers, suggesting tenure might not be a major factor in churn.

Balance:

- Mean: Churned (91,108.54), Not Churned (72,743.37)
- Median: Churned (109,349.29), Not Churned (92,072.68)

Higher median balance in customers who churned, indicating a possible relationship between higher balances and churn.

Number of Products:

- Mean: Churned (1.48), Not Churned (1.54)
- Median: Churned (1.00), Not Churned (2.00)

Customers with more products (especially 3 or 4) tend to churn more, as seen in the previous analysis.

Estimated Salary:

- Mean: Churned (101,465.68), Not Churned (99,730.23)
- Median: Churned (102,460.84), Not Churned (99,595.67)

There's no significant difference in the salaries of customers who churned versus those who didn't, suggesting salary might not be a strong predictor of churn.

Customer Segmentation

Customer segmentation is the process of dividing a customer base into distinct groups of individuals that are similar in specific ways relevant to marketing, such as age, gender, interests, spending habits, and so on. This approach allows businesses to tailor their strategies and communications to meet the unique needs and preferences of different segments, ultimately leading to more effective marketing, improved customer service, and increased sales.

In the context of churn analysis, customer segmentation can be particularly useful in identifying which segments are more prone to churn. This allows businesses to develop targeted retention strategies for these high-risk segments, thereby reducing overall churn rates.

Python code

```
# Age Segmentation
# Creating age groups for segmentation
age_bins = [0, 25, 35, 45, 55, 65, 100]
age_labels = ['0-25', '26-35', '36-45', '46-55', '56-65', '66-100']
churn_data['AgeGroup'] = pd.cut(churn_data['Age'], bins=age_bins, labels=age_labels, right=False)


# Analyzing the Churn Rate within each demographic segment
# Pivot table to analyze churn rate by Age Group, Gender, and Geography
pivot_table = churn_data.pivot_table(values='Exited', index=['AgeGroup', 'Gender'], columns='Geography', aggfunc='mean')


# Visualizing the Churn Rate within each demographic segment
plt.figure(figsize=(10, 7))
sns.heatmap(pivot_table, annot=True, cmap='coolwarm', fmt=".2f")
plt.title('Churn Rate by Age Group, Gender, and Geography')
plt.xlabel('Geography')
plt.ylabel('Age Group and Gender')
plt.show()


pivot_table
```

Output:

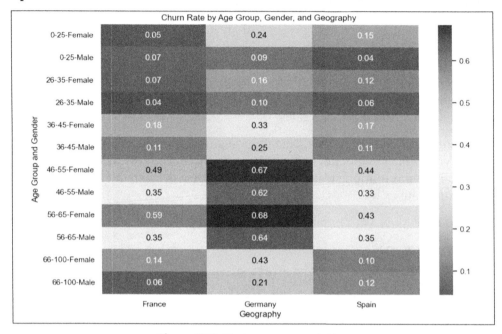

Figure 11.12: *Customer segmentation*

Age Group and Gender Influence on Churn:

- In most age groups, female customers generally have higher churn rates than male customers. This trend is particularly noticeable in the 46-55 and 56-65 age groups across all three geographies.

- The churn rate seems to peak for both genders in the 46-55 and 56-65 age groups, indicating that middle-aged to older customers are more likely to churn.

Geographical Variations:

- Germany shows significantly higher churn rates across almost all age and gender groups compared to France and Spain. This suggests that geographical factors, possibly local market conditions or competitive pressures, significantly influence customer churn.

- The lowest churn rates are often observed in Spain, especially among younger customers (0-25 and 26-35 age groups).

Targeted Retention Strategies:

- Banks may need to develop targeted retention strategies for middle-aged and older customers, especially females, as they are more prone to churn.

- The high churn rate in Germany across various segments suggests a need for market-specific strategies, perhaps focusing on improved customer service, tailored products, or competitive pricing.

Value-based Segmentation

Value-based segmentation involves categorizing customers according to their financial value to the bank, typically assessed through variables like account balances or estimated revenue generation. This type of segmentation allows for identifying high-value customers who may require special attention to retain or potential high-value customers who could be targeted for additional services. Let's perform value-based segmentation on your dataset focusing on two key variables:

- **Account Balance:** This is a direct indicator of the financial value a customer holds with the bank. We can segment customers into different groups based on their account balance ranges.

- **Estimated Salary:** Although not a direct account metric, a customer's estimated salary can be a good indicator of their potential value. Similar to account balances, we can create segments based on estimated salary ranges.

Python code:

```python
# Value-Based Segmentation based on Account Balance and Estimated Salary


# Creating balance segments
balance_bins = [0, 25000, 50000, 75000, 100000, 125000, 150000, 175000,
200000, float('inf')]

balance_labels = ['<25k', '25-50k', '50-75k', '75-100k', '100-125k',
'125-150k', '150-175k', '175-200k', '>200k']

churn_data['BalanceGroup'] = pd.cut(churn_data['Balance'], bins=balance_
bins, labels=balance_labels, right=False)


# Creating salary segments
salary_bins = [0, 25000, 50000, 75000, 100000, 125000, 150000, 175000,
200000, float('inf')]

salary_labels = ['<25k', '25-50k', '50-75k', '75-100k', '100-125k',
'125-150k', '150-175k', '175-200k', '>200k']

churn_data['SalaryGroup'] = pd.cut(churn_data['EstimatedSalary'],
bins=salary_bins, labels=salary_labels, right=False)


# Analyzing churn rates in balance segments
balance_churn = churn_data.groupby('BalanceGroup')['Exited'].mean().
```

```
reset_index()


# Analyzing churn rates in salary segments
salary_churn = churn_data.groupby('SalaryGroup')['Exited'].mean().reset_
index()


# Plotting churn rates for balance and salary segments
fig, axes = plt.subplots(1, 2, figsize=(18, 6))


# Balance Segments
sns.barplot(x='BalanceGroup', y='Exited', data=balance_churn, ax=ax-
es[0])
axes[0].set_title('Churn Rate by Account Balance')
axes[0].set_xlabel('Balance Group')
axes[0].set_ylabel('Churn Rate')
axes[0].tick_params(axis='x', rotation=45)


# Salary Segments
sns.barplot(x='SalaryGroup', y='Exited', data=salary_churn, ax=axes[1])
axes[1].set_title('Churn Rate by Estimated Salary')
axes[1].set_xlabel('Salary Group')
axes[1].set_ylabel('Churn Rate')
axes[1].tick_params(axis='x', rotation=45)


plt.tight_layout()
plt.show()


balance_churn, salary_churn
```

Output:

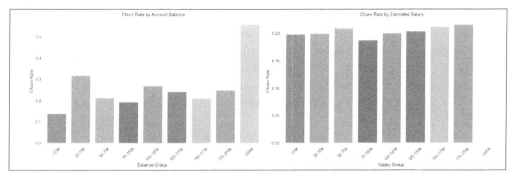

Figure 11.13: *Value-based segmentation*

The visualizations and data for value-based segmentation based on account balance and estimated salary reveal the following insights:

Account Balance Segmentation:

- **High Churn in Lower and Higher Balance Groups:** Customers with very low (<25k) and very high (>200k) account balances show higher churn rates. The high churn rate in the >200k group is particularly notable, though it may be influenced by a smaller sample size in this segment.

- **Mid-Range Stability:** Customers with mid-range balances (50-75k, 75-100k, 100-125k) exhibit relatively lower churn rates, suggesting a more stable relationship with the bank.

- **Variability in Churn:** The churn rate varies significantly across balance groups, indicating that customers' financial value to the bank influences their likelihood of churn.

Estimated Salary Segmentation:

- **Relatively Uniform Churn Rates:** Churn rates across different salary groups are more uniform compared to balance segments. This suggests that salary alone may not be a strong indicator of churn risk.

- **No Clear Trend:** Unlike the balance segments, there is no clear trend of increasing or decreasing churn rate with higher or lower salaries.

- **Missing Data in Highest Salary Group:** The absence of data for the >200k salary group indicates either a lack of customers in this segment or insufficient data to calculate churn rates.

Conclusion

As we reach the conclusion of this chapter, and indeed of the book, it's time to reflect on the journey we have undertaken. Throughout the course of this book, we have navigated the multifaceted world of Pandas, exploring its vast functionalities and how it can be applied to real-world data scenarios. This final chapter, focusing on the analysis of Bank Customer Churn, represents the culmination of all that we have learned.

As we close this chapter, remember that the field of data analysis is ever-evolving. The skills you have acquired through this book are a strong foundation, but continuous learning and practice are key to staying adept in this dynamic field. Keep exploring, experimenting, and expanding your horizons with Pandas and beyond.

Index

Made in United States
North Haven, CT
08 January 2025

64151725R00200